The Consolations of Philosophy:

Hobbes's Secret; Spinoza's Way

THE CONSOLATIONS OF PHILOSOPHY:

Hobbes's Secret; Spinoza's Way

Henry M. Rosenthal

Edited and with an Introduction by
Abigail L. Rosenthal

Temple University Press
PHILADELPHIA

Temple University Press, Philadelphia 19122

Published 1989

Printed in the United States of America

The paper used in this publication meets the minimum requirements of American National Standard for Information Sciences—Permanence of Paper for Printed Library Materials, ANSI Z39.48-1984

Library of Congress Cataloging-in-Publication Data

Rosenthal, Henry M., 1906–1977.
The consolations of philosophy: Hobbes's secret; Spinoza's way/ Henry M. Rosenthal; edited and with an introduction by Abigail L. Rosenthal.
p. cm.
Bibliography: p.
Includes index.
ISBN 0-87722-610-5 (alk. paper)
1. Hobbes, Thomas, 1588–1679. Leviathan. 2. Spinoza, Benedictus de, 1632–1677. Ethica. 3. Ethics. I. Rosenthal, Abigail L. II. Title.
JC153.H659R67 1989
320'.01—dc 19 88-24927
CIP

CONTENTS

PREFACE

The Consolations of Philosophy may be considered a piece of philosophical writing in the meditative tradition. It was not intended as an instrument for pressing forward toward imminent resolution of the current controversies surrounding its subject matter. It is, rather, an occasion for the reader to confront himself in the course of working through its argument about two classic and still-influential philosophic texts.

What is here confronted in the text of Hobbes's *Leviathan* is the problem of being an individual and a moral agent within the constraints of social and political life, and of history. Confronted in Spinoza's *Ethic* is the same problem, of being oneself and a moral person, but this time in the context of private life, with the focus on those special features of private life that deserve to be called eternal.

In both parts of this two-part study, the development of the argument is quite unconventional, often unexpected, yet reliably unstudied in its ways of securing its effects.

That being the character of the present work, my task in the Introduction was to make the whole course of the argument a bit more accessible to the reader who would be going through it for the first time. I thought it might help also to make some attempt to *place* certain moments of the argument in the context of current approaches to Hobbes and Spinoza that do differ from the approach taken here. The author of this work did not do that himself except very occasionally. I have done a little of it, however, sometimes defending his argument from opposition that arose later, or on other tracks, and that the author himself does not take into consideration. My purpose in doing this could not be to provide an exhaustive comparison of this work with the contemporary literature on the subject. It could only be to help readers to keep their philosophical bearings while crossing new territory.

The present work was substantially completed in 1976, one year before its author's death. Certain further additions and corrections were supplied by him in the course of 1976–77. Once I have provided the promised review of the argument and also drawn the relevant philosophic comparisons as well as I am able to, it will be appropriate to say something more about the process of readying the manuscript for publication. That account will be found in the last part of the Introduction, where it will also be time to tell something of the author's life, and of the kind of man he was.

Largely out of a concern for scansion, I have settled on the traditional masculine pronoun as the pronoun of common gender in my own introduction and editor's footnotes. There was one allied consideration as well. This book reflects, in illustrative excerpts, the style of Hobbes, and of Spinoza in translation, in addition to the style of its author, HMR. The two seventeenth-century writers appear here to have made unselfconscious use of the masculine pronoun to express indifferently concerns that were either specifically male or generically human. HMR tended toward a somewhat more differentiated use—now of the masculine pronoun, now of the feminine, now of both, now of genderfree terms like "humanity"—depending on his sense of the context. If I in turn have seemed to revert to a certain seventeenth-century mode in my own contributions, it was also for the sake of stylistic simplicity, so as not to impose on the reader of this book yet another stratum of intuitions on this subject.

A word about Boethius's title, and this one. In the face of the painfulness of human experience, our tendency is generally to cope by *rushing away* from whatever has happened that is painful—toward abstractness, toward premature and unearned transcendence, or into emotional oversimplifications of various kinds. Against all these dogmatic, losing strategems of consolation (which may indeed produce *something* worthwhile, but lose us most of ourselves), Henry M. Rosenthal's *The Consolations of Philosophy: Hobbes's Secret; Spinoza's Way*, offers a corrective that is incessant, pointed, and—in its leisurely way—self-directed. The "consolations" of this corrective are necessarily *plural*, rather than singular as in Boethius's title, because no reductive simplifications—Stoic, Neoplatonic, or other—are allowed by HMR to be consolatory. (Cf. Part Two, p. 136.)

About Boethius, however, and *his* conviction that true philosophy would have to be consolatory, HMR had penned these admiring lines, for a preface (unfinished) to the present work: "In the year 524 of the current era a man named Boethius wrote a book entitled 'The Consolation of Philosophy.' He wrote it"—being then imprisoned and under threat of execution—"at the behest of the then emperor, whom he had served long and faithfully, it would appear, and in high degree. He wrote it to attend to his disappointment, and to bind up the wounds of that disappointment with what he believed to be an overpowering salve."

Many people helped, and urged me along, in the task of bringing this work to publication. They have my tremendous gratitude, and to some of that number I can give at least this word of public thanks and acknowledgment as well.

Among them were my father's classmates of the Columbia College class of 1925: Clifton Fadiman, James and Elsa Grossman, Lillian and Meyer Shapiro shared with me detailed recollections of the era, and of my father as they knew him then. David Pearce, who—many years later—had been his philosophical junior colleague at Hunter College, was good enough to give me his graceful impressions of a Louisville upbringing, and of what one may salvage from it in the thoughtful afteryears.

Others either read the manuscript and discussed with me the specific requirements of its introduction, or else—without having necessarily seen it—guided me to specific references, clarified hard questions, and just gave sustaining encouragement. For having furnished some or all of these manifold kinds of helps, I am exceedingly grateful to Thomas Altizer, John Bacon, Henry LeRoy Finch, Joel Friedman, Frank and Ada Graham, Barry Gross, Elizabeth Knight, Charles Landesman, Arlene Lev, Donald Levy, Dan Lusthaus, Peter Miller, Lucy Rosenthal, Milton Schubin, Elmer Sprague, Joan Stambaugh, Mary Wiseman, and Edith Wyschogrod.

Sandy Deak brought to the typing of my introduction her usual easy rapport with themes and with style.

At each stage of the project, since I first approached her with it in the spring of 1987, Jane Cullen, who is senior acquisitions editor at Temple University Press, has been an inspired and unusually effective editor. I am grateful for her guidance, for the work of the two anonymous referees, for the support of David Bartlett, director of Temple University Press, and for the myriad expert contributions of the staff.

Abigail L. Rosenthal

INTRODUCTION

On The Consolations of Philosophy: Hobbes's Secret; Spinoza's Way

Hobbes's Secret

It is the view of Henry M. Rosenthal that Hobbes has solved most of his own problems, even if he has not solved the main problems with which his commentators have encumbered him. "We impute to Hobbes . . . a thoroughgoing ontological coherence that governs his text esoterically, but unmistakably" (p. 40). "Hobbes's Secret," the first part of this two-part study, accordingly begins with a refusal of the various labels (egoist, authoritarian, determinist, pessimist, if not possessive individualist) under which Hobbes has usually been classified.

These labels have led to the great, more or less insoluble problems of Hobbes interpretation, that is to say: How do you get rights and duties out of generalized egoism, social responsibility out of the values of the market, moral accountability out of mechanism and determinism, fair checks on government out of centralized state power, a political and moral theory out of the contingent, topical constraints on thought and discourse that were around in Hobbes's day? The answers would seem to be that you can't and you don't. So, at the start of "Hobbes's Secret," it is claimed that Hobbes is *not committed* to drawing his consequences out of any of the antecedent conditions mentioned above.

Further, "Hobbes's Secret" marks off the Hobbesian enterprise from the enterprise of any sort of divinity, whether of the religious mainstream or of the seventeenth-century margin. Hobbes's God, it's here claimed, is in a radically different sector of the real from the moral-political sector. If one wanted to come face to face with the Almighty, one would have to step outside the moral-political sector. That in itself would be an act potentially disintegrative to the polity, because it would multiply authorities in private and public life, while destroying the jointly reasoned, communal basis for any given authority. (That Hobbes was laying the foundation of his political theory on ground cleared and leveled by his drastic *repudiation* of religious politics has been maintained recently by David Johnson in *The Rhetoric of Leviathan: Thomas Hobbes and the Politics of Cultural Transformation* [Princeton, N.J.: Princeton University Press, 1986]. And, as far as it goes, this seems to be HMR's view as well.)

If Hobbes is not a politicking religionist of some stripe, should he not after all and once again be restored to classification as a born-too-soon reductionist, with all the problems, iterated at the outset, that will inevitably accompany that position? But no, since HMR does not take the Hobbesian enterprise to be hopelessly problematic. He takes it that Hobbes *more or less realized his intention*. His view is that the Hobbesian enterprise cannot even be seen clear till it has been separated from all the reductionist programs, seventeenth century and contemporary. This is not because Hobbes was presciently aware, back in his own time, that the reductionist programs were going to prove hard successfully to complete at any time. It is not HMR's view that Hobbes held back from reducing commonwealth and reason to mechanism and sense because he was able to preview the difficulties that would crop up in the course of later, systematic endeavors to reduce, say, the social sciences to psychology, mental events to brain events, brain events to their biochemistry, and biochemistry to physics. Rather, the argument in "Hobbes's Secret" is that what is primitive for Hobbes is a certain kind of human experience.

All other human experiences, from the simplest ones marked out and delivered by the linguistic distinction between subject and object to the experiences covered by Hobbes's mechanistic account of nature, are held by HMR to have been extrapolated out of Hobbes's primitive human experience, to which they are held to have in-built reference. Note that this is rather different from the mixed remarks on mechanism in C. B. Macpherson, David Gauthier, and, most recently, Gregory S. Kavka (in *The Political Theory of Possessive Individualism*, *The Logic of Leviathan*, and *Hobbesian Moral and Political Theory*, respectively), to the effect that Hobbes may be in part a *failed* reductionist, but that nevertheless his moral and political philosophy can and ought to be evaluated independently of his mechanistic psychology and physics. On HMR's view, Hobbes is not in part a failed reductionist. He is simply not a reductionist.

It would be a mistake, I think, for this Introduction to assign to itself the highhanded role, going considerably ahead of my competence, of describing and adjudicating these fine, complex, and important differences between Hobbes commentators. It will be assignment enough here just to point out the originality of HMR's interpretation of Hobbes, leaving it to the reader to weigh that interpretation against others in terms of its capacity to shed unexpected light on the language and thought of Hobbes and, I should think, on the human situation more generally. Where we get different questions addressed to a text, it is not surprising that we should also get different answers. The real question I think HMR brings to the text of Hobbes's *Leviathan* is, what sort of human experience has occasioned Hobbes's sort of writing?

The experience imputed by HMR to Hobbes as primitive in the sense of originary is internally a complex one. It is a human experience of struggle against human usurpations. The background is an external reality that is not going to be *mastered* by any of the contenders, whether the contenders work singly or in combination. "Within" and "without" are the two terms that divide reality primitively for Hobbes, and both presuppose a participant witness that is conscious and (since this is Hobbes's thought we are talking about, not the thought of Leibniz or Berkeley) *human*. "Within" and "without" are not terms that work in the service of a neutral description of nature as she may purportedly be found when we conscious beings are not there, *or* when God alone is there. Rather, they play something of the roles filled by Sartre's "for-itself" and "coefficient of adversity." They belong to the human scene.

On this account of Hobbes, we will never, in our long human careers, overcome "withoutness." It's all that we're overwhelmingly up against. All our particular struggles, in the course of which we aim at definite achievements, are projected against this backdrop. When all is said and done, "withoutness" remains vastly larger than anything *we* can achieve.

Given the fact that we cannot overcome the world (i.e., the intra-human struggle for advantage and its infinite backdrop, both comprised in "withoutness"), two options remain. We can either integrate this primitive grappling into the theoretical, technical, and social practices of an accessible and defensible culture, or else we can try mistakenly to exit from the forum, exit from culture that is, and put our petition directly before the infinite ("withoutness" as such). The second course, anarchic or seditious, would be seen by Hobbes as potentially dissolving both of the person and the body politic. But, whichever course we pursue, making "mechanism" the motivating force gets the explanation backward. On HMR's account of Hobbes, putting the explanation frontward summons us to notice how "the 'laws of motion'" turn out to be "metaphors for existential passions either sanctioned by or outlawed from the commonwealth" (p. 39).

Putting temporarily on hold the material question of how HMR works this out, let us first of all forbear to confuse the line of thought followed here with another line to which his bears superficial resemblance. For a great many modern readers, making a philosophically primary pair of terms dependent on a given human experience relativizes the meanings of the terms and likewise the whole structure raised on them.

If Hobbes's thought were supposed to rest on a primitive human *experience,* for example, the experience of human struggle against usurpations, the tendency would get activated to read Hobbes from inside the constraints of his topical political concerns. From there, it would be just a little step for the commentator to read Hobbes as an ideologue who—consciously or unconsciously—put his pen in the service of a special-interest group, which it then becomes the task of the commentator–historian to try to identify.

In the wake of C. B. Macpherson's *Political Theory of Possessive Individualism: Hobbes to Locke* (Oxford: Oxford University Press at the Clarendon Press, 1962), a number of commentators have seen Hobbes and later contract theorists as witting or unwitting advocates for manufacturing classes in need of a strong, central government to police their private property and their market transactions.

A related point has to do with autonomy and equality. These modifying properties of the parties to a social contract are first found imputed to the parties to contracts in the market sense. Market relations themselves are supposed to appear historically only after European feudal relations have been overtaken by the development of commercial manufacturing. (Here one must tactfully bracket the memory of Plato's *Republic*, apparently a counter-example to such Marxian interpretations of contract theory, in that it contains its own social contract theory, although Plato wrote it about twelve hundred years *before* the period of European feudalism!) In any case, whether the relativized reading of Hobbes is fully Marxian, or just more generally historicist, such a reading will continue to see contract theory as contingent on phases of human development the experience of which is by no means universal and only occasionally necessitated.

Thus Hobbes is read as a child of his times, and the kind of struggle he experienced as one that would not be experienced by all men. It's both plausible and informative to try to read Hobbes that way. Nevertheless, and because he has something quite different to attend to, HMR does not read Hobbes that way.

Instead, and just where a human experience has been made primitive for Hobbes, HMR's narrative takes a Platonizing—or perhaps Kantian—turn. The claim is that Hobbes's social contract has an *a priori* status for the human agent, although, like many other items that have been thought to have that status, the social contract must incessantly be reconstructed, or poeticized into actual existence, on the human historical stage. The social contract is an *eidos*, an eternal model for our ramshackle civil arrangements.

Now, this is exactly the sort of claim against which the relativized reading of Hobbes turns all its heavy guns. If Hobbes's model society is extrapolated out of a primitive human experience of struggle, and (as the relativists hold) that experience *must vary* with the changing character of human society and history, then the appeal to the model cannot be necessitated by any and all experiences. Therefore, according to the relativized reading, Hobbes's social contract cannot have *a priori* status.

Just in order to bring out what is meant by HMR's claim about an *a priori* social contract, I will run through a few of the counter-examples to the claim of universality and necessity for Hobbes's social contract theory, which have been recently brought forward, and also mention one possibly favorable example, which is really a counter-example, too. At that point, with the territory and the opposition surveyed as completely as I am able to do at present, the real basis of HMR's argument for an *a priori* social contract can be made apparent.

If the social contract is taken to be Hobbes's remedy against total war, then it has only to be pointed out that there are many social and historical conditions in which total war would neither happen nor tend to happen. For example (this counter-example is mine), in the case where the technology is rudimentary and the natural environment proportionately threatening, sustained intra-cultural or inter-cultural predation wouldn't be practicable. Again, if the population size of would-be contenders hasn't swelled to the point of critical mass in a given locale, semi-nomadic would-be contenders could avoid war by moving on to emptier country. (This last point is one of many concerning such preconditions, made by Gregory S. Kavka, in *Hobbesian Moral and Political Theory* [Princeton, N.J.: Princeton University Press, 1968], pp. 124, 175.) And, as has been noted by Macpherson (*Political Theory of Possessive Individualism*, pp. 47–50), in a "status society," where members are assigned their roles and qualities in advance, the escalating competition of all against all cannot occur either.

Apparently, then, the Hobbesian free-for-all can happen only in conditions of temporary social breakdown, when pre-established power relations de-congeal. These are not universal conditions. They are exceptional. (The planetary condition of *nations* racing toward feared mutual annihilation is, however, not exceptional. Be it noted that, for a long time now, albeit with less effective arms, that condition has been the human norm. So David Gauthier finally concedes in his appendix to *The Logic of Leviathan: The Moral and Political Theory of Thomas Hobbes* [Oxford: Oxford University Press at the Clarendon Press, 1969]. On the international scale, pre-established power relations have *always* seemed to de-congeal, sooner or later. At least, so far they have, and for roughly Hobbesian reasons.)

Whether the human context is planetary or more restricted, given the requisite conditions of social breakdown, we do find decision theory apparently tending to support Hobbes's picture of the dynamics of human conflict. What I would term the "Hobbesian outcome" of decision theory is described by David Gauthier (*Logic of Leviathan*, p. 85), also by Robert Nozick (in *Anarchy, State and Utopia* [New York: Basic Books, 1974], pp. 12–25). The gist of it is that any private or *ad hoc* defensive organization will clash with other such groups in a way that tends to give the advantage to the aggressor and lead to escalating aggression, unless the parties agree mutually to forfeit their aggressive option and transfer it to an authority that they have entrusted with the defense of all. Though noting that decision theory's dictate as to the most reasonable course presupposes that human beings have the material conditions and psychological makeup that will get them into this fix and then get them out of it in the prescribed way, Kavka seems otherwise to agree that this is the finding of decision theory (*Hobbesian Moral and Political Theory*, pp. 132–36, 171–78).

That said, we do not have, even in decision theory, an example favorable to the claim that Hobbes's social contract theory applies universally and necessarily in human experience. For there are still the frequent conditions already cited, where external restraints, social or natural, prevent the escalation of aggression. And there are also instances where nothing prevents, but, as it happens, aggression still does not escalate. It is logically possible that, under any given set of human conditions, the Hobbesian worst case would not be realized. In every condition except the international one, based on the historical record it is in varying degrees probable that the Hobbesian worst case will not be realized. That being so, we still do not see what leads Hobbes to postulate the worst case as underlying all human conditions and to refer all the presumptive sufferers, that is, the whole human race, to the social contract as the only remedy that is universal. When the same question is turned toward the present interpreter of Hobbes, we do not see what leads HMR to assign to the Hobbesian social contract the *a priori* characteristic of applying necessarily and universally to human experience.

Musing about the "thoroughgoing ontological coherence" (p. 40) that, mixed with "his net effectiveness in . . . the transvaluation of labels" (p. 38), HMR finds in Hobbes, I will offer some introductory suggestions of my own, leaving the reader to discover the rest of the story as it discloses itself in "Hobbes's Secret."

Hobbes begins at the worst case imaginable, from the interpersonal and political standpoint, and that is why most people have raised their objections. That is why he is called a "pessimist." After all, whether we start from Hobbes's time and place or from our own, it is logically possible and (barring a nuclear war) empirically likely that the worst case will never be realized. *But it is morally impossible that the choice of it, or of actions that conduce to it, would go absolutely unconsidered by human beings, if by human beings we are to understand moral agents.*

Take a simple and familiar example. A shopkeeper shows faint contempt, by an edge in the voice or a slightly hooded, veiled look. In return, one is tempted to assert oneself, to lower the barriers of civility still further. It is a moment. It will be over. The barriers will hold. But suppose, on one's own side, it were *not* over? An ordinary act of introspection will quickly disclose that contempt is violence veiled. If the veil were dropped, victory (in the short term, anyway) would go to the more aggressive contender. (Hobbes's unsteady, sometime conflation of introspective experience and self-evidence is described, with citations, by F. S. McNeilly in *The Anatomy of Leviathan* [London: Macmillan, 1968], pp. 71f., 90f., 249.) The veil may lie over humanity for millennia. Still, escalating violence remains everywhere and at all times a human possibility. What sort of possibility? Not just a logical possibility, for there are too many of those to call for mention. Once again, escalating violence is a moral possibility.

Here is where HMR's contention that Hobbes is not a mechanist takes on its real, intended significance. As we have seen, HMR holds that Hobbes's description of all things begins with the human experience of struggle against usurpations, *not* with a morally neutral account of insensible matter in motion. It is that human experience of struggle which, from the start, is pervaded by the options of the better, the worse, or the worst course for a struggling human being to take. "All these positivities or credit features of the human condition —which we begin with some knowledge of, if we begin with anything —call for description: *because nothing can be described at all* unless it is morally described" (p. 50).

To sum up: before we have fully launched our careers as human beings, and incessantly along the way, we have a choice of good and evil. The social contract has a synthetic *a priori* or transcendental status for our human experience because we are moralized, confronted with the very worst—and with the social contract as the modest best of human antidotes—before experience can be denominated ours, and human, at all. It is only if we choose evil that the very physiognomy of the choice disappears, the way the sea may erase our signatures in the sand. "Our indefeasible 'natural right' is, as it were, our indefeasible love of sin" (p. 66). It is along these lines that the empiricist objections to the universality and necessity of the social contract would, I think, be handled in "Hobbes's Secret."

Without my anticipating, in a page-by-page way, the rest of the plot of "Hobbes's Secret," several more questions that it attends to may be mentioned at this point, questions that may occur anticipatorily to the reader and that have tended to haunt Hobbes interpretation. The questions concern the mechanism or efficient cause by means of which the *a priori* moral order arises in the midst of the empirical order. For example: how can one get from the universal egoism of Hobbes's state of nature to a humanized or a moral condition? How can one get from the state of nature as a general condition to the particular pre-conditions for a social contract (and are these pre-conditions capitalist, or proto-capitalist, necessarily)? Again (we keep asking roughly the same question but shifting the vocabulary), how can one get from actual history to conscience, from natural mechanism and its determinism to persons and the free moral agency of persons?

Perhaps these are enough to suggest the general tenor of the puzzles about Hobbes, his extraordinary, Jacobean prose and the two unconscionable monsters, the state of nature and the Leviathan, which he seems to be fashioning with it, the bitter realism of his "facts" and the strangely compelling tendency of his "values." How can one get from Hobbesian facts to Hobbesian values, and, incidentally, *are* there any Hobbesian values worth naming?

In a preliminary way, it is possible to flag HMR's strategem with regard to all of these puzzles of Hobbes interpretation. The strategem works like this. Since the condition of fully exploded natural aggression is not a condition in which distinct motives can be discerned or traced at all, it is not rightly called a condition of "egoism." Since, in the (counter-factual) state of nature, nothing is characterizable as mine or thine, instrumental or final, there are in that state no ascertainable "facts" upon which "values" may be called to supervene. Rather, what HMR finds in Hobbes is that the moral constraints on behavior are generated *together with* the condition of obedience or compelled order, without the former being reducible to the latter. It is as if human fear had made contact with itself through "a feedback loop" (i.e., inexplicably) and become, for the first time, reflexive, self-conscious. This condition, of fear turned against itself, might be described (if we were to pretend to stand outside human experience), as a quantum jump *in nature*. As with certain recent descriptions of the origins of consciousness, reflexive fear is not to be traced to any single, designated series of pre-conditions, political, economic, or other.

Reflexive fear or conscience, and socially directed force, thus arise together and are "two different ways of looking at the same moment of human existence" (p. 70). It is as if those who can agree to form a commonwealth can arise only through it. Those who can make a contract have already been constituted by one. And it is as if any "action theory" that tried to account for moral agents and moral persons in abstraction from this *original correlativeness* of social force and conscience would be taken by HMR to be either willfully or carelessly abstract.

The paradoxically non-local character of the contract and the parties to it is another aspect of what is being signaled when the contract is assigned an *a priori* rather than *a posteriori* status, in HMR's reading of Hobbes. In no set of predisposing conditions does the contract arise to set conditions for us all. In no space and no time, prior to its already being there to divide up the times and spaces, does the contract come to be. The contract and the contracting parties are close to being legal fictions, like the "We the People" of the Preamble to the U.S. Constitution, but, without such near-fictions as these, nobody *can* make claims of fact—and make them stick, that is.

It is along the same lines that HMR gives his response to the objection frequently leveled against Hobbes, that his indivisible sovereign admits of no checks and balances in the exercise of the powers of state. HMR's response would be that in the *Leviathan* Hobbes is refining a preamble to all past and future constitutions, not drawing up a particular organization chart for the distribution of power, as would be done in any actual constitution. The latter, HMR calls "philosophy of administration," and he does not think that Hobbes is writing that. The former, which he thinks Hobbes *is* writing, covers the extremely subtle relations between "ontology" and "sociology."

To put this another way: before we write a constitution that divides and allocates privileges and responsibilities, *we have to be in a position to do that*. And before we get into that "original position" (which would be considerably more originary than John Rawls's), there can be no one to be checked, nor any discrete quanta of powers to be balanced. There can only be self-consuming, undifferentiated, acted-out fear, that is to say, aggression, potential and actual. Afterward, but only afterward, one can assign times and places to separate responsibilities and persons.

This, the concretization phase, is also the last phase of HMR's argument with respect to Hobbes. What must be borne in mind is that, up to the present point, no locus of responsibility has been found for the contract and the parties to it. Rather, what is taking place in the discussion of laws one through three is a kind of creation (of reflexive fear and socially directed force) out of the unformed and void. Something fully formed, locatable, and accountable is not yet in the narrative. (The trouble with the whole controversy about whether or not the social contract is a function of capitalism is that it gets rather far ahead of the Hobbesian narrative. In the view of HMR, neither capitalist nor wage earner is in the narrative yet, neither feudal lord nor peasant, neither Roman senator, nor client, nor slave, neither hunter, nor gatherer. Before any of them can appear, first we need for it to be possible for agents to be there in any capacity, and for goods and services to be distinguishable at all as products of human agency.)

So persons have to be argued into being, for someone must take responsibility for whatever has happened and whatever is going to happen. Also, someone must have witnessed it. But nobody knows what the words "person" and "moral responsibility" mean, unless they take their meaning from moral constraints, and vice versa. *Therefore* the next laws of nature, laws four through nineteen, must be touched upon and explicated sufficiently so that persons get something to do and moral responsibility gets some beings to care about it. This is in marked contrast to David Gauthier's suggestion that the next sixteen laws are peripheral and mostly "need not concern us" (*Logic of Leviathan*, p. 56).

On HMR's reading, the Hobbesian "person" is not just a function of the concentration of power in a sovereign, but is also a being who tends teleologically toward the accomplishment of moral ends. The closing discussion, of laws four through nineteen, plays over these simultaneous meanings of "person," politico-judicial and teleological, in sovereign and citizen alike. Here it becomes manifest that no one, sovereign included, can be a "person" alone. Personal *authority* is likewise both representative and delegated. Only as such can it assume the mask of the provisionally disinterested third party, or fourth party, the moral person, to whom private quarrels can be turned over for arbitration.

The upshot is that neither "egoism" nor "altruism" will be starting places for the serious moral philosopher. Egoism is a retrospective posture. (Only after the contract is in place can we tell who has failed to respect it.) Altruism is a derivative posture. (Only after people's interests have been sorted out can we tell who has acted or may act in a disinterested fashion.) The whole discussion of the moral order has to start earlier and go deeper.

As was noted at the outset, "Hobbes's Secret" is a piece of philosophical writing in the meditative tradition, in that it does not so much drive forward toward wrap-up solutions as ask the reader to confront himself in the course of confronting the text. The demands that we have made on Hobbes, that he bridge the imagined worst case of the fact-value gap, and of the behavior-agency gap, are turned back on ourselves as readers. Who and what are we? How did we *get in a position* to make these territorial-classificatory or philosophical demands? What, by the way, is the difference between the terminological-territorial and the philosophical? Is it Hobbes's fault, or the fault of capitalism, or of Cromwellian England, that the demarcation lines between each kind of claim, behaviorist and moral, tend to look wavey and moveable, as one draws closer to them? Or do the very questions exhibit, to the meditative questioner, these moving lines of demarcation? "Hobbes's Secret" thus plunges the sensitized reader into a more focused and enlarged reflection on the very conditions that make possible these old and unfinished controversies.

Spinoza's Way

Toward their close, the several discussions in "Hobbes's Secret" converge toward a brief account of the sorts of acts for which people can take responsibility, because in the social contract there is to be found an instantiated moral order. "Spinoza's Way," the second part of *The Consolations of Philosophy*, is a deeper examination of those acts. It is deeper in the vertical dimension, looking to discern their relation to realities that are absolutely ultimate. It is deeper in the experiential dimension, attending to their textures and cadences, and the sense that such acts make concretely. It is thus the completion of the work of the first part. There is a story of the interrelation between the first and the second parts that HMR did not live to underscore, but I think that without disturbing the text it can be lifted out of this second part of *The Consolations of Philosophy* and studied here.

As to the history-of-ideas side of the question, whether Spinoza and Hobbes *meant* to imbue the notion of agent responsibility with the same meaning when they separately investigated it, and whether the real-life, historical man-without-a-country Benedict de Spinoza thought that in his *Ethic* he was continuing the same line of inquiry pursued earlier by sometime man-without-a-country Thomas Hobbes in his *Leviathan*, well, the following excerpt from HMR's inquiry may help to establish its genre, and to put such questions inside temporary brackets.

> The word "responsibility" would be an uncomfortable word in the context of Spinoza's thought. I do not know whether the word would have a legitimate status in purportedly faithful rendering of a significant term in Spinoza's Latin and/or Dutch text. Nor does it matter. What we are dealing with here is the problematic of convergent tendencies in the history of moral ideas. That history is more like a geological scenario than like the saga of the strife of concepts. When the tendencies are not convergent, then they are stratified one upon another, and thus spiritually cognate to one another, when they are not igneously fused to one another, yet discernible to introspection, in the heat of historical action. (p. 128)

Evidently rejected here is a Hegelian reading of such texts as showing forth "the saga of the strife of concepts." Rejected as well would be a [Lewis S.] Feueresque, Freudian reading of the works of major philosophers as exhibiting symptoms of involuntary influences. Rather, I think this says that, before he wrote this book, HMR had found out the following experimentally: If one starts trying to practice Hobbesian "political responsibility . . . toward our parthenogenetic commonwealth, and social contract" and Spinozistic "responsibility toward ourselves, and our duration" (p. 129), one will find them in tandem, as practices. If one then looks vertically "upward" and "downward" at ultimate explanations, one will see why. And if, while engaging in them, one attends to the practices themselves, dispassionately, as kinds of awareness in motion, one will see why again. "Spinoza's Way" is, then, HMR's attempt to make these experimental findings more generally accessible.

Now, it is a fact in the history of ideas that Spinoza believed Hobbes to have made a mistake when he, as Spinoza thought, had citizens transfer their natural right to the sovereign irrevocably. From this it is clear that Spinoza did not *take himself* to be working in tandem with Hobbes in the sense of HMR's finding to that effect. But whether, had he read "Hobbes's Secret" (where the transfer of natural right is found to be contingent on the sovereign's incessant submission to the moral laws), Spinoza would have stuck by the interpretation of Hobbes that is on record for him is not a question that stops HMR from saying what he has to say—though he is certainly not unaware of those kinds of unanswerable questions. (See HMR's note 8 to Part Two.)

Similarly, whether Hobbes would have congratulated HMR on his fine interpretation of the *Leviathan*, or speedily disavowed it, belongs partly to the biographical question of what a controversial author, beset by his times and his troubles, permits himself in the way of gratitude toward his appreciators.

In *The Radical Spinoza* (New York: New York University Press, 1979, p. 50), Paul Wienpahl maintains that "we do not have a definitive text of the *Ethic*." If this is so, then it would not be possible, where there are textual ambiguities, finally to settle the question of what Spinoza intended. If, however, one imagined, counter-factually, that a definitive text of Spinoza's posthumously published *Ethic* were available, which would settle for the warring translators such problems of ambiguity as, say, the number of the attributes of Substance (either infinitely many infinite attributes or—as some commentators hold—two attributes infinitely spread out), I think that "Spinoza's Way" could live with either such settlement, having generally made sufficient advance provision for either.

So, without suggesting that the nice questions of translation, author's conscious intent, and history of ideas are peripheral to the serious study of Hobbes and Spinoza, or that HMR thought that they were, finally one reads philosophers in the light of what one thinks important and true in philosophy itself. For example, Jonathan Bennett, in *A Study of Spinoza's Ethics* (Indianapolis: Hackett Publishing, 1984), reads Spinoza as *instructively failing* to solve the hard problems of the relations between necessary truths of logic, mental terms, causal laws, and contingent facts. He reads him that way partly because he just does, and partly because Bennett thinks that those would be among the more interesting and deep questions for philosophy to tackle. As he notes wryly, "I am not writing biography. I want to understand the pages of the *Ethics* in a way that will let me learn philosophy from them" (p. 15). On the other hand, when the time at last comes for Bennett to take in Spinoza's view of the mind's eternity, the third kind of knowledge, and the intellectual love of God, Bennett's philosophical conscience forces him to decry all that as "an unmitigated and seemingly unmotivated disaster" (p. 357). He does not pretend that Spinoza would follow him here. And he does not see how he himself can possibly draw back.

From the standpoint of HMR, on the other hand, the fashionable approach to Bennett's questions, concerning the relations between necessary truths, mental terms, causal laws, and contingent facts, turns them all too frequently into filing and sorting operations, which would be assigned by Spinoza to the second kind of knowledge, the kind concerned with getting things done just the way we want them done. While there is nothing inherently nasty or shallow about procedural knowledge—indeed, it's indispensable—for HMR the philosophically interesting questions are about *what to do with ourselves* when we have provisionally finished with our instruments and laid them down. Addressing this question to Spinoza, HMR finds in him not just instructive failures but a method and a way. It's a way to discover "why and how we are alone with what we are" (p. 102).

From the start of "Spinoza's Way," it appears that we are in a more enlarged world than we were in "Hobbes's Secret." In the latter, social contract, conscience, and collected government power appeared together, more or less *ex nihilo,* and on these depended persons, the social order however it might be structured, and the natural order under whatever theory it might be described. The point of this Hobbesian sequence can be expressed as follows: Unless people are going to treat each other with minimal decency, nothing else can possibly be figured out or put in its proper place.

Hobbes's is creation out of chaos, but the Hobbesian chaos is not the primeval *apeiron*. Rather, it is the ever-present possibility of *human* moral and prudential breakdown. In HMR's "existential" reading of Hobbes there is no account of what exists outside of the social contract and the black hole into which man, with his better hopes, can always disappear. But something must exist, after all. The big metaphysical texts may all be human artifacts, the questions and the answers in them human artifacts likewise, but if there is any objective truth about the external world, it would still have to be *discovered*, not willed. The good news is that the natural order is still infinitely sustained. Outside the circle of the social contract, there is a larger circle.

In the course of "Spinoza's Way," one finds progressive clarification of HMR's view of the relations between the two circles, one of which is completely inside the other. The social contract is seen by HMR as an act of self-insertion of the humanized or moral order into an infinitely regnant divine order—*not* itself notably moralized. Both of these orders, the moral and the divine, are, however, eternal. They are not a matter of "framework" or "point of view." When in Genesis 18:25 Abraham asks God, self-insertively, "Shall not the Judge of all the earth do right?" he shows that he has seen the eternal objective relations between the two circles, and seen how to affect those relations. Namely, *insistently*, self-insertively. This—though not HMR's example—carries, I think, something of his point here.

Now to apply such a thought to Hobbes's *Leviathan* and Spinoza's *Ethic* is new for Hobbes interpretation, as we have seen, and rather new for Spinozism, so far as I know. To cover the areas described by his Hobbesian and Spinozistic circles, however (his wheel in a wheel), HMR advances by tracing the meanings and purposes that Spinoza attaches to the different grades of *knowledge*. In pursuing this course, he does just what any serious Spinoza commentator would have to do, since Spinoza's way is incontestably a way of knowledge. There is in any way of knowing a built-in progression. One knows more or one knows less. One moves away from ignorance. So the question is, what sort of progression is built into Spinoza's way of knowing?

From the commentators, there are answers on offer to the question of the kind of way or progression traversed by Spinozistic knowing. Many have taken the Spinozistic progress to a scientific one. They read Spinoza as implicitly endorsing the ideal of a technically improved and rationalized social order, where ignorance and superstition have finally gone down for the count. That would be a pseudo-Rosicrucian or proto-Masonic ideal of progress, which certainly belonged to the imaginative iconography of Spinoza's forerunners, Bacon and Descartes, and of Leibniz, his philosophical descendant. Nor is there any doubt that Spinoza himself was a strong polemicist for the Modern, as opposed to Aristotelian, findings and method in the natural sciences. So, to take the scientific approach to the knowledge question in Spinoza is to do something that, on its face, looks in line with Spinoza's own thinking.

Furthermore, the science-minded approach to Spinozistic knowledge affords these sophisticated commentators a field (philosophy of science) for their works of clarification, here brought to bear on Spinoza's supposed seventeenth-century confusions. For example, there is Spinoza's famous confusion of contingent causal and necessary logical relations, and this can perhaps be cleared up. It is sometimes said of Spinoza that he did not fully face the truth that many particular facts or items are not as such directly deducible from whatever is most general or necessary or law-like in nature. (Why the broad Spinozistic distinction between finite modes and the durational order on the one hand, and infinite modes and attributes and the eternal order on the other, doesn't take in this truth, isn't fully clear to me. But it's clear enough that Spinoza had not taken in the aforesaid truth in the language used currently by philosophers of science.)

The last defect gets remedied, for example, by E. M. Curley, in *Spinoza's Metaphysics: An Essay in Interpretation* (Cambridge: Harvard University Press, 1969), who writes that contingent facts may be subsumed under "accidental generalizations," and these in turn under "true nomological generalizations," the latter ranging over "all members of some class of objects . . . not defined with reference to some particular time and place" (pp. 51f.). A similar reheating of Spinoza for contemporary appetites is done by Jonathan Bennett, by whom the contrast is drawn between "the infinite chain of finite items" and "a finite chain of infinite items" (*Spinoza's Ethics*, p. 113).

Once these confusions imputed to Spinoza have been straightened out by the science-minded commentators, the knowledge progression becomes likewise a straight one, going from first-level "vague experience" to third-level "scientific intuition" in Spinoza, and, in contemporary paraphrase, from *ad hoc* explanations to "accidental generalizations" to "true nomological generalizations" or the "finite chain of infinite items." In consequence, the only truly puzzling thing in Spinoza for these readers would tend to be the exalted, climactic tone of the last book of the *Ethic*. They might be inclined to suppose that in making his high claims for the results of effective self-therapy, Spinoza was either exaggerating, self-deceived, or had got hysterical. (A clear exception is Stuart Hampshire, in *Morality and Conflict* [Oxford: Basil Blackwell, 1983], p. 56, who seconds what he believes to be Spinoza's recommendation that we try where feasible to enjoy the free aspect of our psyche, which is able to contemplate the "intelligible connections of thought," and also the aesthetically satisfying relations between micro-structures and macro-structures in nature. But this rare enjoyment would be more nearly accessible to specialists in the intellectual disciplines, in the view of Hampshire.)

By contrast, HMR sees Spinoza as addressed to everyman, not merely to the specialist, be that specialist scientific or mystical. So all this, the view of humanity as progressing toward a science-based utopia, the view of third-level knowledge as equivalent to comprehension of established scientific theory, and the view of self-therapy as leading to detached enjoyment of the world disclosed by science, all this would be part of what HMR's interpretation is contending *against*. It *must* be contended against if HMR is to make the case for Spinoza's way as a way of being oneself in the first person (not, as in scientific description, the third person), within the eternal, moral constraints of the social contract, constraints to be insisted upon by each one of us, again in the first person, in the face of the whole divinity-filled universe.

In other words, in the science-minded approach to Spinoza, HMR sees evasion. And, of that kind of evasion, he finds Spinoza himself *not* guilty. For example, for the science-minded, one's present situation can be evaded in favor of the improvement-saturated future (or, more recently, the technologically menacing future). The dangling threads and general cloudiness of one's present moment can be evaded by focusing on the technical proficiencies that one is about to acquire. The foreseeable boomerang effects of these improvements can be discounted until the day of moral reckoning, which is to say, until later. Of course, all these evasions need not take place. But if they don't, another outlook is required, supplementary to the science-minded one. One has to pull out of the fast lane. By contrast, it can be said that, wherever Spinoza's way is heading, it is not heading into the fast lane.

What, then, is one supposed to *do* with oneself, in between bouts of technical proficiency? Or, to put it another way, how is one supposed to *be* oneself? What does art have to do with this question, or physical fitness, or yogic practices that purportedly conduce to paranormal powers and the divinization of consciousness? These are among the questions addressed in "Spinoza's Way."

Let us begin with the last-mentioned option. If there is something non-technical to be known on Spinoza's way, is it that all subjects and objects within the multiplicity of nature are "really" one and "divine"? For there are commentators, for example Wienpahl is one, who have taken Spinoza to be a philosopher in that mystical tradition. Wienpahl's view is that, at some point along his way, Spinoza's increased self-understanding disclosed to him "that there are not Substances. Particularly he saw through the idea of his own soul or identity. In a word, he was an egoless man" (*The Radical Spinoza*, p. 94). Of third-level scientific intuition Wienpahl writes that it is the "awareness of a thing with the cloud of words and other images removed. . . . One who knows intuitively may be likened to a Buddha" (p. 116).

For HMR, there is also evasion in this. He was not so much sceptical about the promised rewards of meditative practices, or reports of paranormal phenomena, as *resistant* on other grounds. One has to be oneself, bliss or no bliss, cosmic consciousness or no cosmic consciousness. When all is said and done that can be done along those lines, the moral order has still to be defended, distinctions of mine and thine have still to be respected, slanders have still to be detected and exposed, and credit has still to be given where credit is due. If one does all this, does all that belongs to virtue, one is not beyond good and evil. If one fails to do all this, on the ground that one has risen beyond good and evil, one is (or is becoming) evil. These determinations cannot be evaded. Cosmic consciousness may be a great thing, but it is not an excuse.

As to whether personal identity is real, or made up, the answer here seems to be that it is both. It is real *when* it is made up, but one can decide to forgo one's identity, leave one's boundaries undefended, one's obligations unmet, and slide all the way toward a oneness with everything that is strictly speaking slovenly. One's identity is composed partly by making the decision *for* an identity, and by all that follows from it. The social contract comes into one's decision to have an identity, since these boundaries and obligations are *or eternally ought to be* mutually recognized within a human community. Whether *en tant que philosophe* one concedes this or not, the body makes these admissions, and gives one away, by looking conscious when one pretends that one "meant nothing" by what one did.

> The locus of the real action can only be adjudicated by human conatus; and this will be an ethical decision. What did I mean when I raised my arm? Did I mean anything? Granted that I am not to be burdened with precising a meaning that I do not yet know, and perhaps am afraid to know, nevertheless I am not allowed to take refuge in the posture that I did not mean *anything*. Who or what does not allow me? My body does not allow me: the object of the idea that my mind is, that does not allow me. (p. 139)

What there is to know, then, is this: "knowledge of the third kind is a mere luminosity, astigmatic or otherwise, of the presence of the social contract in the order of human determination" (p. 157). By "astigmatic" is meant perspectival, biased, with human interests to defend, interests disclosed and interests as yet undisclosed. God, being infinite, has no limited perspective on things and has no particular interests. But, for all that, he does not swallow us up in his irresistible largeness. He vouchsafes us, rather, the causal order, within which our own meaningful resistances can be effectively moralized. God, being innocent, has no internal reason to be moral, unless, perhaps, by our efforts, we have given him a reason. ("Shall not the Judge of all the earth do right?" *we* have said.)

If we have tainted God's innocence and our own by the effort of self-moralization, one thing would be worse than what we have done by spoiling paradise. "Take the taint away from it, as the metaphysics of radical purification or salvation would seek to do, and that individual loses the coherence essential to the very concept of himself, and Substance becomes a history of tiredness; ultimately of self-exhaustion" (p. 170). If, by the yogic practices of divinization of consciousness, or kabbalistic practices for the divinization of the world, we *could* literally overcome the world, we would also overcome ourselves, and with us, all the possibilities of differentiation. God himself may thus have a moral stake in our keeping him at a certain distance. If we disappeared into him, good and evil might disappear with us.

If a mystical divinization of human consciousness has been ruled out as the goal of Spinoza's way, what about the goal (or subsidiary goal) of optimal physical fitness, within the very causal order to which we self-individuating human beings have been assigned? "As for the simple ideal of good health, there was of course no reason for Spinoza to be opposed to it, since he did not have it, and had an early death, like many of his contemporaries, from lack of it" (pp. 159f.). On HMR's view, the body "fitted for doing many things," which Spinoza praised, is a body whose actions are fitted into the self-given constraints of the social contract. It is not HMR's example, but one may think of the nicely balanced ledger books, for what was due one's neighbors, for what was due to life in the wild, for personal expenses, kept by Henry David Thoreau, who never jogged or lifted weights, who was ailing all of his adult life. One tends to approach one's invisible ledger books with especial reluctance, but, as they say in the physical fitness business: no pain, no gain.

Is art also among the evasions? Art is among the examples, or preferred illustrations, by means of which HMR takes us close to the kinds of things Spinoza means, and does not mean, by action. But it would be perhaps unnecessarily anticipating his narrative to say any more about it than I have already said here. There are climactic discussions of *rites de passage*, weddings, deathbed scenes, and of pain, which come even closer than art to presenting us with examples of what is meant here by the kinds of action that coincide entirely with

Spinoza's ways of knowing. But I think that the subtleties of these discussions can now safely be left to the reader to follow.

Henry M. Rosenthal

I was in Louisville, the Old Kentucky Home, my father's birthplace, for the first time in October of 1985 to read a paper at the Forty-Third Meeting of the American Society for Aesthetics, being held that year at the University of Louisville. Professor Charles Breslin of the Philosophy Department there had most kindly consented to drive me around those streets of the town that would have been familiar to my father when he left Louisville in 1921, at the age of fifteen. Alone of four brothers and a sister he had been sent—not to the University of Louisville or Chicago—but to New York City, to begin his college years at Columbia University. He had been marked out by his parents for the seminary, which among other things might possibly have been the payment on that ticket to Columbia.

We stopped at 1211 Second Street, the narrow, unassuming, three-story brick house where he had grown up. Professor Breslin stepped back quietly and waited, head down, while I stared at it, and the dark red roof corners self-adjusted, imperceptibly, into eternal congruence with the frame of my father's almost-comical, sad memories. "They kept collie dogs," I muttered, inconsequentially. Henry M. Rosenthal was one of five children of immigrants who were part of a transplanted Lithuanian-Jewish community within Louisville. The elder Rosenthals had had few illusions and many painful experiences. They had been factory workers in their youth and small business people in their best days. They had by no stretch of the imagination realized the American Dream. Professor Breslin drove to the banks of the Ohio River and explained to a puzzled New Yorker how the flood of 1937 could have done what it did do to their small family business, which is to say—wash it away.

In my father's mind there was blended an association between civic responsibility and metaphorical power that was, I believe, typical for boys who had grown up in Kentucky when he did, and for some decades after that. Fellow Louisvillian David L. Pearce, who had been his philosophical junior colleague and had also shared, at a distance of three decades, the same English teacher at Male High School in Louisville, William F. Bradbury, has talked with me of the way the nineteenth-century American literary tradition was conveyed then so as to show, in the English language, the convergence of "the sacred and the common powers." My father could read the Bible in Hebrew, but if it came down to English translations, he had a strong

Kentucky bias in favor of the King James Version. Standing with my host on the steps of the courthouse square, the jailhouse across the street as hardfaced southern reminder of where you went when you lost the case, reading the long paragraphs of graceful, eighteenth-century Jeffersonian prose incised in stone there, "I see," I laughed to Professor Breslin, "when you've got Kentucky in you, you *never* get it out."

Elinor Grumet's article, "The Apprenticeship of Lionel Trilling" (*Prooftexts* 4 [1984]: 153–73), gives a picture of the brilliant Columbia class of 1925 that matches to the letter such family lore as I had assembled, with the additional help of conversations with Meyer and Lillian Shapiro, Clifton Fadiman, and James and Elsa Grossman shortly after my father's death in 1977. Grumet's article is about the intense, dialectical friendship, and dialectical parting of the ways, between Henry Rosenthal and Lionel Trilling,

> both seniors at Columbia College, and best friends. They served together on the staff of the *Morningside*, Columbia's literary magazine, under the editorship of fellow-students Clifton Fadiman and Victor Lemaitre. The magazine had quality; Whittaker Chambers, Jacques Barzun, John Gassner, S. Guy Endore, and Meyer Shapiro were writing for the *Morningside* those same years; Louis Zukofsky and Mortimer Adler had appeared in its pages several years earlier. Trilling, Rosenthal, Fadiman, and Herbert Solow were known as campus intellectuals, and meeting often in the Hartley Hall dormitory, came to be called the Hartley Corporation. . . . The members of the Hartley Corporation brought one another into Elliot Cohen's circle at the *Menorah Journal*.
>
> The friendship between Lionel Trilling and Henry Rosenthal was especially significant in Trilling's development at this time. Their long conversations confirmed them in the values they shared: respect for excellence and critical intelligence; faith in the primacy of literature and works of imagination, and the fresh superiority of their own observations about cultural life. They were also bound by the issue on which they finally differed—the implications of being Jewish. First Rosenthal, then Elliot Cohen, were Trilling's Jewish higher education, and Trilling's later public pronouncements about Jews and Judaism were the heuristic observations of these friends adopted by Trilling as conclusions. Their fiction and essays in the *Menorah Journal* show that young Trilling and Rosenthal encouraged each other's tendency to ground their work in autobiography. (p. 154)

> . . . The young writers on the *Menorah Journal* considered Henry Rosenthal their mad genius, their James Joyce, the one most marked for literary success. (p. 157)

My father's correspondence and diaries of the period show an extraordinarily self-sure intelligence operating within a circle of friends who were marking themselves out for what they expected might well be something very notable. They sent each other short stories, literary pieces, for suggestion, for criticism, for reaction. They reported to each other on crises of health, of mood, and of confidence in their shared vocation. They pooled triumphs and hopes. They honed each other's prose and moral sensibility. They sharpened each other's taste in friends. They seemed to have been aware not only of a general level of talent, even brilliance, but of a shared passion. It was not just the passion for "excellence" and for authentic self-expression. Almost all of these men, and some of their equally gifted wives, had an ethico-aesthetic passion of a quite particular kind.

Almost all of these people in the inner circle, future taste makers to some part of this nation, were as it happened Jews. (They appear described under code letters—Rosenthal is "A" and Trilling is "F"—in an article by Mark Van Doren published in the *Menorah Journal* in 1928 that is actually *titled* "Jewish Students I Have Known"—13 [June, 1927]: 264–65.) Being Jewish apparently accounted in part for the shared problematic of their young lives, and in part for their eventual divergence from the author of this book. The problem was not just one of careers, of being the first Jew who had to walk through virtually any door that was worth walking through. The problem was a problem of *voice*. What was one supposed to say, in an English-speaking culture where the Jew was universally deprecated, in one's own voice, and how was one to retain its timbre? America undeniably opened opportunities to young Jews, but it did not automatically take away the denial of worth that Western culture more generally still insisted upon. It is only intellectuals or perhaps religionists who can face such a problem, because it is a problem of the spirit.

As Grumet notes, the men of this group did consider my father to have been their "genius," to have had the most talent. Whether they retained that opinion in later years, or decided that he must have burned himself out, I don't know. No doubt their opinions varied. In any case, it is absolutely not for his daughter to enter into those comparisons. But I suspect that he naturally commanded their moral center of gravity *then* because of them all he was the most American, in grain and tone and culture, and also *then* the most believing a Jew, the only practicing and believing one, I think. And he was absolutely serious, absolutely sincere, almost beside himself with seriousness and condensed, articulate passion.

In 1925 he entered the Jewish Theological Seminary of America. In that era of self-conscious enlightenment, the line between the secular and the parochial was very broadly drawn. Having once stepped over it, from the career standpoint it would be considered very hard to come back.

In those years he met Rachelle Tchernowitz, the (beautiful) daughter of the authority on Talmudics and Jewish jurisprudence, Chaim Tchernowitz, who was known by the pen name Rav Tsair, "the Young Rabbi." She was passing through New York because Rav Tsair had recently been invited to come to New York from Lausanne, Switzerland, to join the faculty of the Jewish Institute of Religion as professor of Talmud. My father had been introduced to her only briefly but wrote in his diary the same evening, "I have met the woman I am going to marry." As was generally the case in respect of the essentials, he wasn't wrong. They talked about Proust and things like that. He had no money. They took long walks. So, on September 15, 1927, my father married the girl that he loved, and his marriage gave him a certain personal equilibrium that is perhaps the celebration in the world of the devotion of the private heart. But his peers, the stellar members of the class of 1925, some of whom would have pretty happy marriages too, were going on without him to five-star American careers.

The relations between success and integrity, success and authenticity, are not that easy to sort out. It has been my no doubt limited experience that most very successful people are not very interesting. Henry M. Rosenthal, to the last day of his life, was very interesting. Those in the philosophic profession who loved him best have suggested to me, not so much with a word as with quickened undertone and furrowed expression, that I had best not touch on this matter, that I had best gloss it over somehow, in presenting the story of his life. But it *is* the story. It can't be glossed over. On the other hand, the theologian Thomas Altizer has said to me about my father, "Goodness is the real scandal of the world."

Perhaps as his death, and other people's relative successes, recede from the present hour, the scandal too will subside.

In 1929 he graduated from the seminary and became first Religious Director of the 92nd Street YMHA in New York City, and then founder of its well-known Adult School of Jewish Studies. A program announcement of 1938–39 lists Paul Tillich, Reinhold Neibuhr, John Herman Randall, and others of like eminence among the speakers. He received the Ph.D. in philosophy from Columbia in 1940 with a monograph, *On the Function of Religion in Culture*, published by Columbia

University Press in 1941. His advisor at Columbia, Horace L. Friess, wrote in a Foreword, "One has to go back to Emile Durkheim's work to find comparable reflections on the basic relations of religion and society." In the same period he wrote with Horace Friess an essay titled "Reason in Religion and the Emancipated Spirit: A Dialogue," contributed to *The Philosophy of George Santayana*, The Library of Living Philosophers, vol. 2 (Evanston and Chicago: Northwestern University Press, 1940), which was singled out for praise by Santayana in an essay in the same volume, "Apologia Pro Mente Sua."

In the years that followed, before and after he left the rabbinate, there were continuing contributions to the *Menorah Journal*, essays, reviews, and short stories. There was an occasional piece on Jewish themes in *Conservative Judaism*, or in the *Reconstructionist*. Later, when he had become a professional philosopher, there were introductions to Plato and to Berkeley, in *Foundations of Western Thought* (New York: Knopf, 1962). To read almost any of these scattered evidences now is to be struck by their extreme sophistication, and by their high historical authority. There is also, in all of the earlier essays, a quality of quasi-deliberate inconspicuousness, a typical avoidance of finality, a refusal absolutely to declare oneself. There is an apparent decision to live alongside others in the world of shared partial realizations, where everybody had better muddle through, without the mirage of excessive clarity.

In 1945, with two small children and no long-term prospect of gainful employment, he left the rabbinate and didn't look back. It had given him intellectual access to the letter of Jewish thought, and to the practical and public implications of religion in the hard world of fact, during the war years. He and my mother had brought over ten refugee families, despite the State Department and everything else. He would remain, thus, out of touch with the requirements of an American career of the period, but in the deepest touch with his times and what they required. Besides, he *was*, as Thomas Altizer has also said on another occasion, "a man of God." Whatever one means by that saying (he believed in God, but as a saying its accents are a bit more southern than my father's were ordinarily), there was no mistaking the reality it referred to when one was around him. He was extremely modest. He was extremely truthful. Whereas numbers of academics have egos about as big as Texas, he did not have an obtrusive ego at all. He had none of the usual male solemnity about being male. He was often extremely worried that he might not get to do, with his talents, whatever those talents were meant to do. But, on the other hand, he was temperamentally unable to accommodate to any purpose whose shape was not natively fitted to his original purposes in life. Sometimes he was naive, in thinking he saw affinities where there were none, or in refusing to notice affinities where they might safely have been acknowledged. But the intransigence was not a put-on. It belonged absolutely to his structure, and he was rather light about that. He was radically unpretentious, yet gentlemanly.

Between 1945 and 1947 he was Extension Lecturer in Social Philosophy at the Cooper Union. During the following year, 1947–48, he was named a Guggenheim Fellow. He joined the faculty of Hunter College to teach philosophy in 1948, retiring as Professor Emeritus of Philosophy at Hunter College of the City University of New York in 1973. He had been a loved and demanding teacher, with a resolved sense of pedagogic honor, a stabilizing and a civilizing influence on several generations of students. He had, as one of his students wrote at the time, "an intelligence that I for one shall never see again."

He was never president of the American Philosophical Association. He did not publish a long list of combative articles on the most controversial issues of the day. He did not chair national committees to look into this or that. My sister (Lucy Rosenthal, the novelist and literary critic), has said of him, and it is perhaps his finest epitaph, that "he never made a useful friend." He was not a materialist. He was never a positivist. He was never a linguistic analyst. As to the successor movements, those he had not yet heard of, it is conceivable that some of them would have roused him immediately to prepare the most exquisite feasts of irony. If he was an existentialist, he was not anybody's existentialist in particular. While he cared all his life, and with great intensity, about Jewish existence, its defense, and its intrinsic vocation, to say he had not cottoned much to Jewish organizational life at the period (World War II) when he had best known it is to put it mildly, and he detested the clergy of every stripe. He was not a practitioner of any mystical discipline that I know of, but he believed "that it was blasphemy to believe it possible to blaspheme God" (Grumet, "Apprenticeship," p. 157).

He did not believe that the race was to the swift. Though in his youth he had been capable of a painful sense of frustration, eventually that too was sublimated and transcended as, in later years, he came to understand what one pays for what one gets. He offended many people, though not deliberately.

In 1973, the year of his retirement, he began the present work. The original typescript was completed in May 1976. That summer, he gave it to me to read, in the small town in northern Maine where he and my mother had their summer home. Over the winter of 1976–77 we would meet to discuss the Hobbes section. Where I raised questions, and he agreed with the sense of them, he would rewrite a passage here or there, add a note, or expand a particular argument. When he died in the summer of 1977, this editorial conversation about

Hobbes had been about concluded, but a similar conversation about Spinoza had not yet begun.

During the year following, 1977–78, I reworked the Hobbes manuscript, with his additional interpolations, into a finished typescript again. At that time I also included a number of editor's footnotes and appendices to Part One. Some of these were interpretive, but mostly they contained excerpts from HMR's 1973 and 1975 longhand drafts and notebooks for the Hobbes essay. I added them at points in the text of *Hobbes's Secret* where the earlier material seemed to me to give interesting supplementary insight. Although I reviewed the notebooks and longhand drafts from which he prepared the Spinoza essay as well, those preparatory materials did not seem to me to contain illustrations that would make the finished argument more visible. So I left the Spinoza essay to stand as he had left it.

As it happened, it was not feasible for me effectively to pursue the project of getting that manuscript published at that time. It was not until the spring of 1987, ten years later, when I had a more solid philosophical foundation on which to stand, that I could reread it with fresh eyes and really see what kind of a book it was. At that time, it was also clear to me that his 1976 version had been the more integral and in that sense correct version.

Accordingly, in preparing the manuscript for its present publication, I dropped all but one of the appendices and some of the earlier editor's footnotes. However, there now had to be occasional new editor's footnotes, incorporating some of the material from the 1977 version of the Hobbes essay. A few of HMR's responsive editorial interpolations were left in the body of the text, where they appeared to read more smoothly and to be more clarifying there. Elsewhere, wherever it seemed to me to be the version most faithful to the book's style and intent, I restored the 1976 version of the Hobbes essay.

In going over the Spinoza essay, I continued to agree with my earlier decision not to use editor's footnotes incorporating earlier supplementary materials. But I did decide, finally, to add editor's footnotes of an interpretive kind to that essay, adding them at transitional points where—had he lived to continue our conversation—I would have liked now to ask him to elaborate or to clarify. The purpose of these footnotes is simply to supply the reader with arrows or road signs at intervals where the argument on the page appears so highly condensed and subtle that one wants to remember and to flag the unbroken continuity of the path it traverses. Overall, however, what became clear to me as I reread the book in 1987 was that death had not interrupted his work, merely punctuated it.

A word about that last event, to which eighteenth- and nineteenth-century biographers used to give their deepest attention. He had been idiosyncratically "failing" over his last winter and spring, although an exhausting series of medical tests were turning up negative results. Occasionally I would see him at a distance, coming across a room, and think, "Something is terribly wrong. He looks almost transparent." But then I would forget the feeling. I was to come up to Maine the week of July 25, and was speaking to my mother long distance the Sunday morning before. I was then embroiled in a long union grievance that had gone to arbitration that spring, and expressed to her the sad sense that my father's failing health was somehow "my fault," that is, one consequence of that struggle in its effect on him. When he was told what I'd said, he turned to her, saying emphatically, "It's not true. But even if it *were* true, it would be worth it."

In the same conversation I mentioned that a number of collegial and other friends were expressing their concern about him. When that was relayed, instantly he suggested the following mail notification: "Family of Rosenthal happy to announce obsequies for Professor Rosenthal postponed for a little while, but will keep in touch."

Watching his face, getting, as my sister said, "younger and younger" in that week that he was dying in the Maine Coast Memorial Hospital, I jotted down in my diary, "How palpable are the considerations of the spirit. How insignificant are all these venal and perverse life structures."

The last complete sentence that I heard him say was in answer to the intelligent young physician at the hospital who had just begun to give him oxygen and was then asking him how he felt. In one of his unfathomable remarks, this last time about life and death, and resurrection, and medical technology, my father drawled, . . . "I feel *real* resuscitated."

PART ONE

Hobbes's Secret

Hobbes's secret is that he is not a political philosopher; nor a mechanist–materialist; nor a royalist, that is to say, not a die-hard one; nor a philosopher of law, natural or unnatural, in the way in which these oblique contraries have been traditionally implied, nor a religio-political scientist of Euclidean method who eventually finds himself in equivocal advocacy of a "divine" polity (this has been long ago suggested[1]); nor most of the several other roles imputed to him by the variety of learned and able commentators that he has had the benefit of. That is, he is not *characteristically* any of the things aforementioned. He sometimes slips into one of those roles, and therefore for a time, in one or another of his texts, wears the mask appropriate to it, and even gets to look like the mask worn. But this is an occupational hazard of a seventeenth-century thinker, when the party lines in the republic of ideas were not as strictly drawn as they later became.

Lines were drawn, strictly and consequentially enough, on the field of civil war, or when it came to a question of money; but not when it came to such puzzles as First Cause and what a man ought to do to avoid despair. As to the first question, God, on the thresh-hold of deism, became a blanket to cover it, rather than an answer to it. And as to the second, the question of despair, people began to be unsure that there was anything to be done.[2] So it was not unusual, it was almost inevitable, for a gifted and fertile rhetorician like Hobbes to try on various broad-brimmed ideas as if they were hats. Monarchism (or the fusion of "natural" and "feigned" personhood defended in *Leviathan*, chapter 19)? Of course. Where else should it be lodged, what later came to be known as executive power, with its requisite omnicompetence and charisma, if not in a crowned king, exempt from regicide? Money-power? Where else should it be lodged, if not in them that have it, namely, in the peers and commoners of any realm, who, having relative freedom from the overwhelming burden of the social contract, have had the time and the wit to get money and hold it? And what makes men move? Why, motion of course, as Dr. William Harvey has so well shown in his treatise on the motion of our most moveable fluid. Spare the rod, and the man, who moves anyway, will not move civilly. So let it not be spared.*

A seventeenth-century philosopher—with one or two quite rare exceptions—is thus spared the necessity of follow-through: he need

---

*Later, HMR will argue for the dependency of Hobbes's theoretical account of motion on those absolutely primitive social arrangements that will apply the rod to potential predators. Once kept in line, the potential predators can if they like become theoreticians, whether of the mechanistic or some other bent. This is an allusion to that argument. Page references for HMR's citations from Hobbes's *Leviathan* are to the Michael Oakeshott edition (Oxford: Basil Blackwell, 1946).—*All and only the notes at the foot of the page are the editor's.*

not, in fact he almost dare not, be consistent, for if he tries to be consistent he will end up with nothing to say, it having all been said, either by the Schoolmen or by Aristotle, and none of these great-voiced mouthpieces is to our liking. They have made it difficult for us to breathe. Far better, then, Dr. Harvey and the laws of motion that have taught us, once more, how to breathe.

But if Hobbes is not, in any satisfactory sense, what we have said he is not, what is he then, and where is his ill-kept secret to be found?

He is, of course, a *metaphysical moralist,* long after Plato and long before Kant, and precisely in their line, in that the label applied to him (since nobody likes to use the label, it has to be applied) means just what it optimally would when applied to them—namely, no more and no less than the refusal of reductionism. Morality doesn't come from below and cannot be read back down there; it comes from nowhere. A metaphysical moralist and an inspired, ironical, scolding prophet, which suggests that he was also something of a mystic, if quite a hardheaded one; that is to say, neither orthodox nor a roundhead. But a hardheaded mystic was the easiest thing of all to be in the seventeenth century, when people were really scared; and Hobbes, by his own account, the most scared of them all, from earliest on.[3]

This secret of his is hidden, from himself provisionally, in the thirteenth to sixteenth chapters of his rhetorical masterpiece, *Leviathan: or the matter, forme, and power of a commonwealth ecclesiastical and civil.*

Note two things about the bravura of this title, typical for its time, and being itself, as titles then tended to be, a substantive statement. One: that the commonwealth to be described, that is to say, produced for us, will be a true Aristotelian individual, a substance of matter and form, and self-moving—that is to say, having power. As political rhetoric it has no great point other than as metaphor; and as metaphor its functions will be something of a surprise, when they come.

Two: that the flourish of this title is truly esoteric; it conceals by revealing. For there is no such thing, not really, and not truly, as an "ecclesiastical" commonwealth. If it's a commonwealth, it's not ecclesiastical but civil; and if it's literally ecclesiastical, that is to say, if God is there or purports to be there—as the emperor's new clothes purport to be there—then it's not a commonwealth, but . . . . But what? It depends. If the purporting of God to be there (in the commonwealth and either homogeneous with it, as in most allegedly "peaceable kingdoms," or supervening to it, as when God's vicar summons an emperor to Canossa) is through a self-styled churchdom of God, why, this is truly regrettable: it is no less and no more than a veritable kingdom of darkness. This is the obverting of commonwealth; it is worse than the state of nature because it is a *compact* with darkness, and *in* darkness, if that be possible. But if God is there, in the commonwealth, in the broader and more diffuse sense of the metaphor of God's being anywhere, then that commonwealth in which he is there in that sense is no commonwealth at all: it is merely the realm of Infinite Power. One does not talk about that realm, except in the language of the theological physics of the Book of Job, which is a poor substitute for silence, though perhaps the best we can do, and not very good physics at that.* For physics, too, and its ordinary language, must wait upon the covenant and remain derivative from it.

So it is clear that our commonwealth, if it is to be one, has to be civil; not otherwise.

And the civil commonwealth that Hobbes is talking about is something less and something *more* than Infinite God. It is less because it is *mortal;* and, God knows, the one true infinite God is by no means mortal. But it is *more* because it has *initiated* and, for all we can know to the contrary, thereby *created* the world that we know, and insofar as we know it; and sustains us, insofar as we are sustained, in our knowing of it.

There is no *empirical* evidence whatsoever that the immortal God, the infinite One, can be credited with anything like that. On the contrary: so far as our empirical evidence goes—and it is the only evidence that counts—the truly infinite and immortal God seems to be given over to *counter-productiveness*. What he is directly, visibly, and overwhelmingly responsible for is *death*. In the phenomenology, so to speak, of that, above all, is Infinite Power made manifest.

Hobbes does not say that; but then his own theological physics is largely unexpressed and has to be read between the lines of his *political* physics—which supervenes upon and in the upshot entirely supersedes the theological physics it recoils from. If we try to reconstruct what the ontology was like before the recoil, we get the dim outlines of an ontological field in which there are two poles: commonwealth and death. Where, then, is God, with his infinite (and "immortal") power? If we place him in commonwealth, where, in a well-ordered ontology, he belongs, then he knows his place, all right, and had better keep to it; or else. But then he is not so infinite, is he?, except in the emptiest of metaphors. So we place him elsewhere, in the non-time and non-place that surround commonwealth, that were before it, in

---

*HMR is not suggesting here that the author[s] of the Book of Job would have done better to observe a discreet silence. In the face of Infinite Power, we do protestingly "express ourselves." The difficulty is that, when we do so, it is never quite satisfying, nor quite to the point. We are, so to speak, out of our depth.

the preternatural state of nature that came before commonwealth, and that will come after it, if there is really any before and after outside of commonwealth. But this non-time and non-place, whether before or after, or neither, they are where death is. So the un-covenanted, pre-political, and a-political God is, for Hobbes, never "dead": he *is* death. "All other time," says Hobbes, in chapter 13 of *Leviathan*, "is PEACE" (p. 82). Our problem is to *make* that other time, for there is none of it by God or by nature.

Whence, then, the origin of this cosmogonic, proto-physical, city-building commonwealth? We know well enough that it sometimes *looks* as if it originates by "mechanism": from motion to aggression to death wish to quantum jump to peace wish and life force and covenant. (If that be mechanism, then all you have to do is let Michelangelo's Sistine God be reduced to his jointed parts, as in Vesalius's overgrown anatomical drawings of human figures, and he too will be a mechanism.) But this disguising look comes simply from the rhetorical necessities of having a beginning, a middle, and an end. And to put your alleged beginning back in the laws of motion—inertia, acceleration, collision, and composition—effectively disguises the fact that there *is* no beginning: the beginning has no beginning; the origin originates, but has no origin. Nobody made God—every child knows that, once he has asked the question—*but nobody made the commonwealth either*. The commonwealth was always there.

We are prepared, then, to see *Leviathan* in its true literary perspective: *Leviathan* is a *commentary* on the self-defining origins of things. Like most such commentaries, it reads backward as well as forward, and eventually comes to supersede the significance of the thing commented upon. In the end we shall read this, philosophically, in a syntax that is structurally analogous to the sophisticated, recently provenient, translations of the first lines of Genesis in the Hebrew Bible: "In the *beginning* of God's creating of the heavens and the earth . . . etc." So Hobbes's *Leviathan*, read backward: "In the beginning of Leviathan's (i.e., commonwealth's) creating of the *eternal laws of nature* . . ." and, for that matter, of anything else you can think of.

The commentary (i.e., our text of *Leviathan*) begins, innocently enough, with praise of sense, motion, and externality. Of these three prime objects of Hobbes's metaphysical respect, sense is clearly derivative and perhaps of no ultimate importance. For soon sense becomes phantasm or imagination, then memory, and soon thereafter passion, and after a while, forgetting what it was to begin with, it becomes *reason*—denying its origin, and unable to account for itself. Unless reason, like other things in these elusive and perhaps ambivalent ontologies, has all along been its own reason for being: in that, for instance, sense is *speech;* it is that which makes sense.

If sense is to be a problem for a philosopher, it is an insoluble one: problems that swallow themselves are always insoluble. Hobbes, who has openly admired Plato above all other philosophers, must know this discouraging fact about the problems of sense. But condemned, like all others, to deal with the five operators of being—seeing, hearing, touching, tasting, smelling—under one manageable general name for them, he chooses, purposefully enough, the name sense. Give it a name and, like the animals in the Garden, it will make sense.

What is sense derivative from? Ontology is much given to the dyadic form of reproduction, and here, as elsewhere, it takes two to make a derivation: in this case, motion and externality. Hobbes's word is "without." Note, then, that we are not dealing, not yet, with "subject" and "object," but with "within" and "without." Is the difference crucial? It might be. If one is a radical ontological egalitarian, as Hobbes is, it might be important, consciously or unconsciously, to eschew any distinctions which have the taint of the morally or politically invidious about them. One must wait for the commonwealth, or the laws civil, to introduce such distinctions; and then they are all right. When there is a *motion* of the without upon the within, then you have sense; and the rest (including "subject" and "object") follows.

But what is the difference between the within and the without? Are we involved, all at once, in pre-physical metaphysics, in such questions as what, or when, is time? and what, or where, is space? As if everybody does not know the difference between here and there, then and now. And Hobbes knows the difference as well as anybody: time has to do with before and after—before and after what? "Before and after" one occasion or another within the absolute framework of moving occasions guaranteed by the covenant. Motion by itself establishes no sequences, since you would not know whether something is going backward or forward until you have a position whereby to judge the matter. Such a position, and its relation to the motion which it observes, is the "occasion" one must have in mind. One takes a position as a decision in time. The reliability of this temporal position-taking is guaranteed by the covenant which, like common sense itself, knows nothing of an "uncertainty principle." Before and after are now both inexorable and indefeasible.

Motion and withoutness fall quietly into place, dialectically speaking: The without is the viewpoint of the other, one being always other to the other. And motion has its laws, of course, complex but harmonious: the first law being inertia. Inertia is the inclination to stay where you are, or, much the same, to move where you are going. And from the viewpoint of the other, whose occupancy might be threatened, however remotely, this looks like a resolve to go faster than you have a right (by nature) to be going, or in other words, *acceleration*. So that the first two laws of motion—inertia and acceleration—are the same as themselves. Collision is natural and inevitable. The composition of forces, or their vectorial resolution into an accommodation—would this already mark the inception of "covenant"?—does not seem quite so inevitable. But then the *a priori* never does: notice the interminable length of its usual demonstration, as in Kant; and neither does the commonwealth. Nevertheless, there, all at once, it is.

I have made short shrift—for that is what it amounts to—of Hobbes's cool clichés about body and space, time and motion, because they take one nowhere—if the destination be physics, whether astral or terrestial, and in my opinion cannot be supposed to be taking one anywhere—except, through the state of nature, that Slough of hardheaded Despond, to the very brink of commonwealth.*

It is my further belief that this road was mapped only after one had traversed it. Everybody in the seventeenth century knew that the world—meaning by that, everything in it and on it, since the world as the notion of a physical globe is a mere "phantasm" (pending the materialization of a space ship to view it from) of the geometer's or navigator's calculus—"still does move." What difference did it make? It made a difference, then as now, to such men as Huygens, Harvey, Galileo, Leibniz (who was quite capable of denying it while, at the same time, making the most of it), and Newton, to name a few of many. And it made, or might have made, a difference to Aristotle, Ptolemy, Aquinas, Dante, and the others to whom is variously imputed another "phantasm" about these matters. But to Hobbes, and his most serious purposes, it made, so far as I can see, no difference whatsoever.

---

*This non-derivation of the commonwealth from Hobbes's mechanism is discussed at greater length in the 1977 version, where HMR argues in more detail for the following points: "From the standpoint of the later history of scientific mechanism, Hobbes was not a contributor. . . . Whether he knew it or not, Hobbes was in principle unable to describe and explain the cosmos in accordance with a theoretical model. . . . So Hobbes's motion is filtered through experience, and even if it were not so filtered, is not in its origin quantifiable. . . . Committed as he is to the principle of *order*, as the final cause of an existence worth the name, Hobbes . . . in the nature of his case, must be equally committed to an explanation of the cause of order; since the concept of order, being a concept of beginning-middle-and-end (even if the termini of the series are located at infinity), demands that it either contain or be invested with a first agent of order, the god, mortal or immortal, of the series in question. And if the series be the 'series of all series'—such as, e.g., motion—the demand that the series at all costs *begin*, is all the more urgent.

"Nothing less than *Leviathan* itself, the logical redeemer from the 'state of nature,' is competent to provide this genuinely causal beginning to the series of interminable 'accidents' (for such they are in Hobbes's physics) called motion."

If the world did not move, as it does, the state of nature would still be there, ready for postulation. Close-packed inertial occupants of "phantastick" spaces would still, and then, be in the stasis of absolute collision. The argument for commonwealth would still be there.

Hobbes's concept of motion, such as it is, is a sub-argument in the great argument for the commonwealth.

What about his concept of "withoutness"? What is it an argument for?

I submit that it is not an argument for something else. It is the argument, in the form of a productive though provisional metaphor, itself.

Withoutness is Hobbes's great reminder, contributed to human forgetting, a forgetting that goes on all the time in accordance with natural law. It alone, this ontological dimension of externality, survives all projects of nihilation of the world. So it is affirmed in the first paragraph of *Leviathan*, where, with a backward glance, no doubt, at Descartes' specious project of nihilating the world by taking inauthentic thought about it, Hobbes reminds us that the putative otherness of our project survives its hoped-for success.* The without is there; it does not matter where; it could even be here; but it is still there. So a holy moujik like Tolstoy, having seen the light, might argue that the kingdom of God is within you, but God is still king. So the withoutness of Hobbes's careless mechanism might be anywhere, but it is still beyond you. You can't reach it to snuff it out, not even by taking thought. After all, thought is only the phantasm, or side-effect, of motion; and motion needs withoutness even to have become what it is.

Do not confuse—one soon becomes tempted to do so—withoutness with space. Space needs an occupant to be what it is, and for lack of a better name we will call that occupant, any occupant, body. But what, or who, is the occupant of the without, of withoutness as such?

This is the productiveness of Hobbes's metaphor: ostensibly mechanistic, but quickly assimilable to the ontology of reverence. Out there, in withoutness as such, is Infinite Power. Infinite Power is also overwhelming, but that is only because and when one happens to get in its way, as we all do. There is another name for Infinite Power. We

---

*The first paragraph of *Leviathan* reads: "Concerning the thoughts of man, I will consider them first *singly*, and afterwards in *train*, or dependence upon one another. *Singly*, they are every one a *representation* or *appearance*, of some quality, or other accident of a body without us, which is commonly called an *object*. Which object worketh on the eyes, ears, and other parts of a man's body; and by diversity of working, produceth diversity of appearances."

all know that name. We do not speak it lightly. We should not speak it at all, except by covenant, except under commonwealth. At that point God, if it seems convenient to metaphysical speculation, can be said to have an invisible body, and can be said to occupy the space of infinity, wherever that may stretch or contract. All this speculation, however, under the laws civil—which are competent to see to it that doctrinal passion does not become subornation of subversion.

At this early stage of our anxiety by nature we do not "clearly and distinctly" see or know the difference between God and death. They are both quite overwhelming, and both in total and exclusive occupancy of their respective domains which seem, to the mortal eye, to overlap somewhat.

These matters are given to us as too much for us, except by revelation, which, if it is to happen has "already" happened and is therefore under authority. We do not seek, or pray, so much for enlightenment as for an opportunity to be obedient. At all costs it is necessary to conquer our fear of death, and our fear of God. We shall therefore construct a mortal God, its name *Leviathan,* and endow it with sufficient immortality for its purposes by renouncing any right to revolution—the democratic form of regicide—so long as *Leviathan* preserves and protects our natural right, which had better remain a little bit ambiguous and a little bit obscure.

Such, in brief, and roughly paraphrased, is the short happy course of Hobbes's metaphor of mechanism: from the phantasm of body without, to the phantasm of sovereignty, mythic author of the laws civil, by which we keep death temporarily without, at bay.

Hobbes's peculiar power as a philosopher is not simply the power of his rhetoric, in itself no mean power, but, more substantivally, his net effectiveness in what may be called the transvaluation of labels. This, of course, is what I mean by his secret, and, so viewed, it hardly matters whether he intends his secret or whether it is there in spite of himself, and hidden from himself. Perhaps this transvaluative efficacy is what distracts some of his commentators, and draws them into controversy about his alleged psychology of self-interest and power, for instance, and its frustrating or even nihilating influence upon his alleged moral doctrine of self-abandonment to obedience; or the incompatibility of his moral doctrine, such as it is, with his political notions ("obligation" or "sovereignty," but not both; or could it be a weak alternation in this case?); etc.

With regard to such issues I am, in effect, submitting that it is a philosophical displacement to impute to him a "psychological" doctrine at all. Aristotle has one, John Locke may be said to have one, David Hartley had one, the Mills, father and son, had one or two, etc.; but Hobbes doesn't have one in the self-standing and more or less technical sense in which these others have. What he has is a *doctrine of man,* in the sense in which Plato had such a doctrine (though not exactly Hobbes's), and if anybody wants to call that a "psychology," he is of course free to do so, for one purpose or another; but it would not, on the other hand, be at all helpful to think of William James's *Principles* . . . as a "doctrine of man."

In Hobbes's case the doctrine of man falls between, and is the product of, his ontology—commonly spoken of as his mechanism—and his social contract, commonly spoken of as his politics.

And it is in his doctrine of man, as well as in his proto-physics, or doctrine of "body," that his transvaluative touch shows itself. Is Hobbes a "mechanist" in his psychology? Well, why not? Who wasn't? But mechanism is a two-forked word. On the one hand it is a mere label for the descriptive mode. Describe anything so that you can in principle quantify it, or diagram its identifiable units and subunits, or reproduce the description for the purposes of application—and that is all it seems necessary to mean by describing it mechanistically. In this sense, angelology—but not theology—can be as mechanistic as anything else. But mechanism also suggests, and this is its more serious thrust, the mode of *derivation.* If one consistently (more or less) derives from *below,* one is a mechanist in the more serious sense.

And if one derives (whether consistently or merely persistently is here of secondary import) from *above*—what is the appropriate label for that mode of derivation?

It is in this sense—questions of strict consistency apart—that the case of Hobbes demands to be labeled, if not exactly a case of transcendental idealism!, at least as a case, in his doctrine of man, of Platonism. Hobbes's doctrine of man *derives from above;* from the parameters of the covenant—in the last long run these will turn out to be the "eternal laws of nature"—and not from the "laws of motion," which are neither physical laws nor physical motions, but metaphors for existential passions either sanctioned by or outlawed from the commonwealth.

The case of Hobbes might turn out to be even worse than that —worse, that is, than a case of Platonism—when we get to Hobbes's "eternal laws of nature." But one thing at a time.

Are we to conclude, then, that the covenant is the final cause of Hobbes's "nature"? And of all that moves in it?

We remind ourselves that if covenant, or commonwealth, is a final cause, it must also, in some appropriate sense, be a first and efficient cause of those effects, physical and otherwise, that we are seeking to account for. It will now be helpful in the further diagnostic of Hobbes to bring into the picture two other metaphors of analysis: one from Plato and his mythic ontology in the *Timaeus,* and the other from Durkheim's sociology of knowledge as in *The Elementary Forms of the Religious Life*.[4]

The name for the artificer, or maker, of the ontic world in Plato's *Timaeus* is *demi-urge*. The sybilline, rather gnostic, sound of the word does not fool the dictionaries: it means, they say, "public craftsman." What "public craftsman" meant in the ordinary language game of Greek usage I do not profess to know. But I do not see what in the nature of the case precludes *demi-urge* or "public craftsman" from meaning "hired hand," or conceivably "mortal god," or *agent* of our own ontological *authorship*. The swift dialectic of relation between *author* and *agent* is one of the basic operators in Hobbes's scheme of things that he will come to later: in and after the covenant, when it is about to move across the instant of transition, from *in foro interno* to *in foro externo*, from the interiority of conscience to the exteriority of armed and resounding might.

If Plato's *demi-urge*, manipulating the forms, the harmonics of the cosmic tonic, and some exudate from the receptacle as well, may be plausibly offered by Plato as a "public craftsman" to us all, it is not evident why Hobbes's "mortal god" cannot serve as a *demi-urge* in buskin. He is certainly public enough. Our question up to now has been, is he, or it, the craftsman of the order of existence? And our answer has been, with repetition, affirmative. The difficulty that might lie in seeing Hobbes in the light of Plato's metaphor is that Hobbes's artificer—as I claim—of the order of existence has done his job retroactively: at least so it would appear from the order of exposition in Hobbes's text.

But this is an old story: that the order of exposition is the reverse of the order of ideas. And it would be bold indeed to argue that the case is any different, most of the time, in Plato's text.

What now does Durkheim contribute? What he contributes has an unsurprising explicitness: so much so that one might think my argument, hitherto, has been more apropos of Durkheim than of Hobbes, and that relating one to the other is mere extrapolation.

But that is not the case. It should not astonish us to have to maintain that the sociology of knowledge is only implicit in Hobbes, but that to find what is implicit in his epistemology is the only way of making it coherent; that is, of making sense of it. Otherwise, his epistemology, such as it is, falls radically apart into two helpless halves: one half being, as alleged, a mechanist (or perhaps materialist?) sensationalism, and the other half an *ad hoc* rationalism, brought up out of the blue to ground the social contract on.

We impute to Hobbes, on the contrary, a thoroughgoing ontological coherence that governs his text esoterically, but unmistakably. Why it should be esoteric—that is, in need of hermeneutic surfacing

—seems to me a secondary question, having to do with psychological and linguistic factors perhaps endemic to the century, or perhaps peculiar to Hobbes's time and circumstance, talent and temperament, but not decisive for our main question: Does the *order* of existence in Hobbes make sense on any grounds other than those of derivation from the formed commonwealth, or from its "Form"? That is to say, from the archetypal or prototypical *Leviathan,* the primary and most primitive occupant of Hobbes's ontological space? In Hobbes's ontology the difference between archetype and prototype would not matter.

Durkheim has helped our argument when he concludes, for instance, that the idea of *physical force* is of *social* origin.[5]

What, then, has Durkheim meant by "social"?

He has been describing certain pre-literate ("primitive") people of the Melanesian archipelago and related regions, and precipitating his "elementary forms" out of the sediments of aboriginal culture available to an anthropologist's inspection. These sediments seem to be safeguarded by the religio-specialist custodians of these cultures, as if on reserve for preferred anthropological tourists. The forms of preservation are for the most part *ritual* forms: that is, they are modes of public agitation, in which a formalized theatrical method is at work, alongside an exploratory intention—in effect, a kind of "waiting for Godot," the *deus absconditus* of the human psyche, who makes everything happen, provided only that it does not matter.

The technology of action in the ontological realm of Durkheim's "elementary forms" is expressed by a great, whirring, noise-making device called a "bull-roarer."

The "bull roarer" works no miracles and makes no magic. It is merely a reminder of a primordial ontological covenant that is always taking place.

Out of the ritual of enactment and activation, climaxed in and by the great, humming roar of the "bull roarer" (as if the people of Durkheim's islands were committed to showing how Vico's cosmogonic thunderclap really comes about), out of this and sundry such rituals there derive all the categories and sub-categories of conceptualized effectiveness: specifically, such notions as force, cause and effect, space and time, power, control, etc.

Who and what is this "bull-roarer," both the peculiar, louder-than-life whirling-and-whirring wind-instrument that is used in the ritual, and the ritualist who "roars" through it?

Is he or it the social contract? Is he mortal god or demi-urge, artificer and manipulator of the phantasms that are to be denied, that is to say, brought under rational control?

How far do the phantasms, the working myths and metaphors,

the "pre-scientific" constructs of primitive cultures, go in their hermeneutic possibilities? Do they go as far as making contact in their phenomenological significance with the mythic dialectic of Plato, with the impatient pseudo-mechanism of Hobbes?

Hobbes thus requires us to attend to the relations, presumptively intrinsic, between sociology and ontology; one might go so far as to say, between poetry and truth.

It does not in any way alter our question, as it comes into focus, that the relevant sociology is a proto-sociology, as in Hobbes as well as Plato, and that the relevant ontology is implicit and to that extent esoteric, as at least in Hobbes.

In considering the question, certain reminders will be helpful: One, that Plato's all-out excursus on ontology, the *Timaeus*, was a sequel to his all-out address to sociological and "political" questions in the *Republic*. It was a sequel in conception, in Plato's mind, in the setting laid out for the discourse, and, so it is alleged, in the continuum of theme.

Just why these ontological phantasms of the *Timaeus* should be offered as a sequel to the rise and fall of ideality in the City, as well as to the subsidence and eruption of continental island-masses—give or take an Atlantis or an Athens or two—is not altogether clear; but that is more or less our question; just what is the relation of administration to ontology?

This leads us to another reminder: that neither Plato nor Hobbes is in the strictest sense a *political* philosopher, if by that is meant a philosopher from whose ideas, such as they are, one can develop an architectural rendering, if not a blueprint, of the actual, conceivable workings of a political community, large or small. In other words, concrete political philosophy is philosophy of administration: what you do when, and how you do it, and *who* or *what* has the doing of it.

In this sense, John Locke is a political philosopher; so, probably, were Calvin, Machiavelli, and Marx, at least in his *Civil War in France*, *Eighteenth Brumaire . . .*, and *Critique of the Gotha Program*, if not in the *Communist Manifesto*.*

---

*HMR's 1975 longhand draft extends these remarks as follows, in part:

"The moral, perhaps, is not to be a 'political philosopher,' but if you are interested in *government* above all, as some people are quite innocently interested in pipes and valves, in the strategy of position of a raised hammer, in the angle of least friction of a sharpened edge, etc., then your proper field is not philosophy but what has been called political science, or even political economy, or even that branch of social psychology called the theory of justice.

"My argument here is that Hobbes is not *essentially* interested in any of these matters, though of course he is secondarily and inadvertently interested in them all. We are all interested in everything, and spend half our wasted lives sweep-

There are no doubt numerous other political philosophers, and it is not claimed that they are a highly select company. The claim is that Plato and Hobbes are not among them, though it may well be that Plato is such a little bit more than Hobbes is (in *The Laws*, for example). The test is a simple one: *not* what is the first step, *but what is the second step?*

There are lineaments of that second step, and perhaps even of a third one, in the *Republic*, as well as of the crashing fall that comes after; but there are no second steps discernible at all in the *Leviathan*. The mortal god takes only the first step, howsoever "giant" that first step might be.

This, then, may serve as our clue to the relations between sociology and ontology.

If philosophy, in its traditional self-assertion to be first or prime science, is making a meaningful and to that extent indisputable claim, then there can be no ultimate and no hard-and-fast distinction between the sciences. Let us pursue the truism a step or two. Tennis and billiards are worlds apart, but they are both games. It is only when we get to an action like chess that the question becomes obscure. There might be some question as to whether chess is truly a game, or merely a form of savage, if non-traumatic, competitiveness: a kind of bloodless war. But about tennis and billiards there can be no serious question: they are both games, in a sense in which language is *not* a game.

In a roughly analogous sense, ontology relates to the specific, and subordinate, sciences as genus to species. What is the genus about? For lack of a better word, let us use Hegel's word, *Geist*, or spirit. One could offer a neologism, such as self-consciousness about one's relation to reality, or to history (again Hegel's), but neither the

---

ing our interests under the rug. Hobbes is no exception. How can he help being interested in the mystery and horror of regicide and decapitation, in the poisonous rage of near neighbors against one another, in treachery and flight, in the difficulties of personal hygiene under the circumstances of relatively impoverished exile? Of course, he is interested; as who of us would not be? But it is not these and such interests that drive him to philosophize . . . to raise up an ontological construct called Fear Itself, or Infinite Power, and refuse it any role in our lives, and derive the world from it.

"What drives Hobbes to philosophize is a crucial moral impulse: to rescue human existence from madness. This is achieved by laying down clear categories [as they are called] of difference, and maintaining them. Existence is by no means an impossible Cartesian dream; but very conceivably it is a nightmare. The question whether we are not really dreaming is a ridiculous question that has never been asked in good faith. But the question of how to wake from a nightmare is a very serious question indeed.

"Hobbes's motivation in philosophy is to show us the grounds of wakefulness."

circumlocution nor the clumsiness would provide any particular advantage.

From the viewpoint of philosophy, then, all things, of both life and art, address an ontological question to the mind: political theory and sociology more than most, since in them both the synthesis of life and art is conspicuous, in the one case in respect to the efficient and formal causes—the organization chart of social, i.e., human, actions, and in the other case, the material causes, or the concrete results of human actions and relations as they crystallize and petrify.

In originating minds, like Durkheim's, a close study of the second steps inevitably leads back to an all-out suggestion as to how the first step was taken: sociology becomes a clear case of ontology —a case study in *Geist*—without quite realizing that it was speaking prose.

So much for the general, and unfortunately rather abstract, question of the relations of ontology and sociology.

The digression was unavoidable. If we are to place Hobbes's intention, whether esoteric or avowed (and from the point of view of what he actually made happen the difference is not all that important), and the execution of that intention in their proper case, we must maintain that Hobbes is not a political philosopher, but a sociological ontologist. Or, in short, an ontological thinker through and through. He lacks, in *Leviathan*, all concern with administrative substance. What he is concerned with is the substance of the *first step*, and the nineteen "eternal laws of nature."

Hobbes's ontologism, to make no further bones about what it is, comes out unalloyed and unmistakable in the pervasively *qualitative* character of his thought. If thinking, as, in his nominalistic mode he seems to want us to understand, is but pragmatic counting—what is the sum that our counting aims at, or the real limit which governs it, other than, say, the infinity of methodological regress or the infinity of omnipotence by nature? If Hobbes's rational counting, that taking of prudent thought which is the best that sense can finally do, is a species of archetypal utilitarianism—what are the cardinal quantities which are manipulated in this unflagging operation of the mind by nature: are they units of happiness? But happiness by nature is a null factor, except in the form of power: and units of power cannot be counted any more than units of infinity could be counted (except in the same absurd non-sense in which Hobbes had tried all his life to get the incommensurate circle commensurately squared). So that, in the upshot, there is nothing for thought to count up, or to count toward; and all these fumblings of the mind by nature will acquire meaning only in that far-off but quite imminent event of the social contract, which comes to receive and absorb the collapse of nature, hardly to compute it. The awful distance between nature and covenant is infinite only until the one collapses into the other.

We have been toyed with. There are no quantities we are destined, or condemned, to live in. In human destiny, given that we are going to have one, there are only qualities: that is to say, absolute differences of kind, not of degree, these absolute differences being quite capable of shading into each other, should occasion require.

I do not mean my interpretation of Hobbes to be more sybilline than his circumstance warrants. But what is at stake here is the fundamental, and if needs be, the underlying, character of his thought, which turns out to be uncommonly without benefit of numerical parameters: more so than Plato's. Plato had Pythagoras to be indebted to; Hobbes had, if anybody, only Plato.

The point is not that there are no "checks and balances" in Hobbes's political system (which, of course, is no system); it is, rather, that the "system" cannot be put on any kind of abacus at all. How many, or how much, is there—of what, in this alleged system? It is immune to statistic, or census, or computation. In it, there is only the grand and indivisible, pre-Platonic, pre-Socratic, Parmenidean One: the mortal god of sovereignty that does not allocate anything to anybody, for the anybodies that might conceivably exist under it do not count.

These matters are not merely the accidental results of the grandeur and carelessness of Hobbes's philosophical rhetoric: they are the result of something deeper than that, namely, his radical philosophical *egalitarianism*.

By nature, or in the state of it, all men are *equal*. And some are by no means more equal than others, because the differences, if any, do not count. In ultimate effect by nature, I am not only as good as you, I am better than you, which means that you are nothing; there is only me. The indiscernibility of differences is their equality.

One must seek an analogy, however imperfect, for the case, and the analogy that comes to hand is that of color, where the differences *are,* but do not count. The analogy is imperfect, because in the case of colors the differences are susceptible of reduction to angstrom units, and the like, but in the case of men, as of other components of Hobbes's ontological realm, if there are any other, the differences are equal absolutely, and irreducible.

Take, for instance, the case of *time*.

One is accustomed nowadays to make certain easy distinctions between various kinds of time: sidereal or geometric time, biological time, such as birds and reptiles have, psychological time, such as novelists and poets deploy, and existential or phenomenological time, as recently exercised by a variety of writers. There may, indeed, be many other possibilities of classification.

Traditionally, the time that is taken to be basic to the others is the first kind, sidereal or geometric time. One way or another this time is always expressed as a function of motion. Thus Aristotle's familiar paradigm on the subject, as cited, for instance, by Hobbes: ". . . *time is the number of motion according to former and latter*."

Hobbes takes his own definition of time to be close enough to Aristotle's, by which he means, presumably, that they are both definitions of *physical* time. In respect of time, Hobbes and Aristotle should both be mechanists. Thus Hobbes: "Wherefore a complete definition of *time* is such as this, TIME *is the phantasm of before and after in motion;* which agrees with this definition of *Aristotle*, etc."[6]

One could find a dialectical pathos in this kind of "mechanism," except that the mechanism imputed to Hobbes has never been self-imputed, and might even, perhaps, be disavowed if the issue presented itself to him, as it is alleged, historically, to present itself to us. What is evident, first, in Hobbes's short-shrift formulation of the matter (or "problem") of time is that all the varieties of time—specifically, the physical and psychological varieties, which in Hobbes's time would be inclusive of other sub-varieties—collapse into one: time is the phantasm of the motion of successiveness. But motion itself, at this stage of its being, is a phantasm of . . . .

We need not belabor the regressive redundancy. It is not peculiar to Hobbes, and in any case Hobbes is neither a mechanist, nor a metaphysician of time. That is to say, he has no special responsibilities to the category, and is not to be faulted for not having met them.

The significance of his remarks on time lies elsewhere.

Time for Hobbes does not appear to be that parametric constant which it ought to be, if one is going to stay out of epistemological trouble. Time is more like a dependent variable. The dependency, to begin with, is on the two quasi-constants: motion and its own phantasm, which is a by-product of more ultimate motion; or so one must, up to this point, assume.

But we have already seen that the parameters of motion, such as they discoverably are, are legislated into being by the social contract, to give the matter its short rubric made normative by Rousseau.

The best and the most that one can at this point say, then, is that in the underlying system of Hobbesian premises, time, motion and mental life are revolving functions of one another, with no one of these having a dialectical primacy over any other; or a more primitive explanatory status.

I believe that one is in effect saying that Hobbes's philosophical world is a world of *qualities*. Quantities, even a fundamental quantum like time, are for Hobbes quite derivative. It is not that "quantity becomes quality," as Hegel is sometimes read to mean, but that *quality* —if one keeps to the moving-staircase image of the matter—descends into quantity. The echo of neo-Platonic emanationism here is unmistakable and, to be sure, altogether unwelcome. But ontological types of thinker are open to this kind of contamination, and are answerable for its consequences.

Here is how, in an unguarded moment, Hobbes will use the word "time."

Hobbes is speaking, in chapter 13 of *Leviathan*, "Of the Natural Condition of Mankind as concerning their Felicity, and Misery" (p. 80).

"*Out of civil states*," he says, and the saying is to be graven on the mind,

> *there is always war of every one against every one*. Hereby it is manifest, that during the time men live without a common power to keep them all in awe, they are in that condition which is called war; and such a war, as is of every man against every man. For WAR, consisteth not in battle only, or the act of fighting; but in a tract of time, wherein the will to contend by battle is sufficiently known; and therefore the notion of *time*, is to be considered in the nature of war; as it is in the nature of weather. For as the nature of foul weather, lieth not in a shower or two of rain; but in an inclination thereto of many days together: so the nature of war, consisteth not in actual fighting; but in the known disposition thereto, during all the time there is no assurance to the contrary. All other time is PEACE. (p. 82)

Very well. Let us consider the notion of time.

The notion of time that underlies the "nature of weather" consists in an "inclination . . . of many days together," or, as in "the nature of war," in a "known disposition" toward an actuality, or actualization, that must, in the nature of the case, be already known to the mind.

It is evident that one cannot use the language of "potentiality–actuality," or the language of a developmental but pre-established metaphysics, without at the same time falling into that usage in which the priority of final and formal causes is necessarily assumed.

The underlying premises of the passage quoted from Hobbes sum up as follows: A "tract of time" is not a tract of before and after, which would have no identifiability at all, but is a segment of a certain kind of potentiality. It is the same thing, for discourse, as a *nature*.

The nature of the potentiality in question is known to us by virtue of our knowledge of the relevant actuality: whether war or peace, rain or shine. In the matter that really concerns us, the matter of war and peace, we know everything that is possible to know only under the condition of peace. For in the condition of war, there is "no knowledge of the face of the earth; no account of time; no arts; no letters; no society; and which is worst of all, continual fear, and danger of violent death; and the life of man, solitary, poor, nasty, brutish, and short" (p. 82).

Hobbes somewhat overstates his case. In the condition he is indicating—since it cannot really be described—we would not even know enough to be afraid. There is, I believe, a fairy tale of the brothers Grimm to that effect, concerning the unfortunate who did not know fear, but *our* awakening in the case Hobbes has in mind would not be so simple.

In short: time is a quality of existence. To speak of time in quantitative terms, a "tract of time," for instance, is mere metaphor. Literal usage is qualitative. "All other time," says Hobbes, "is PEACE." The meaning is that in the state of nature there is no other such time at all; and there would be, in effect, no meaning to the parameter "time" at all.

It is hardly necessary to add that this is not a physical doctrine. If it aimed to be such, it would be quite useless. It is, indeed, a *political conception of time*.

It is in that sense that Hobbes is a political philosopher. But this sort of political theory is the merest ontologism.

My argument simplifies as follows: Hobbes's social contract is not a decision about government—its origin and more plausible form —but a decision about the world.

Before the social contract there was, of course, some sort of world, since nothing can come from nothing (it would be hard to find in Hobbes as theologian any considered assurance to the contrary).

Hobbes's notion of transit from the state of nature to covenant has sometimes, and otiosely, been taken to be a historical passage. Taken that way, several familiar options would confront a philosopher. For example, shall the philosophy of history, which would now be entertained either explicitly or implicitly, be a philosophy of progress, either of linear or of spiraling development? History as the story of liberty, as in Croce? Shall it be a philosophy of recurrence? Or shall it be a philosophy of revolutionary, "bombs-bursting-in-air" self-transformation? Meteoric history, flashing across the sky into disappearance, as in Toynbee? Decline history, as in Tacitus, or decline-and-fall history, as in Gibbon? History, in the spontaneous theory of the man in the street, as the chronicle of the regrettable? Shall it be providential history, with eschatalogical possibilities at the farther end, and so forth? If any such options were present to Hobbes's mind at this point, they were well eschewed.

His thought has chosen not to be a philosophy of history. It would follow from that alone that the concept of state of nature is not historical, any more than the passage to covenant can be assigned a date. Hobbes's thought about the periodicity of human life is strictly qualitative and immanentalist. Human life becomes sociable and civilized in a way that is neither linear, nor successive, nor cyclical, nor extrusive from ulterior situations into the life of people. That desired state of human relations called covenant can erupt at any time and under various (if not any and all) circumstances, having always, when it does erupt, the character of spontaneity. A peculiar character that Hobbes sometimes calls "Reason." This spontaneous eruption is from an eternal threat, the name for which is "state of nature." The asymmetrical equipoise between "state of nature" and supervening covenant is all the philosophy of history that Hobbes's ontology enjoys.

Thus the some-sort-of-world before the social contract was and is unformed and void. The two tenses of reference—was and is—must both be invoked, since the world as formless void is neither a historical situation, though it might be considered a pre-historical one, nor a vanishing present. The world as formless void is more like time's potentiality as such. We have it always with us. It is the potentiality of time incompletely politicized. Give it a name in the language of psycho-drama and it is called the death wish. The final cause of the social contract—and that, of course, must also be its first cause—is to keep the death wish at bay.

It would be a mistake to assume that in the formless void of the world there are no human relations. Of course there are. We simply give to the category of human relations a Pickwickian extension, so that it comes to include—or, rather, becomes coextensive with—the world of non-relations, or of anti-human ones.

It would be a mistake to say that in the state of nature there is no morality. On the contrary: the state of nature exhibits the only truly universal morality that empirical speculation—and Hobbes's ontology is always quite empirical—can discover: the morality of *power*. It is not true, for Hobbes, that "power always corrupts," and absolute power corrupts absolutely, as Acton pointed out. It is rather the case that power is always by nature; and if it follows from that that corruption is the most natural thing in the world, that is merely the triviality of an enthymeme.

It is not that there is a "will to power" in the state of nature, but rather that even in that state—insofar as it is a "state," that is, a state of affairs, in any degree at all—there is a "will" to be *moral*.

Therefore the fundamental ambivalence of the first twelve chapters of *Leviathan*, and, more particularly, of chapters 6, 8, 10, 11, and 12: ranging broadly apropos of the ". . . Passions," of the intellectual ". . . Virtues," etc., of ". . . Power, Worth, Dignity, Honour, and Worthiness," "Of the Difference of Manners," and "Of Religion."

All these positivities or credit features of the human condition—which we begin with some knowledge of, if we begin with anything—call for description: *because nothing can be described at all* unless it is morally described.

This is the case even before the fiat of the social contract has made itself known, which it does not do until chapter 14 ("Of the First and Second Natural Laws, and of Contracts"). But the true state of affairs—the requirements of any given case—is known to description even before it is experienced by the senses.

In the older language of such matters, one tends to say that any *logos* is inseparable from the "value system" that is coextensive with it. But neither the venerability nor any possible upstart quality of the language of the matter alters the nature of the case: we cannot describe the world without, alas, moralizing about it. And if the world includes physics, as it is generally held to do, then we cannot describe physical relations without moralizing about them too. So much the worse for physics, as for us. If Hobbes were a classical Chinese cosmographer—which he happens not to be: he is only a political, or ontological, physicist—he would no doubt describe the laws of motion as being examples of good and bad manners, or even of morbid and healthy *yin* and *yang*.

(It has never, so far as I know, been made clear to us what happens to *yin* and *yang* in their ultimate exponential phase; but conceivably they do not issue in a social contract. It is equally conceivable that *yin* and *yang*, skipping the social contract, might come to rest in Hobbes's "nineteen eternal laws of nature.")

But it is the greatness of Hobbes as philosopher that his entire argument is that we skip the social contract at our eternal peril. If we skip it, we have nothing: not even physics, not even theology.

The ambivalence of chapters 6, 8, 10, 11, and 12, mentioned above, consists in this: If human reality is to be described at all, in any phase of its actuality or at any stage of its so-called development, it has to be described in moral terms. One does not falsify the matter if one puts it with utmost bluntness: *Conditions for description are always moral conditions*. In the chapters in question we are dealing with human reality before the social contract. In principle, we do not yet know that there is to be one, or that there *can* be one. The case thus far presented to us is one in which the "laws of motion" are governing. Never mind the hidden, Durkheimian question—how can there be "laws of motion" before there is a social contract, or without benefit of one? We have not yet come to that wisdom that enables us to see the hidden provenance of that question, no matter how or where we turn. Motion alone is, motion is as motion does; and what motion does, as soon as there are those lay figures called human beings on the set, is produce a peculiar human posture or expression called *hypocrisy*.

What could be more moral than that? Our rhetorical question is, of course, one that has the full benefit of the hindsight of the social contract. Before we are endowed with that hindsight, we do not quite know that "hypocrisy" is the name for it; and not knowing that, the only name we have for it is "virtue." E.g.: "power," "worth," "dignity," "honour," "worthiness" . . . and whatever else there is, such as "manners" and "religion."

But as we read the text, of the chapters mentioned, in which these excellences of the moral life are set forth, it turns out that they are all simply *different lines* (perhaps different frequencies) *on the spectrum of power*.

Now we know where we are at: power is of course just a somewhat resonant, shorthand metaphor for motion, seen from the standpoint of the "law of acceleration," which is merely inertia in a hurry. So that the excellences of the moral life just described are simply more-or-less convenient metaphors for the *power drive,* as it is sometimes called. Hobbes could have called it that; because the only function that these unabashed "moral excellences" have, at this stage of Hobbes's account of them, is to bring human lay figures into proper placement for the drama of the *state of nature;* that is, to show how their by-nature irrepressible and uncontrollable power drives lead all men, in the state of nature, to grasp for everything in order to secure for themselves the least of anything; so that if you cannot postpone the fear of death, you can at least ride that fear, or try to, against all others.

What is going on here? What kind of moral doctrine has been given us? A moral doctrine of ambivalence? Well, that would be one way of dodging the question, with a soft answer.

I consider that Hobbes's ambivalence, when he has it, is always, or nearly always, superficial. He is an incomplete philosopher—perhaps to be a philosopher is to be incomplete—but his doctrine always knows where it is going, even if he, its author, does not.

Where the moral virtues of the above-mentioned chapters are going is straight—as straight as the circumstances permit—into the state of nature. It is no different, in the dialectical principle of the matter, from having to pass through the Slough of Despond before arriving at the Heavenly City. I doubt that Hobbes wanted to arrive *there*. He only wanted to get to the social contract.

The ambivalence of an argument is merely superficial when it does not seriously entertain, and would ultimately refuse to accept, the eventual dualism that seems to be called for by ambivalence. In this respect Plato's *Timaeus*, for instance, is more seriously ambivalent, because the "Receptacle" and the Forms have a polarity to one another that is not easily subject to dialectical conciliation. It can be done, but it is somewhat forced. So one has few qualms, if a few regrets, about typing Plato, for trivial purposes, as a dualist.

Hobbes will resist such typing. Or at worst his argument easily by-passes the issue, and does so without embarrassment to its own substance.

This is what an uncompromising ontologism will typically do. It will have no traffic that can possibly be avoided with such topological formalisms as dualism versus, or in uneasy tandem with, monism; and the like. Ontologism that really means it will thus head as directly as possible toward either some sort of emanationism (of which neo-Platonism is merely an antique and more picturesque example, there being many others, both then and now) or toward a doctrine of *ex nihilo*.

A sociological or political ontologism has a third option, which Hobbes instinctively—that is, in the nature of his own case—has chosen: to stop short of both emanationism, which is poetic but absurd, and *ex nihilo,* which is agitating and empty. When you stop short of these two options, you are left only with human reality and its metaphysical possibilities. That is where Hobbes has come to rest. Averse as he is to philosophical melodrama, and altogether serious about the social facts of life, there is no possibility of a collapse of his argument into such eccentric, and sometimes hysterical, forms of human metaphysics as, say, the existentialist varieties of a recent day.

If we must type Hobbes—and there is only a quite provisional need to do so—we propose that his type is at the farther boundary of ontological humanism: where philosophy becomes strategy, and the strategy has to do with survival.

The mortal god wishes at all costs to endure. If it were mere *Geist*, or if, *per impossible,* it were immortal, it would not have that problem. But the mortal god is content with the problem that it has.

The problem is that of order. And the problem of order is complicated by the fact of equality.

That philosopher whose project of thought is necessarily an ontological one has two things to do in connection with the problem of order. The first is to assert, and if feasible to describe, the order of physics, or the natural world. Some philosophers do this last—Plato is an example, in his "later" dialogues, and sometimes at the end of a middle one—and some do not do it at all; as if it goes without saying, or is not as important as all that; or perhaps a desiccated state of empirical knowledge leaves them little to say.

Hobbes asserts what he knows, or what he must, about the order of physics with a spirited confidence that suggests enthusiasm. It belongs to the *Geist* of his time to be enthusiastic about mechanism; and, after all, few serious thinkers have been enthusiastic about God, or about the State, even when they believe in one or both of those metaphysical entities. In the age of Harvey and of Galileo it is both natural and hygienic to be enthusiastic about mechanism; but that does not mean that you are a mechanist.

The *Leviathan* has asserted the order appropriate to the natural world in its first eleven chapters. The abruptness and somewhat dismissive character of the assertions need not detain us. We are hastened along to the second aspect of the problem of ontological order: the order appropriate to, and required for, human existence.

As usual: what is second in the order of exposition has been first in the order of thought.

It is the covenant, or the social contract, that has *legislated*, or evoked by its logistic fiat, the parameters of motion, the structure of outside-and-inside for the housing of "psycho-physics," carried us across the paradoxical field of "virtues" that are merely by-nature, and brought us to the terminus of physics unredeemed: the state of nature as seen by a conscientious ontology that has seen the next step from the beginning. *A priori*, as it were.

What is the nexus for a conscientious ontologist between the order appropriate to physics and the order appropriate to man?

A myth will do, or an aesthetic conceit; but better than a myth is a fact. The fact, once more, is that of *equality*.

I would assume as a working hypothesis that the main function of mechanism for a political ontologist is to provide an underpinning from physics for the notion of equality.

A main difficulty in verifying that hypothesis would be, of course, that there are few, if any, examples of political ontologists to put alongside Hobbes for historical comparison.

There is Democritus, a relatively early example of a man who is ontological, or structurally radical, in his thinking, as well as mechanistic.

But Democritus can hardly be said to have a social contract in his thought—those early philosophers like Empedocles who manipulated enlarged constructs like "love" and "hate" came nearer to the idea of social bonding, or at least to a metaphor of it, but not near enough—and so the ancient atomist cannot serve, exactly, as a control on our hypothesis. We note that any interpretation of a proto-philosopher like Democritus is necessarily speculative, because of the fragmentary and sparse character of the texts attributable to him. In the last analysis the speculation has to rest on such thought attributed to Democritus as "Poverty under democracy is as much to be preferred to so-called happiness under tyrants as freedom to slavery" (fr. 251); as well as on the not-to-be-despised intrinsic nature of the case. Democritus's mechanistic materialism—that imperceptible but ever-present event of generative atoms in swift motion—goes hand in hand with, and would form the basis of a tendency toward, a sociological egalitarianism, or at least a leveling tendency toward ataraxia and away from hierarchical "excellence," in the implications of his thought for human existence; but a political configuring in this thought, if he had one, eludes our recovery.

If a thinker's motivation is an ethical one—that is, an agitating conviction that people should be better toward one another than they are—it is quite possible that his ethical egalitarianism comes to be extrapolated into his physics, rather than the other way round. This may well have been the case with Karl Marx, at his somewhat patchy ethical best, or, rather, with the satellite combination called Marx–Engels.[7] Their physics—whence this materialistic physics of theirs? is it a most peculiar mixture of Hegel and Baron d'Holbach?—renders one consistently uneasy, but their ethics makes all things purposeful, even their physics.

The case of Hobbes is unique.

My hypothesis, therefore, if it will not do for others, must at least do for him.

The contract, as we have seen, is not constructed by accretion out of its physical elements, but supervenes to make sense of nature in accordance with its own self-given and *a priori* requirements. The nearest philosophical companion to this way of approach from above is, as we have seen, Plato. In Plato's case there is no prior contract, because there are not any "equals." And, asymmetricals or unequals cannot compact with one another. If they did, it would not hold up, because people would continue to obey their innate tendencies, which are up and down, superior to inferior, with the psycho-social distortions that follow from that. Plato doesn't investigate these distortions. He's intuitively aware of them, and therefore arbitrarily organizes a society to control them. The founding philosopher, or philosophers, who starts the only true community, corresponds to what in Plato's physics is the demi-urge, the artificer god. Plato's structural dependence on a super-natural ordering of the controls of power relations accords with his schema of better and worser elements in nature.

In Hobbes, by contrast, the physics of equality follows from the prior assumption of compact. People are either actually equal by nature or must be hypothesized to be so. Why? Because only on such a basis can one have a compact. The high contracting parties in compact with one another are none higher than the other, so far as the transaction of contract is concerned. Just as Hobbes's physics is impossible "before" or without compact, so the character of the physics which follows exemplifies the axiomatic egalitarianism of any social compact.

(It is in the nature of such arguments—as for instance in the Kantian "Deduction" of the synthetic *a prioris*—for the derivative case to support, like a power behind the throne, the alleged originating premise.)

In sum: the state of nature, which is the argumentative *sanction* for the social contract, is characterized in an absolutely unique degree by the *equality of its members,* and has to be so characterized, because as soon as physics takes the human shape all powers, and the moral "excellences" strictly derivative from those powers, are equal, even if some are provisionally more equal than others.

We attend now to the memorable egalitarianism of Hobbes's world.

All men, it was said, in a later time and another country, "are created equal."

Yes, in "the opinion of mankind," of course; but by what or by whom created?

The contradictions of Jefferson's personal life, and those of many of the circumstances and dispensations of other Founding Fathers, are reflected in the Declaration of Independence or very shrewdly evaded by the Declaration and consequently persist in American history till there is a terrible and bloody calling-to-account in the Civil War of nearly a centennial later.

What was wrong?

The Declaration did not mean what it said. It was silent on the question of slavery. We did not do it, the Founding Fathers suggest. God did it, and in God's good time it will be undone.

But notwithstanding its evasions that subsist on the buoyant surface of ambivalences, the Declaration has remained the document of indisputable first influence in the matter of where we get our equality from. We get it, according to the Declaration, from God. As a secondary grace from the same source, we also have our liberty. (It does not seem much to the point that after having created us, He also gave us life. Could He have created us lifeless? The phrase is probably an encoded one. In giving us the "right to life," God has authorized us to rebel against those who "tyrannically" interfere with that right. It is an attempt to read the right to revolution as an integral part of God's creation of man.) And as for the pursuit of happiness, there seems to be no reason why it should be a primary or incontestible derivative from equality. We could, for instance, very easily have been created equally unhappy and given equal right to pursue our salvation in unsuccess, suffering, and purification.

But for Hobbes equality is by-nature, and it has all the relentlessness and ferocity that nature has.

It would be wrong, when speaking of Hobbes's nature, for any reflex of piety to add to nature the thought, for instance, of ". . . nature's God."

Hobbes's nature, like everything else in Hobbes's world, has two gods: the mortal one, and the one who is immortal.

About the latter, the less said the better; for He speaks to us, if He speaks at all, only through revelation and by authority; and we do not under any circumstances grossly presume to usurp that authority as private persons and reveal our knowledge of Him back to Him.

But the fiat of the mortal god has called into being the category of nature itself, as it will in due course transform nature into commonwealth, delegate to sovereignty a circumscribed omnipotence, and direct the sublation of categories whereby natural right comes to be called natural law—as if the new name makes it eligible for further transformation—and natural law rises to the quite redeemed form of "law of nature."

This is the source of the continuing ambiguity—not quite ambivalence in this case—that attends the deployment of terms in chapters 11 and 13, as well as subsequently, in connection with the absoluteness of sovereignty, when the indefeasible *reserve* that pertains to natural right even under sovereignty is called to our attention; and we are left to make of it what we can, or will.

In what circumstances is there an actual right of revolution against the state? The circumstances are indiscernible, because the right of revolution is identical with the state itself. The state is the right of revolution arrested.

Thus: each and every natural right, obtaining for us all in the state of nature, is transferred to sovereignty, when that has sprung full-blown from the act of compacting; and yet the natural right we primordially made do with remains inalienable. Let sovereignty impinge on it—or, at least, significantly impinge—and the revolutionary situation is established *from above*. Sovereignty has abdicated, and we are back where we were, if we ever were. These paradoxes of the argument of covenant no more trouble the mortal god than they would the immortal one, if He were interested. In what other way could an *a priori* of the political life work, if it is to work at all?

But we have not yet *faced* the fact of our equality by nature.

The face of this fact is both monstrous and bland. We are equal to know, we are equal to fear, and we are equal to kill.

I have deliberately chosen this way of putting it, which may appear to strain grammar, in order to bring out that, since (*a*) equality is our condition by nature, therefore (*b*) we *act out* our equality in our epistemic, feeling, and moral relation to other "equals" and to the world, and (*c*) that the acting out of that equality takes the form of knowing acts (prudential cunning), fearful acts (defensiveness), and the supremely pragmatic act of homicidal war.

Hobbes means that it is not just a flaw of our structure that we are born fearful and not courageous. We had better fear.* Fear is a strategy of our nature whereby we are goaded to exploit the fear of others to the utmost and outwit their fear with our own. Hobbes's doctrine of knowledge, insofar as it is a doctrine in the *Leviathan*, is a strictly and absolutely pragmatic conception. It has nothing to do with what is traditionally meant by "Reason." "Reason" in Hobbes is a name for the calculation of effects. Reason, or knowledge, is not *scientia intuitiva*, not *theōria*, not illumination. It is knowing how to obtain sufficient advantage to survive. The only way to get sufficient advantage in the state of nature, before there is a social contract, is to get absolute advantage, which means that everybody else has to be absolutely disadvantaged. The grim consequence is that our project by nature has to be relentless denial to our "fellows" in that same condition of the minimal possibility of retrieved advantage which life itself might offer to the other. This abstraction is conceivably absurd but quite inevitable.

Hobbes has put the thought just paraphrased in the following way.

"Nature hath made men so equal," he says, at the beginning of chapter 13,

---

*HMR's 1975 longhand draft adds: "When death establishes its own covenant absolutely, we are no longer even afraid." And, from the 1973–74 longhand draft: "The alternative of auto-genocide was—let us not say attractive, but let us without fear of contradiction say *compelling*, so that there does not, offhand, appear to be any reason why the half-man, the irresolute sub-monster in a treacherous league with death, should not have gone all the way: to kill *and* be killed. The sub-monster's finger is on the button, and his whole nature, such nature as he has in the state of nature, has only one message for him: namely, to press the button. . . . Why not? What fun to sweep the chessboard clean, to topple the ridiculous building blocks into their warm and welcoming dust. . . . There is a reason, and an answer to these rhetorical questions. The reason is *fear*. [Man's unhappiness must be the grace of his original fear.] Man is afraid. He has been afraid all along. His fear is the same as his hope. What does it mean to be the 'same' as something? It means to be productive of the same result. . . . And that is precisely the sense in which man's fear—as Hobbes has just about noted—is the same as his hope: it is going to lead him, or drive him, or seduce him into commonwealth. He will always regret it. But he will be unable to help himself. His fear is stronger than death."

> in the faculties of the body, and mind; as that though there be found one man sometimes manifestly stronger in body, or of quicker mind than another; yet when all is reckoned together, the difference between man, and man, is not so considerable, as that one man can thereupon claim to himself any benefit, to which another man may not pretend, as well as he. For as to the strength of body, the weakest has strength enough to kill the strongest, either by secret machination, or by confederacy with others, that are in the same danger with himself. (p. 80)

The argument is, thus, in its principle an argument of *potentiality,* analogous to the argument about the "nature of time" in that same state of nature, that Hobbes will be making a few paragraphs later. In effect he is saying: men in the state of nature are *potentially* equal; and no doubt the formalism would be implicit here, that in Hobbes's ontology "nature" is Aristotle's state of pure potentiality as such.

But by the same token, if, in the state of nature, we are potentially equal, in body and mind, we are also potentially *unequal;* a consummation or actualization which we will realize only under the *laws civil,* in and after the covenant; upon which we depend with our whole being to render us unequal.

So that we confront once more, in the reading of Hobbes, that irrepressible ambiguity, verging perhaps on ambivalence, that we have already observed in connection with his notice of the virtues, or moral excellences, that are merely by-nature: men-by-nature are and are not moral and/or immoral. In the same way, men-by-nature are and are not *unequal*. This kind of ambiguity may well be inseparable from ontological types of argument that very much aim to be descriptive and empirical as well: the *a priori* of such ontology must, in the nature of the case, be both before and after. The *déjà vu* of the case, like your *a priori* of the Kantian Understanding, has never been altogether *experienced*.

In the text just cited, the opening lines of *Leviathan* chapter 13, the distinction between faculties of "body" and "mind" must be held to be an indiscernible. It is evident that whatever else he is, Hobbes is not a Cartesian "dualist." So clear is it that the body *knows,* that we are impelled to doubt whether there is any other way of knowing except as the body, in its self-transcending career of phantasms, comes to know, or has already known.

We need not press the doubt. It is at once mollified by the suppressed but irrepressible ambiguity of Hobbes's next paragraph. "And as to the faculties of the mind," he says,

> setting aside the arts grounded upon words, and especially that skill of proceeding upon general, and infallible rules, called sci-

> ence; which very few have, and but in few things; as being not a native faculty, born with us; nor attained, as prudence, while we look after somewhat else, I find yet a greater equality amongst men, than that of strength. For prudence, is but experience; which equal time, equally bestows on all men, in those things they equally apply themselves unto. (p. 80)

The ambiguity here is quite innocent: men are both equal by-nature, and also, in a degree, unequal. The inequality—perceptible in a small but presumably elite minority—has to do with science; *but science arises only in and after the covenant,* as is evident from the nature of the case, but is made explicitly clear a few paragraphs later in the same chapter 13. For in the state of nature,

> there is no place for industry; because the fruit thereof is uncertain: and consequently no culture of the earth; no navigation, nor use of the commodities that may be imported by sea; no commodious building; no instruments of moving, and removing, such things as require much force; no knowledge of the face of the earth; no account of time; no arts; no letters; no society; . . . (p. 82)

An *a priori* is, so to speak, ambiguous by nature. The social contract was there, so to speak, before time; but before there was "account of time," all times were *equal,* that is to say, the same as no-time; and in this state of equal-time, men too were quite equal; *by-nature;* except for those few, already touched by the grace of science, who are potentially *unequal;* at least they are such *in foro interno.* But by the same token, it must also be true that all others, being in the state-of-nature, are in that state *in foro interno,* and not particularly in any other way. Neither anthropology nor history will argue us out of the state of nature, as they do not essentially demonstrate our being in it—so Hobbes will half-heartedly imply, when he comes, half-heartedly, to suggest an anthropological-historical "proof" for the actuality, if not the historicity, of a state of nature—and we shall be argued out of it only by the legislation of a political ontology, presenting itself as "eternal laws of nature"; as we are argued into it by the forcible persuasion of hypothesis.

Very well; we are then equal by-nature; and our recidivist reduction to equality, when that happens—either improbably and very briefly in history, or in the hapless souls of men self-victimized by their received assurance of equality—will be, in effect, a reduction to the state of nature.

And being equal by-nature, we are equal in both body and mind, for by-nature they are equal to each other; the times of them both being equal; and our more significant equality is an equality, with our knowledge, to *perform*.

Performance, in the state of nature, has not merely ambiguity but also desperation in it: there is only one thing to do with your knowingness in the state of nature, and that is to kill with it. In the state of nature, killing is knowing, itself. The courage to kill is, in its highly distilled essence, the "courage to be."

We are reminded of Hegel's chapter on "Absolute Freedom and Terror," in the *Phenomenology*. There, most notably in the literature, an inexorable dialectic of hopefulness, called freedom, leads to the absoluteness of doing-to-death. It is the only thing left to do, provided it were well done; and it is always well done, if not by the fall of the guillotine, then in some other way.

Hobbes's dialectic, in chapter 13, is not inspired by a philosophy of history, nor enlivened by a contemporary apocalypse like the Terror of '93. The episodes of his own history and reading—the regicide of his time, the fitful leveling movements of English history, the wars of the Fronde, when he was there; these do not add up to Apocalypse; nor does he seem to have endured them in that spirit, as Hegel must have endured in spirit the giant historical stalking of Robespierre and Saint-Just, and the decapitate pantheon of all the others.

But though without benefit of the marvelous enrichment of terror that Hegel enjoyed, Hobbes's argument is equally forcible, and persuasive. It would be, being an argument that arises, like Hegel's, from an ontological ground.

"*From equality proceeds diffidence.* From this equality of ability," note that the difference between mind and body has already been forgotten, if it was ever in mind at all, "ariseth equality of hope in the attaining of our ends. And therefore if any two men desire the same thing, which nevertheless they cannot both enjoy, they become enemies; and in the way to their end, which is principally their own conservation, and sometimes their delectation only, endeavour to destroy, or subdue one another . . .

"*From diffidence war* . . .

"Again, men have no pleasure, but on the contrary a great deal of grief, in keeping company, where there is no power able to overawe them all . . ." (p. 81).

Does it then follow that even in this condition of mutual aversion by-nature, there is co-present with the aversion the "hope" of soon being compelled by the covenant to love one another?

Such questions are necessarily rhetorical. Because at this stage of Hobbes's world the distinction between motives has not yet arisen. It is not so much that hope and fear pass into one another—and Hobbes, like most psychological analysts of the seventeenth century, can be read to mean that they do—as that they *are* one another. And where the distinction between motives has not arisen, there are no motives. This, perhaps, is Swinburne's moment, "From hope and fear set free"; but this motiveless world has come *before* the fact, not after.* In a motiveless world, the social contract is the one last hope of being motivated.

Let us sum up.

Hobbes's state of nature is that entropic condition of man's existence, which is to be read, can only be read, retroactively.

The motion that goes on in it is random motion, and is perceptible only by courtesy.

The so-called laws of motion are extrapolations after the fact. They are by-products of the "arts grounded upon words," and the "rules called science," which severally proceed from the social contract, once that is known and has been called, or has called itself, into being.

From the legislative eminence of the social contract, we survey the conditions precedent.

We note, with amazement, and, in due course, with some horror, that we were once quite equal.

Taking further note of the three strands of this equality—to

---

*HMR's notebook number 1 transcribes several stanzas of Algernon Charles Swinburne's "The Garden of Proserpine," from which this line is taken.

From too much love of living,
  From hope and fear set free,
We thank with brief thanksgiving
  Whatever gods may be
That no life lives for ever;
That dead men rise up never;
That even the weariest river
  Winds somewhere safe to sea.

Then star nor sun shall waken,
  Nor any change of light:
Nor sound of waters shaken,
  Nor any sound or sight:
Nor wintry leaves nor vernal,
Nor days nor things diurnal;
Only the sleep eternal
  In an eternal night.

HMR then remarks in part: "Is this the 'pre-political-state-of-nature,' where, allegedly, even *motion* is motionless, or has been absorbed into 'pure potentiality' . . . 'absolute rest'?"

In HMR's apparent view, Swinburne in the poem would not so much be "facing facts" as describing the "motiveless world" that comes "*before* the fact, not after." In other words, he would be facing *away* from the facts.

know, to kill, and to fear—we observe that these strands tend to converge, or, as it were, sublate, into a single *equality of obligation*.[8]

From the much later standpoint of a constitutional emotion one could be tempted to think of the equal obligation that now becomes manifest, as an obligation of, or to, citizenship.

But the premature, or impulsive, invocation of the category of citizen in the case of Hobbes—though he himself is not radically averse to the word—can be misleading. There is, of course, nothing in the nature of the word "citizen" that makes it inapplicable to the members of the commonwealth instituted by the mortal god. But there is that in the history of the word that would tend to obscure Hobbes's meaning, and force him back into the routine of political thinking. Citizens have rights, as well as duties, in the history of their own category, and if they do not have clear rights, and duties that are better than self-evident ones, then at least they have functions, as in the case of Plato's citizens, as Hegel's citizens have both rights, duties, *and* functions. Locke's citizens, and Jefferson's, package various assortments, in varying proportions, of rights, duties, and/or functions. Rousseau's citizens are a special case: they wish to be born, but they are not yet born, and never will be, remaining forever dissolved in the amniotic fluid of the "general will."

Hobbes's citizens have no precedent in the history of the category.

They have no rights.

Rights are precisely that which the citizens of the Hobbesian commonwealth *renounce*.

One might speak of the Hobbesian citizen as having a single over-riding, and perhaps overwhelming, *duty*—of obedience to the instituted sovereign; but essentially this duty of obedience is a way of being consistent in the comprehensive renunciation that one has obligated oneself to. The duty of the Hobbesian citizen is a duty to remember *that* one has renounced, and *what* one has renounced, which is simply one's *natural right;* or, in other words, everything.

One cannot renounce everything unless everybody renounces it equally.

The Hobbesian citizen is the prime mover, as well as absolute beneficiary, of this equality of obligation to renounce.

There is a metaphysical immediacy, or instantaneity, of this manifestation in Hobbes, that makes it difficult to speak of it as a proper dialectic. That requires mediation. There is little such mediation to speak of, and perhaps none whatsoever, in the case of the transformation in Hobbes of the omni-killing by-nature into that radical renunciation which Hobbes comes to know as "the first law of nature."

Here is what Hobbes has to say about the moment precedent to the transformation: We quote from the well-known last two paragraphs of chapter 13:

> It is consequent also to the same condition [namely, the state of nature] that there be no propriety, no dominion, no *mine* and *thine* distinct; but only that to be every man's, that he can get: and for so long, as he can keep it. And thus much for the ill condition, which man by mere nature is actually placed in; though with a possibility to come out of it, consisting partly in the passions, partly in his reason.
>
> *The passions that incline men to peace* . . . are fear of death; desire of such things as are necessary to commodious living; and a hope by their industry to obtain them. And reason suggesteth convenient articles of peace, upon which men may be drawn to agreement. These articles, are they, which otherwise are called the Laws of Nature. . . . (pp. 83f.)

Edification and grand rhetoric combine in this passage to give us one of the great sleight-of-hand performances in the history of argument.

Fear of death inclines men to peace? But it is precisely fear of death that has (up to now) inclined men to war; has, indeed, activated them to kill, comprehensively and without let. "Desire of such things as are necessary to commodious living"? Whence, in the history of universal war by-nature, has arisen knowledge of such a category as "commodious living"? Is there a sociology of knowledge operative in the state of nature that insinuates this refined and exalted anticipation even into the *gestalt* of brutishness? And as for "hope . . . to obtain them," it has already been told us that hope is merely the obverse of fear: the rictus upon the face of that master passion.

Finally, *reason* itself, with its far-fetched suggestion of "articles of peace," upon which men may be drawn to unprecedented agreement: whence this reason? In what eddies and currents of motion-by-nature has it had its hiding place?

These rhetorical questions have obvious non-answers: no-where, and by-no-means.

No possibility has been made evident for extracting desire-of-commodious-living, or the syndrome called hope, and the meta-passion or counter-passion called reason, from the war-of-all-against-all. Nor is it manifest how the fear-of-death suddenly ceases to be both death wish and death deed, and becomes, in preparation for covenant, libidinal.

We are reduced, once more, to our sole option: this is not a dialectic of a historical, or even a quasi-historical, development, or even a dialectic of process in Whitehead's sense of process, where "novelty" is a good-enough word for any further stage that is the next-stage-but-one. What Hobbes is giving us is dialectic without mediation: that is to say, a dialectic of an *a priori*. What Hobbes ought to be giving us—if he were that kind of writer—is an argument of "deduction," comparable to Kant's "deduction" of his transcendental logic; that is to say, an exhibition of the modes and possibilities of empirical instantiation. In truth, Hobbes does give us a little of such "deduction"; as, for instance, when he argues that the real proof of the endemic presence of the "state of nature," in our lives as in our being, is the way we lock up our chests and cupboards against our children, when we leave our well-covenanted houses. Cotton Mather would have had no difficulty in understanding the case.

But Hobbes does not bother to give us much of a Kantian "deduction" of the matter, or any other kind, because his *a priori* is more elementary and more radical than Kant's was. It is perhaps more like an Aristotelian "law of thought"—for instance, the so-called law of excluded middle: *A* is either *A* or not-*A;* etc. The qualifications do not matter so much as the fundamental law. And so, for Hobbes, *political man is either consensual by nature,* or he does not exist at all; and neither does the possibility of him. The state-of-nature is an afterthought, and a rabid one. Man entertains it all the time. But this does not in the least mean that it is a founding thought, in the being of man, or even a primordial one, in any ontologically significant sense of the word "primordial."

And so we come to the *first law of nature,* in which Hobbes proposes that *right* and *law,* by nature contrary to each other, shall perpetuate themselves in a dialectical equipoise, by virtue of which a civil order may endure.

First, a definition, cavalier, but for the present purpose sufficient: "RIGHT, consisteth in liberty to do, or to forbear: whereas LAW, determineth, and bindeth to one of them: so that law, and right, differ as much, as obligation, and liberty; which in one and the same matter are inconsistent" (chapter 14, p. 84).

The definition suffices to move us along, but it will not quite stand. In the state of nature, for instance, there cannot really be any right, or liberty, to *forbear*. Motion has no options, no choice of motives; it cannot "forbear" to move. Whatever it is in the state of nature that might, at a given moment, exercise a right, or liberty, to forbear, has in that moment fallen under *obligation*. Such a moment is the moment of the birth of covenant.

The *equality* of this obligation is simply the instant of its universality, or unanimity.

"And consequently it is a precept, or general rule of reason, *that every man, ought to endeavour peace, as far as he has hope of obtaining it; and when he cannot obtain it, that he may seek, and use, all helps, and advantages of war*" (p. 85).

It may be that Hobbes perceives that there is something wrong with this thesis. He hastens to assure us that it is forked: "The first branch of which rule, containeth the first, and fundamental law of nature; which is, *to seek peace, and follow it*. The second, the sum of the right of nature; which is, *by all means we can, to defend ourselves*" (*ibid.*).

The appropriate question here is this:

Does Hobbes's argument know of the principle of good faith? And if it does, where and how is such a principle operative here, at the moment of the birth of the social contract?

For there can be no question that it is precisely that that we have witnessed, like the birth of a male heir to a king of France: the *first law of nature* is as public and as informal as all that. How, then, can there be "two branches" to such a law, or, at least, two branches such as Hobbes has described? Do they not cancel each other, in simple bad faith?

The argument is esoteric, and unabashed. What Hobbes means by the "self-defense" of the first law of nature is the unanimous *disarmament* of the *second law*.

Thus: "*The second law of nature*. From this fundamental law of nature, by which men are commanded to endeavour peace, is derived this second law; *that a man be willing, when others are so too, as far-forth, as for peace, and defence of himself he shall think it necessary, to lay down this right to all things; and be contented with so much liberty against other men, as he would allow other men against himself* . . ." (p. 85). Or, more precisely: no liberty at all.

But Hobbes's argument has not yet come to focus in the paradox of liberty, a paradox that can easily take a brutal form, to wit: that there is optimum liberty when all are absolutely deprived of it. The question is faced, after his fashion, in connection with the question of sovereign-and-subject, and we shall notice it then.

Hobbes's main concern, at the moment, is man's absolute right-by-nature to that totality of self-defense which takes the form of uninhibited aggression. And what he says is plain: at that moment when such abstract essences as "right" versus "law" move into the dimension of human existences, the right of aggression transforms into the obligation to disarm.

I have spoken of this obligation to disarm as an obligation to renounce. The scope of that renunciation should not be underestimated. At this moment of the genesis of covenant, one renounces, (*a*) aggression as the end, or "summum bonum," of human existence;

(*b*) the means, whether natural weaponry of tooth and claw, or hardware of stick and stone, whereby the life of natural right can be lived; (*c*) the posture and intention of natural right—that mode of body-language which in the Common Law would be called "assault," as distinguished from battery; and (*d*) liberty—or, at least, the liberty-by-nature, that with which we are endowed, as we know, by our Creator, along with two other goods.[9]

This, self-evidently, is no small renunciation. It is all that we have hitherto had.

And I have also spoken of this renunciation as a universal renunciation, and equated universality with unanimity.

I shall assume that this equation requires no special defense. There seems no meaning that universality can have other than unanimity, once it too moves along the orbit of instantiation, from ontological essences to human existences; or from prescription to description. If there is a difficulty, one has only to make the effort to take Hobbes's metaphor of the progression of law from law one to law two, concretely as, with J. L. Austin's usage, a "performative" sentence. It is then evident, that no one can put the stone that he carries in his closed hand down—he dare not do so—until the other has done so too. How, then, does that particular moment of Hobbes's new-born, commonwealth "time" become ostensively clear-and-distinct, the moment of not-yet-but-until? It is obvious that the two hands of this particular clock must move together, if they move at all. We must disarm simultaneously, multilaterally, and unanimously, if we disarm at all.*

The nostalgia for the state of nature, now vanished, or *almost* vanished, beyond recall, will, of course, never quite leave us. But we are not to worry. Its persistence in our structure—in whatever hiding place it finds in that structure: in the *id*, or in the back-to-nature fantasy of our souls when we become Hegel's "beautiful souls," or in the permanently reserved right of revolution which Jefferson's Declaration discreetly adverts to; which right is the scandal of all political theory, from Plato to Trotsky—has a constructive significance in the life, henceforth, of the commonwealth. The significance is that of the idea of "hell fire" in more orthodox ontologies. It is the threat of the fate that awaits us if commonwealth should break down. Our indefeasible "natural right" is, as it were, our indefeasible love of sin.

As if to lock out that threat once and for all, or at least keep it in its place, we move as quickly as possible from the first and second

---

*See Appendix to Part One.

laws of nature, to the third and consummatory one, which is *justice*, or keeping promises (chapter 15).

Hobbes has been at pains to assure us, in chapter 14, containing the immediately preceding phases of his argument of the third law, that "*Not all rights are alienable*" (p. 86); and among those that are not, are, for instance, the right to resist an attempt on one's life, the right to refuse to accept, voluntarily, wounds, chains, imprisonment.

The reasoning is obscure, and unsatisfactory.

If we are still in a state of nature, then we are alien to everyone, and we will alienate nothing. If we have left the state of nature, then we have alienated everything. But not quite.

We have not alienated our natural right to self-defense, *but transferred it to the commonwealth.*

It is now the commonwealth, through the sovereignty which will, hopefully, be expressive of its contractual nature, as well as of its absoluteness and irreversibility, it is that commonwealth that will now defend us, if necessary, presumably, against ourselves.

It remains obscure in Hobbes whether we should go willingly to our death at the hands of the commonwealth, acting, of course, through its structured or deputed sovereignty, or must be dragged to it.

On this point, Socrates, in the *Crito*, has been more forthright, and more explicit. He goes willingly—more or less—to his death because above and beyond the city that has nurtured him, there is a city in heaven, that has nurtured all cities. But the ontological premises by which Socrates lives, and dies, are no secret to him, as they may be in the case of Hobbes.

Hobbes does not tarry on these niceties, though he will revert to them, if fleetingly, in connection with such themes yet to come, as sovereignty, liberty, etc. If he paused on them more than at this moment he does, he would no doubt find his secret self-exposed; or, worse yet, he would be entangled in the same scandalous absurdity as the political theorists are, namely: how guarantee to the contracting parties of the social contract, the right to abrogate that contract, or the "permanent" right to revolution?

It is evident that the rhetoric of the Declaration does not *guarantee* that right—in order to do so it would have to set up a Permanent Committee of Public Safety, not to be superseded by any constitutional government, though it might exist side by side with it—nor does a guarantee follow from the Constitution's allowance of the citizens' right to bear arms, since it does not tell us: bear arms for what? No man dare argue that the question is self-answering.

The whole purpose of the social contract has to be to make sure that the question of the right to revolution *does not arise*. And if it should? Then the work of creation, so to speak, has to be done all over again. The demi-urge has made a mistake. The Declaration of Independence, in adverting to the possibility of just such a mistake, is of course dealing with a "counter-factual conditional": lives, fortunes, and sacred honor had already been invested in a new social contract.

What then? Are all governments "provisional," or else "governments in exile"?

Hobbes has alluded to the relations between states—"international relations," as they have come to be known—as the last full measure of proof of the socio-historical actuality of a "state of nature." If revolutionary dialectic were in any sense a natural idiom for Hobbes —as it is not, despite regicide, and Cromwell, and the Long Parliament, and the rest of it—he might well speak of international relations as illustrative, since illustration there must be, of a permanent right to permanent revolution.

But he would regard that right not as the right to advance to the next stage in the history of class struggle, or other struggle, but as the right, so to speak, to enjoy a nightmare. The state of nature is the nightmare of ontology, and though we do well to remember it, having had it, we do ill to settle down with it.

Social contract theory—whether of the ontological variety, such as I have here argued on behalf of Hobbes, or of the more usual form of explanatory political myth—has an in-built tendency to run up against the requirement of world apocalypse, as its final cause. World revolution leads to world order, liberty becomes confluent with absolute sovereignty, whose locus is in principle everywhere, and therefore nowhere; and the revolution is permanent because self-verifying, and dead.

But Hobbes's apocalypse is at the beginning of things, not at its end; and he is by nature willing to settle for smaller gains. As he scales down his demands to a minimal and manageable compass, it turns out that all he is asking for, in his commonwealth-without-illusions, is the governance of the "eternal laws of nature." And thus provokes the thought, in a sympathetic reader, that he might as well have asked for the Form of the Good, or Kant's uncontaminated and uncompromising Good Will, to begin with.

But we are getting ahead of our story. We have not yet experienced the fullness of the claim of the third law of nature.

The third law of nature tells us, to our surprise, that we are now living in a *state*. There is even greater surprise as it gradually dawns upon aroused curiosity that we have been living for some time—ever since the beginning of commonwealth time—in just such a *state*.

Suppose a competent medieval theologian should assure a lucky freeholder, or a just emerging bourgeois, that he is living in a *church*. And suppose the freeholder or bourgeois should only discover much later—whether by letter from the original theologian or whether by anonymous pamphlet from another, is not clear—that what the disputant meant, for it seems to have been a dispute, was a *church invisible*.

There would in all likelihood be some political trouble of mind as to what was meant: just when does a church invisible become *visible*? Does it have a right to enforce its own visibility? Can a universal compel its own (unique?) instantiation! And so on.

The history of these traumatic controversies need not detain us, since Hobbes has made substantive short shrift of them, though with incessant particulars, in his excursuses on religion, and on various kingdoms of darkness.[10]* Hobbes knows exactly how men shall be justified, both men of little faith and of greater faith, and that is by faith in the *state*. To men of religion, as to religion itself, he has the same message: all things are justified by the political order, and whatever is not so justified is *unjust*. Outside the state there is neither justification nor *justice*.

"And whatsoever is not unjust," Hobbes says, in explication of the third law, "is *just*" (p. 94).

"*Justice and propriety begin with the constitution of commonwealth* . . . [but] before the names of just, and unjust can have place, there must be some coercive power, to compel men equally to the performance of their covenants, by the terror of some punishment, greater than the

---

*The following remarks, from HMR's 1973–74 longhand draft, seem apropos, taking note of "Hobbes's marvelous rhetoric" on the subject of "God, man, nature and covenant . . . a rhetoric which beguiles while it also distracts, though no doubt without intention of distraction. It distracts by its use of a language of conformity, or even of piety, and beguiles by attaching that language to meanings of unmistakable unorthodoxy: meanings that might be expected from, say, a mystic, or a Faustian kabbalist, or a clever heresiarch seeking to confuse and evade.

"But Hobbes is none of these things. And if he confuses, it is for two reasons: (1) he is confused, and (2) he is afraid. Not of man, but of God, and of the laws of 'nature's God.' Just as Job was, whom Hobbes cites with confident relish and approval in this same chapter. 'Where wast thou,' God called out to Job, 'when I laid the foundations of the earth?' and the like, both approved Job's innocence and reproved the erroneous doctrine of his friends' (*Leviathan*, p. 235, quoting Job 38:4).

"It is, of course, one of a philosopher's roles that he inevitably plays: God talking, as the next voice one hears; and talking to whom? Why, to him, and to *you*. So it is Hobbes talking to himself: Hobbes as God-maker talking to Hobbes as a thing made, and most fearful. Where was he indeed, when the 'laws of nature,' were, so to speak, propounded?

"Well, right here, where he is now; and he is trying to locate that situation to us, to himself, and, one may dare say, to all mankind."

benefit they expect by the breach of their covenant; and to make good that propriety, which by mutual contract men acquire, in recompense of the universal right they abandon: and such power there is none before the erection of a commonwealth" (p. 94).

Very well: the state is defined as *coercive power*. Coercive power is defined as "the terror of some punishment."

We now have a working answer to the various questions of "when," etc., that have arisen: When did we enter into statehood? When we acquired property. When did we acquire title to property? When we submitted to "terror of punishment." But did we not always live under fear, most of all in the state of nature? Fear of death, or the generalized fear of one's fellow, is not the same as terror of punishment. Terror of punishment is centripetal. The passion of fear has now been given headquarters, so to speak. Those headquarters are precisely where the weaponry has been deposited, according to the first and second laws. In sum: Statehood is always in principle symbolical. The state becomes visible when the symbolism becomes explicit.

In Hobbes this question, of the visible versus the invisible, the explicit versus the implicit, the existentially quantified versus the essentially present, takes the form of a running concern with the difference between *foro interno,* the social contract internalized, and *foro externo,* the same thing externalized.

We can now, if we like, pursue, as in a squirrel cage, what might seem to be the same question: which came first, and when did we, or do we, pass from one to the other?

Let us say that it is not *quite* the same question—that by-now familiar question, which *a priori* came first? Kant's *a priori* of time, for instance, or his *a priori* of space!—since Hobbes's distinction between the internal and external forms of the social contract seems to suggest that in passing from one to the other we pass from the psychological to the institutional, or, say, from the realm of conscience to the stage of history. Surely, in such a passage there are antecedents and consequents to be clearly and distinctly identified.

But, no.

I submit that precisely in Hobbes—or, at least, in his *Leviathan*—there is a refusal to suggest how and when such a passage is possible, a refusal that is even more conspicuous than it might be, for instance, in Plato's *Republic*. I suggest, then, that in the *Leviathan* the argument, or the assumption, is to this effect: when there is a certain disposition of the conscience, or the consciousness, there is, by that same token, an institutional reality, identifiable to an informed, or a candid, inspection, which corresponds to the internal disposition. *The internal and the external forms of the social contract are two different ways of looking at the same moment of human existence whenever that moment arises.*

Therefore, all the questions that arise in connection with the third law of nature have by no means been suppressed by Hobbes, or evaded; those questions are in the nature of his argument, and his case, self-answering.

Thus, for instance: If justice is "keeping promises," to whom and when were the promises made? Clearly, to one another and to ourselves; and as for *when,* they were made at that precise moment when the arms were laid down.* And if the keeping of promises—at least, promises of so grave a nature as these!—depends on a coercive power that represents the terror of punishment, when and where does that power, and its terror, make its entrance? Precisely then and there, where the arms have been laid down. Still we do not see it? Then all we have to do, in the morality play that Hobbes is writing, is raise the trap-door of our conscience, and the terror is there. We still claim that it is excessively invisible? But it is well known, to anthropologists as to us all, that terror has considerable coercive power. Nevertheless, we should like that terror to have the benefit of the form of space, to have, in other words, an institutional definition? The social contract is in search of its own identity as *sovereignty*?

The mantle of sovereignty seems to have fallen upon that person or those persons, of the contracting parties, who happen to be standing nearest to where the arms have been deposited. The custodian, henceforth, of natural power seems to have come into his office by original propinquity. This seems to be all the charisma of "leadership" that the logic of the case calls for. Once the state invisible has become, so far forth, visible, such accidents by-nature as are called conquest, subjugation, cession, and the rest, may follow a normal

---

*This moment of the play is re-described in HMR's 1975 longhand draft as follows:

"What I primordially promise is *non-injury*. I have promised, in the first and second laws, to kill no more; and since every wounding, and every assault, whether or no followed by battery, is necessarily and inevitably *an assault with intent to kill,* I have most literally promised never to assault you at all.

"Can I transmute all at once from the exhilarating, homicidal state of nature to this bland Buddhism of the covenant: do I really undertake to do no injury? Can I keep such a promise?

"Of course not. It is pure grotesquerie, or bad faith, so long as it remains *in foro interno,* that is, as a matter of conscience.

"It would have been no news to Hobbes that the Buddha was in political bad faith. Nor would it have been any news to Hegel.

"The law of non-injury is not yet a law of nature, (1) any more than the law of love would be, (2) and becomes such, becomes justice, when I take up the stick that you and I have agreed that you are to lay down (the first and second laws are operative here), and I *compel* you to do me no injury.

"There is little or no fear that I will, or can, do any to you; *because I am now acting in your name;* you are my author, and I am your agent and your action; and we are both the *same* person, though perhaps hardly one person, as we bounce from role to role in this game that mortal gods play, when they play politics."

course—called history, or even the "cunning of Reason"!—but the ontological requirements of the matter have been met. We are where we were supposed to be.

No doubt, this one or that one of the contracting parties might wish to understand somewhat better why *he* is not the sovereign, but someone else is. We have, of course, been told that, indeed, we *are*. But this does not yet seem to be crystal clear, much as we agree to the justice, and the justness, of the third law of nature.

How did it come about that we, who, from the moment that we entered into covenant, surely meant no harm, have done all this? Namely, that we have produced frankensteins of political ineptitude, as of moral evil, and called them sovereign?

The puzzle is no worse than that of nature itself: out of it came commonwealth, which is as much of a negation as one could ask for, being, as we were, in a state of nature.

The frankenstein, in this morality tale, is ourselves.

By the structuring of sovereignty, in and of the commonwealth, we have become *persons*.

Hobbes fences with the subject: who and what a person is.

"A person, is he, *whose words or actions are considered, either as his own, or as representing the words or actions of another man, or of any other thing, to whom they are attributed, whether truly or by fiction*" (chapter 16, p. 105).

Then, what, or who, is *not* a person, or cannot be one?

There is no one, and no such thing. *Perhaps God is not a person*, for a person is a commonwealth thing, either an *author* or *actor* of sovereignty, or sovereignty itself; and though God is in some sense "sovereign," he is either sovereign under commonwealth, in which case the less said about him as God, the better, or if he is sovereign outside the commonwealth and above it—which, presumably, he is and has to be, insofar as he is immortal—then he is in the same case as any other outlaw; he is not a person; or, perhaps, he is a non-person.

So much for the curious casuistries of the matter, not developed by Hobbes, but implicit in the cat-and-mouse dialectic he briefly offers on it.

"*Person natural, and artificial*," he goes on. "When they are considered as his own, then is he called a *natural person:* and when they are considered as representing the words and actions of another, then is he a *feigned* or *artificial* person" (*ibid.*).

What is notable here, and conceivably distressing, is, in the first place, the radical obliviousness to biology, and, beyond that, the pitfalls of application. It would be reasonably helpful, and perhaps consolatory, to point out to ourselves, simplistically, that the people inside the Houses of Parliament *bleed*, as Charles I, himself, did, whereas the Houses themselves do not. But this, it turns out, would soon not help us at all. For the member of Commons, sitting inside the House, is a *feigned* or *artificial* person, whether or no he bleeds, insofar as he represents, in his vote and other *actions*, a party or constituency.

Who, then, if anybody or anything, is a *natural* person?

The answer seems plain enough: "he whose words or actions are considered as his own . . . is called a natural person."

We are presumably not called upon to locate an *original* person, so to speak, but one whose words or actions are *indefeasibly* or *incorrigibly* to be considered as his own.

It is still not altogether clear why any usurping sovereign, or pirate, could not be so *considered*. One has to say, that once the distinction begins to be made—these actions are in behalf of his private purse and appetite, those actions or proclamations are in behalf of his fellow-conspirators, his crew, and his future subject–victims—the social contract is already operative, if not fully in force. William the Conqueror does quite a good deal for himself, or Robin Hood for himself, for that matter, but he also does something for Norman homeland, and for the England yet to be; or Sherwood Forest.

In our quest for the incorrigible natural person we are not yet, therefore, at the point of no return.

We only arrive at that point when we hold fast to one side of the distinction being made: the natural person, the one whose words or actions are incorrigibly his own, is originally and exclusively the *commonwealth*. *Originally*, because the notion of person has no meaning or provenance before the social contract; and *exclusively*, because once the commonwealth is in being, all words and actions whatsoever are in part, at least, *representative*, and therefore *feigned*.

This of course leaves us with our original ontological ambiguity. But we ought to be used to it, since Plato. To look for the original *natural* person is like looking for the demi-urge. Look through the wrong end of the forms, and one will see the demi-urge, at least sufficiently to identify him. Look through the wrong end of *authority*, and we will see the only quite *natural* person that there has ever been in Hobbes's world, and perhaps in ours. The metaphor becomes complicated, but it is the only one we are left to live with: only the commonwealth, as mortal god, or in some vulgarer manifestation as sovereign despot, speaks and does words and actions that are indisputably his own. And perhaps he does it only once. The best, perhaps, that we can do with the metaphor is extend it, along the lines of its theological paradigm: there is an archetypal *person*, which is commonalty; and the rest of us, as soi-disant persons, or whatever, are derivative.

To try to find a person is like looking to see God face to face.

There are penalties here; and the game may not be worth the candle. It is better, no doubt, to look for something we can see; the phantasm of it being quite actual. For instance, *authority*.

The road to authority is roundabout, and one travels it backward.

First, one encounters an *action;* or one does one, and encounters it reflexively.

And considering an action, whether it be truly such, and not merely a motion, which in its own nature is always merely random, no matter how highly accelerated, one undertakes to identify the doer of the action, or the *actor*. The duplicity of actorship becomes quickly evident. One acts either for oneself, or for another; though in many cases, the one and the other have a single point of origin, one's so-called self. If one acts for another, notably for the wholly other,[11] one is an *actor* strictly; and in that case one's problem is much simplified: one looks for the *author* of the lines spoken by the actor, or the action done by him. Having found the author, one has located the *authority* by which the action was done.

These maneuvers will lead one where one expects; that is, face to face with the actualities of human relations, harsh or approximately bearable, that one already knows. Having come this far, and it is a fair distance, one executes an about-face and perceives one's own starting point: the *commonwealth*.

> . . . as if every man should say to every man, *I authorize and give up my right of governing myself, to this man, or to this assembly of men, on this condition, that thou give up thy right to him, and authorize all his actions in like manner* . . . . And in him consisteth the essence of the commonwealth; which, to define it, is *one person, of whose acts a great multitude, by mutual covenants one with another, have made themselves every one the author, to the end he may use the strength and means of them all, as he shall think expedient, for their peace and common defence*. (chapter 17, p. 112)

The primordial *person*, as the saying goes, is, then, the *commonwealth*. The natural and the feigned come together in *its* singular person. And it is altogether easy for such a singularity of person to be *equal* to himself, to be absolute as well as instantaneous in his *renunciation* of all the rights there are, and to *authorize* to his ecumenical self all the actions yet to be done. If this be tyranny, yet the egalitarianism of it cannot be faulted, nor its voluntarism; and one therefore has to make the most of it.

It is thus a meta-truism—a truism above all truisms—that government *of* the people and *by* the people cannot perish from the earth.

But what of government *for* the people?

The demi-urge, the public craftsman, the mortal god and primordial person has yet this to answer for.

Perhaps he will never quite do so to his and our satisfaction.

For, from the moment of his constitution—this mortal god and primordial person—he dissolves or disintegrates into a multiplicity that can easily become infinite, of actions, all of which have been authorized, but none of which can be incontestably attributed. The moment of his constitution is also the moment of his institution; and the institution that at once issues from the act of covenant, which is the birth of this primordial person, a person both natural and feigned, is the institution of overwhelming and exclusive *force*. The employment of that force by the sovereign commonwealth is necessarily always *just*, and to question it is always unjust. But the mere existence of such force, not to speak of its employment, implies that in the enduring of the commonwealth there also endures a perpetual *adversary* relation.

The powers of the commonwealth are not divisible, says Hobbes, disposing in advance of Locke's checks and balances; *but the commonwealth is divided against itself*. And though this house may very well stand—things with so solid a metaphysical foundation manage to do so—the fissure in its being cannot be patched over, much less healed, with an abstraction. The abstraction in question is that of *natural right*. It is that which we have renounced; it is also the primordial mud which we have used to fashion the primordial person, the commonwealth, endowing it, or him, with our universal and unanimous renunciations; and it is precisely that—the object of our renunciation—that is to be used against us as sovereign force.

But it is also the one thing that, in principle, we retain as unalienable. It is the one thing that will tell us, when the sovereign treads upon it, that—though he acts by our authority and we are the author of his actions—his reign is over.

We conclude, then, that the natural right which Hobbes wishes to use, and does use, as he must, both ways at once, *does not exist*, as genuine abstractions really do not. And we propose for consideration that the only meaning of right is *moral right;* which, being concrete right, must also be by nature, as it is by commonwealth[12]; that what the sovereign has been endowed with is our unalienable moral rights; and that it is these rights that he wields into a sword, until it is wrested from his hand.*

---

*At this point, HMR's 1977 version continues as follows: "We argue . . . that 'natural right,' rhetorically useful though it be in the pilgrim's progress toward *Leviathan*, is pure abstraction; since in the condition where it . . . allegedly obtains, it is indistinguishable from 'natural wrong'; and all such 'rights' by-nature

The thesis is, then, that governments are instituted among men to secure their *moral* rights; that it is only men who have such rights; that governments have no rights whatsoever, except the "natural right" transferred to them at the covenant; that this natural right that government has is the monopoly of force contracted out to it; that this natural right resists absolute transfer, owing to a law of the *inertia of right;* it is therefore to be called *liberty,* which is a *feigned* right, as the absolute owner of liberty, the sovereign, is a feigned person, and becomes *naturalized* only to the extent that he dissolves in the *moral rights* enjoyed by men. This is as much as to say that positive law, or the commands of the lawgiver, are viable—in theological language, or the language of salvation, are justified—only to the extent that they become identical with the moral law.

Hobbes's name for the moral law is "the eternal laws of nature." These are the last sixteen of the nineteen laws of nature that Hobbes enumerates, the first three of these nineteen being simply the foundation stone that the builder, so to speak, having used, has rejected. The eternal laws of nature stand in eternal confrontation with the absolute liberty of the sovereign, for this liberty is simply his natural right of the sword; and it is inevitable, and thus proper, that the moral law and the sword stand in confrontation with each other, a confrontation far more serious, and more deadly, than the confrontation of the sacred and the secular arms with one another. For in the confrontation of the moral law with natural right, the king's *alter ego,* [13] it is natural right that stands under eternal damnation. It is possible that natural right is quite cheerful to be relieved in this way of the responsibility for itself.

The circle that we have described, and that we venture to impute

---

are equally and instantly wrongs, from a point of view which, in that benighted state, has to be, by definition, universally shared. Right becomes distinguishable from wrong (or from the 'right' to do it)—and thus not subject to instantaneous conversion to it—only when it becomes concrete as *moral* right, when, as, and if that happens.

"By the same token, the concept 'nature,' or 'state of nature,' which is progenitive to 'natural right,' or god-parent to it, is an abstraction that is even purer, since we do not know that we are in it, or in any condition whatsoever, until we are well out of it. Abstract nature becomes *concrete* nature—that is to say, both subject to internal distinctions, and also distinguishable from what is *not* nature; for instance, the civil or human order—when we have imputed to nature (what we may or may not find there; or both find and do not find) an *equality* of the elemental occupants of nature. It is original *equality,* as we have seen, that has already *moralized* nature, or endowed it with unique eligibility to being compacted, by 'natural persons,' into a civil order.

"It is in this sense that Hobbes's 'nature,' when it becomes concrete, has already discovered itself as moral. The potentiality of the moral, in principle, is all that is needed here."

to Hobbes as his secret, or esoteric, dialectic, is not a vicious one. The circle is merely the outline of the empirical attempt at encounter with the good, there being no other conceivable mode of such attempt: how encounter it except empirically? The empirical attempt necessarily bears resemblance to Lear's experience in the storm, in the wood: there is madness in it, and fear, and thunder and lightning, and folly for company, and much idle exhibition of power. But then the idleness of power is nowhere better celebrated than in the Book of Job, where All-Power itself, speaking to Job, in rebuke of the unctuous, frightened friends, calls upon Job to contemplate the awful idleness of creation. Therefore, in Hobbes, a turning away, as quickly as possible, from the great frustration of the problem of *liberty*, which, it turns out, is simply another name for omnipotence, which we all have a little of, but not enough to speak of.[14]

One is inclined to concede once and for all, to Hobbes, or along with him, that true liberty, like true omnipotence, is liberty of the *body*. More precisely, liberty consists in simply having a body; and the having of it is, of course, always being one way or another interfered with. These facts, as the saying goes, are brute; there are things to be done about them, and Hobbes has some suggestions; but there is no sense denying them. To deny them is to lay claim to the possibility, as the "parapsychologists," or some of them, do, of having an "out of the body experience." From the point of view of an honest ontology, the very making of such a claim has a touch of the obscene in it.*

We have already noted Hobbes's constructive circularity, in defining the "essence of the commonwealth," to consist in "*one person, of whose acts a great multitude, by mutual covenants one with another, have made themselves every one the author, to the end he may use the strength and means of them all, as he shall think expedient, for their peace and common defence*" (chapter 17, p. 112).

It is not unexpected that the same locution of an "essence," also defines for us our *final cause* of commonwealth, to wit: our "peace and common defence."

Here and there, but only here and there, a further word. Thus, for instance, at the beginning of chapter 17, "Of the Causes, Generation, and Definition of a Commonwealth": "*The end of commonwealth, particular security:* The final cause, end, or design of men, who naturally love liberty, and dominion over others, in the introduction of that restraint upon themselves, in which we see them live in common-

*Quite apart from the open question of whether people credibly have them, an out-of-the-body experience could certainly be *regarded* as an avenue of escape from the obligations of the social contract. Clearly HMR is regarding them in that light.

wealths, is the foresight of their own preservation, and of a more contented life thereby." Which omnipotent person, thus created, now ties men "by fear of punishment to the performance of their covenants, and observation of those laws of nature set forth in the fourteenth and fifteenth chapters" (p. 109).

We remind ourselves once more that those laws of nature are "eternal." The Hobbesian meaning of "eternal" will appear hereinafter.

Finally, from chapter 21, "Of the Liberty of Subjects": "The liberty of a subject, lieth therefore only in those things, which in regulating their actions, the sovereign hath praetermitted: such as is the liberty to buy, and sell, and otherwise contract with one another; to choose their own abode, their own diet, their own trade of life, and institute their children as they themselves think fit; and the like" (p. 139). As for instance? Does "liberty" of choice as to abode include the right of exit from and re-entry to the commonwealth state? We cannot suppose so, since this would be a right to traverse the no-man's land, or *actual* state of nature, that obtains between states. We have renounced that right. Covenants made must be kept. This is the third law of nature, soon to be eternal.*

We have, as well, no right to cavil at a flaw in the state of affairs—that flaw being constitutive of international relations as Hobbes knew them—that is acknowledged in the argument, and not falsely covered over by it.

Apart from our non-liberty to have the benefit of international relations that do not exist, is there any other impediment in our liberty to pursue happiness under the sovereign? We are not told whether or no we may choose to vaccinate, or not to vaccinate, in defiance of the sovereign's behest; but the question has not yet fairly arisen; and if it should arise, the only grounds for settling it would be, not our natural right, which we have renounced once and for all, but our *moral rights* . . . which, so long as they remain *in foro interno,* are mere wind.

---

*On the topic of *licensed* exit and re-entry (passports), HMR's 1975 longhand draft adds the following: "He [Hobbes] has, one assumes, no objections to passports, even those embellished by photography, provided they continue to protect our enjoyment of air and water, or put us in touch, for the first time in our lives, with the possibility of such enjoyment. But then passports are part, an essential part, of our reserved natural right: passports for everybody. The denial of a passport, in short, is an instant re-invocation of the state of nature. And that is too bad. By a passport is meant not only the right to arrive, but the far more important right to *depart*. It is *arrogant* to deny us that right. It is only *modest*, on our part, to want to claim it, for ourselves, and for everybody. In asserting that right, and in exercising it, we are only re-affirming our obedience to the commandment of primordial equality. After that, we shall well achieve the inequality we are really interested in: I shall go my way, and you will go yours, and they will be, please God, sufficiently unequal."

It is for that reason that *it is the sovereign's sole and absolute duty to enforce them.*

Thus, having already taken note of the end of commonwealth as being our particular (personal, private, or individual) security, and having further taken note that the substance of the covenant entered into, at the birth of commonwealth, was "observation of those laws of nature set down in the fourteenth and fifteenth chapters," we note in conclusion that the laws of nature, eternal though they be, are not self-enforcing.

Thus: "For the laws of nature, as *justice, equity, modesty, mercy,* and, in sum, *doing to others, as we would be done to,* of themselves, without the terror of some power, to cause them to be observed, are contrary to our natural passions, that carry us to partiality, pride, revenge, and the like. And covenants, without the sword, are but words, and of no strength to secure a man at all" (p. 109).

Ontological arguments are rarely productive of surprises, since they usually declare themselves early on, and thereafter tend to celebrate their own clichés.

One has, however, to acknowledge that Hobbes has here given us his own surprise. *Modesty,* for instance, is an eternal law of nature, and we arm the covenant with a sword precisely for the purpose of enforcing it.

As if to say: we demand of the covenant, as custodian of the promises we have made to one another, that it shall compel us not to walk proudly.

This is going pretty far. But it is as far as that that Hobbes has gone. It is not sumptuary legislation, such as niceties or excesses of dress and adornment, etc., that he has in mind, or the unwelcome and rejected possibilities of a theocratic community. It is something simpler, vaguer, of more general and more open application; one that he has several times referred to, in illustration of his own meaning, as the Golden Rule.

In short, Hobbes is saying that the Covenant with the Sword has been vested with that sword for the purpose of enforcement, by whatever terror, of the Moral Law.

But one had thought that purpose of the much-welcomed terror was to secure us in our natural right.

Yes, of course. The various suppositions are convergent; they are one and the same. Our natural rights are our moral rights, for the ontological reason that there aren't any other.

We now review Hobbes's collation of the eternal laws of nature, as given particularly in the fifteenth chapter of *Leviathan.* There are seventeen of them in this chapter, counting the third law, which is justice, or keeping promises. But the first three laws of nature, the first two of which have been given in chapter 14, are introductory.

They have summoned the covenanters together and have told them what they are come together for, namely, to make a covenant, but it is the next and conclusive sixteen eternal laws that are the *substance* of the covenant. So that the substance of the covenant, both before it is armed with a sword, and after, is the moral rights of man.

We confine ourselves to the sixteen substantive ones.

"*The fourth law of nature, gratitude*. As justice dependeth on antecedent covenant; so does GRATITUDE depend on antecedent grace; that is to say, antecedent free gift: and is the fourth law of nature; which may be conceived in this form, *that a man which receiveth benefit from another of mere grace, endeavour that he which giveth it, have no reasonable cause to repent him of his good will*. . . . The breach of this law, is called *ingratitude;* and hath the same relation to grace, that injustice hath to obligation by covenant" (p. 99).

No doubt, Hobbes does not mean to exclude the principle that the donor of bread to the hungry and water to the thirsty is entitled, by law of nature, to the beneficiary's gratitude. The principle seems obvious, but it does not follow that the law of nature is meant to exclude the obvious.

But the law of gratitude is armed with a sword. And the sword of gratitude is not pointed at the obvious. It is pointed at our natural right; which is, to "*Hate, from difficulty of requiting great benefits*. To have received from one, to whom we think ourselves equal, greater benefits than there is hope to requite, disposeth to counterfeit love; but really secret hatred; etc. . . ." (from chapter 11, p. 65, "Of the Difference of Manners," that is, *before* the covenant).

We are not to be rendered inattentive by the hearty obviousness of examples.

We know that the bread and the water, under the circumstances in which they were given, were a very great benefit, indeed. We are forbidden, by the law of nature, to hate our benefactors. Being forbidden to hate them, we can only be grateful to them.

The sword commands, not to love one another, which the covenant does not seem to be concerned with, but to be grateful *to one another*. Grace was *original,* and it was reciprocal, or mutual. It flowed from the moment of the social contract itself. If we must seek for it a further origin, we have to say that it is nothing more or less than the counter-productiveness, so to speak, of our equality by nature. We shall be proving that equality by nature over and over again. The social contract itself is one proof. Our mutual hatred by nature is another.

Therefore, the sovereign sword: to defend our moral right to one another's grace; or gratitude.

This right is unalienable. It seems absurd that governments, with their armed might, should have to maintain us in this right; but what are governments for, we may ask, in Hobbes's name, if not to protect us against hatred? That this hatred is, of course, the hatred of our equals, makes our right to grace all the more unalienable; that is, imperative.

The fifth law. "A fifth law of nature is COMPLAISANCE; that is to say, *that every man strive to accommodate himself to the rest* . . . a man that by asperity of nature, will strive to retain those things which to himself are superfluous, and to others necessary; and for the stubbornness of his passions, cannot be corrected, is to be left, or cast out of society, as cumbersome thereunto. For seeing every man, not only by right, but also by necessity of nature, is supposed to endeavour all he can, to obtain that which is necessary for his conservation; he that shall oppose himself against it, for things superfluous, is guilty of the war that thereupon is to follow" (p. 99).

Hobbes, for one reason or another, is putting it mildly; or, perhaps, with an unnecessary periphrasis that hedges his meaning.

The necessary meaning, from the dialectic of his argument of nature, covenant and law, is that acquisitive preemption of the things that are to others necessary *is* reversion to the state of nature, and therefore *is* war. The war of one against all—and, in principle, the war of one against another is the war of one against all—is the war of all against all.

The observers of this *fifth law,* Hobbes says, "may be called SOCIABLE . . . the contrary, *stubborn, insociable, froward, intractable*" (ibid.).

The sword of the covenant is, thus, directed against greed.

To be protected against greed—the greed of others, as well, perhaps, as our own, is, evidently, among our unalienable moral rights by nature. The stubbornness of greed is merely greed itself.

All economic orders would derive in Hobbes's view under the fifth law, from that rapaciousness of man-by-nature which Hobbes calls "stubborn" and "insociable" and we call acquisitive. All economic orders are thus, in Hobbes's implied view, acquisitive orders. The rule of descriptive analysis is to read or see the social contract as precipitate from the state of nature *once the latter has been turned against itself.* The rule of therapy for economic disorder is to turn acquisitiveness or rapacity against itself.

The casuisitry of the fifth law, applied to the problems of political economy would then read somewhat as follows: (*a*) since acquisitiveness is by-nature, it is not something that calls for extirpation, but rather something that calls for contractual accommodation between the cut-throat competitors. (*b*) Such accommodation or "complaisance" properly and therefore necessarily calls for the deposit of cut-throat competitiveness into a sovereign system called regulation. This means that in principle under the fifth law the social order has the strategic obligation of imposing accommodation. In practice, accommodation can also take the form of spontaneous cooperative arrangements. But self-regulation, like self-government, is a metaphor, usually a desirable one, for delayed enforcement.

If Hobbes believes in the "free enterprise" of his mercantilist day, it is because no enterprise is really free. It is governed by ontological principle. If Hobbes may be assumed to reject the presumptive collectivism of the "levelers" of his day, it is because it would make greed oblique and obsessional. (*c*) From the standpoint of the citizen as acquisitive for his necessities, this accommodation between the competitors might, by implication and in historical development, take the form of public welfare, the distributive aspect of accommodation. The in-built inhibitory or limiting mechanisms of the remaining "laws of nature" would then apply to the fifth law, "complaisance," as well, since the laws of nature are mutually self-regulating rather than expansive each one against the other.*

In sum, the economic order is not of itself or by definition self-corrective. And if it is not so in practice, it must be subjected to correction by whatever other instruments of the moral order are available.

The sixth law, "facility to pardon. A sixth law of nature, is this, *that upon caution of the future time, a man ought to pardon the offences past of them that repenting, desire it.* For PARDON, is nothing but granting of peace; . . ." (p. 99).

The postulation of our *right* to be forgiven for offenses past, as of our *obligation* to forgive those that privately trespass against us, has no novelty in it. The distinction is elsewhere made explicit between public offenses and private ones.[15] If that distinction is left inexplicit in the sixth law, it must signify that it is not always relevant. When is that? It is not relevant when it is indiscernible, and that can only be at the moment of the birth of the social contract, when we are both authors and actors under it.

The forgiveness here described, however succinctly, contains, or in fact is, a threat. The threat is the "*caution of future time.*" This threat is the sword of renewal. What is being renewed is the covenant itself. "Don't do it again," is an ontological saying. In this context it

---

*The meaning may perhaps be seen more clearly from the following remarks—crossed out in HMR's draft: "But the 'welfare state' is subject to the inhibitor set up by the original covenant, namely, that no man shall have more welfare than the next, and also that social sacrifice is a universal norm in society, equal with welfare. Welfare cannot take the form of a mandate to the state of nature to flourish in the midst of society."

has to do with the nature of time, which, morally speaking, is the uninterrupted demand for renewal, the nature of conscience, which is Hobbes's equivalent of Plato's soul, that is to say, the city within, and the nature of law, whose coherence and incoherence are expressed in those forces and institutions which radiate from the terror of punishment. Hobbes's metaphors re-enforce each other inexorably. They are never trivial, except when he talks about administrative concepts—monarchy, despotism, writs of seizure, and the like, in the faltering role of an early political scientist.

Forgive, then, says Hobbes, and/or be damned.

The seventh law. "The seventh, that in revenges, men respect only the future good. A seventh is, *that in revenges,* that is, retribution of evil for evil, *men look not at the greatness of the evil past, but the greatness of the good to follow.* Whereby we are forbidden to inflict punishment with any other design, than for correction of the offender, or direction of others. For this law is consequent to the next before it, that commandeth pardon, upon security of the future time . . . etc." (p. 100).

What shall one make of this? What kind of originality of magnanimity is here expressed? Hobbes is quite capable of a burst of ethical generosity. His threshhold of tolerance is high—except for forces of disorder and anarchy—and he is a forgiving man. But one expects of Hobbes that he solve a problem of his without *ad hoc* recourse to the available stockpile of attitudes, Classical and Christian, strategic and conscience-laden, that had to do with giving quarter in military operations of siege, or in the exercise of clemency to major miscreants after they have been rendered harmless. It is occasionally difficult to know whether Hobbes is invoking, by way of anticipation, our own clichés, or celebrating his. Not that one demands originality from penological speculation, even Hobbes's. The matter is too serious for mere originality. (The special seriousness of the penal experience is that it is in a unique sense inexpungeable and irreversible, as even severe deprivation, illness, or physical debilitation, is not necessarily functionally irreversible.) But one expects of Hobbes an unwillingness to be taken in by *ad hoc* thoughts.

The speculative confrontation between thoughts of deterrence versus thoughts of rehabilitation, and the like, tend to have just that *ad hoc* character that makes them uninstructive, and sometimes offensive. Who does not believe in rehabilitation, or, at worst, social example? When the Grand Inquisitor burns alive does he not do it for the rehabilitation of the victim's immortal soul, in that domain beyond the covenant?

The instructiveness of Hobbes's seventh law lies in its association of punishment, in principle, with pardon. Pardon is an act of *reason,* and reason is the original instrument whereby the state of nature was rendered into the social contract. This instrument, reason, once the covenant has been enacted, cannot be reduced to a therapeutic methodology for use in prisons or slums, or other circles of social fallout, but persists as Hobbes's formal metaphor for what more nearly resembles a "sacrament" whereby state-of-nature outlaws are brought to grace, that is, rehabilitated into the covenant. The unsatisfactoriness in practice of programs of rehabilitation follows from the difficulties of such a metaphysical undertaking, that is to say, from the programming of grace.

Punishment, too, has to have the benefit of such metaphysics, and that, of course, without mythological assumptions about conditions and immunities pertaining to a state "beyond history," as is sometimes said, or beyond the social contract: ". . . revenge," says Hobbes, "without respect to the example, and profit to come, is a triumph, or glorying in the hurt of another, tending to no end; for the end is always somewhat to come; and glorying to no end, is vainglory, and contrary to reason, and to hurt without reason, tendeth to the introduction of war; which is against the law of nature; and is commonly styled by the name of *cruelty*"[16] (p. 100).

Hobbes's "theory" of punishment serves to remind us that the act of covenant was in its moral import an act of the renunciation of cruelty. He implies, moreover, that all crime is cruelty.

In re-invoking our own natural right against a criminally invoked natural right of another, we are *not*, necessarily, construing the moral law our way, as one might simplistically assume. What we are doing is creating *history*. For Hobbes, history would seem to be the sequence of acts of concrete judgment under the moral law. But this sequence is not by any means a systematic whole. The historical acts of individuals are acts of resistance to the state of nature. And if "history" has any unity of character, it is the unity of continuous resistance.

This distinguishes his view from the view of the exemplary philosopher of history, Hegel, that history itself is a whole, that it expresses a sometimes deflected or circuitous but never interrupted progress toward freedom, and that its internal dynamics are governed by self-resolving and self-transcending conflicts in the spontaneous interpretation of what is going on.

In his nineteen eternal laws of nature, Hobbes is conspicuously more "Kantian" than Hegelian, in that for him there is no history except under the moral law, but not more Kantian in the sense that he would relegate the substance of moral reality to the restricted realm of acts done under the aegis of the "good will." The purity of the "good will" in Kant is not really discoverable, but remains always elusive and obscure to human inspection or introspection. The character of an "eternal act" in Hobbes is discoverable because it's empirically defined. The definition of "eternal" is constituted by the concrete specifications of the nineteen laws as the visible and observable parameters of conscience. For Hobbes, the realm of moral reality is thus coextensive with "eternal" acts under the social contract. The laws of nature, Hobbes is arguing all along, are eternal. Punishment is not.

The eighth law, "against contumely."

With the eighth, ninth, and tenth laws Hobbes leaves the field of social pragmatics—or, perhaps, that gray area where the moral law interposes against social pragmatics, and seeks confederacy with the latter—and enters the realm, as it were, of absolute spirit.

That is to say: whatever hermeneutic of human existence one proposes—whether it be the hermeneutic of absolute spirit, or that, merely, of the requirement of good faith—it will be incorrigible in application, insusceptible of compromises, and, as far as dialectic can see, closed against loopholes.

Thus, "we may in the eighth place, for a law of nature, set down this precept, *that no man by deed, word, countenance, or gesture, declare hatred, or contempt of another*. The breach of which law, is commonly called *contumely*" (p. 100).

The list is short, but exhaustive: deed, word, countenance, gesture; the loopholes for contempt are closed. The sword of sovereignty tilts at windmills.*

The ninth law, "against pride."

This law is the cornerstone of the Hobbesian political ontology, and can easily become its principal stumbling block. It is Hobbes's quite unique egalitarianism: his legitimation of *inequality under the laws civil*, that is to say, *under the covenant*, founded absolutely on the *hypothesis* of our *absolute equality by nature*. It is founded absolutely in the sense that the sword of sovereignty enforces precisely that hypothesis, and no other. The penalty for questioning the hypothesis is instant reversion to the state hypothesized, that is, to the state of nature. The hypothesis must be true, because there is nothing more absurd.

Our inequality is normative for the laws civil. But any particular

---

*The following remarks from HMR's 1975 longhand draft seem apropos here:

"No; we no longer murder; or not so often anyhow; meaning it has become an embarrassment to try to get away with murder.

"But not to murder is no longer enough.

"This is Hobbes's great discovery: as if he had made a breakthrough from his all-too-phenomenal world [an ontological mobile in most agitated perpetual motion] into a 'noumenal' world, where he does not at all belong. But he has no other place to go. And having broken through into this only place, he will, God helping him, not budge from it. This newly found noumenal world is the very substance of our covenant."

condition of inequality or set of inequalities is always remediable by and in the laws civil. What is not remediable is our equality by nature, upon which foundation alone the law civil is raised up.

Thus, further, the ninth law: "The question who is the better man, has no place in the condition of mere nature; where, as has been shown before, all men are equal. The inequality that now is, has been introduced by the laws civil." The exposition of the law is interrupted by a brief refutation of Aristotle's hierarchical counter-thesis in his *Politics*. Hobbes then resumes: "If nature therefore have made men equal, that equality is to be acknowledged: or if nature have made men unequal; yet because men that think themselves equal, will not enter into conditions of peace, but upon equal terms, such equality must be admitted. And therefore for the ninth law of nature, I put this, *that every man acknowledge another for his equal by nature*. The breach of this precept is *pride*" (p. 100f.). Pride goeth before the fall of the commonwealth.*

What does Hobbes mean by the inequality introduced into our existence by the laws civil?

I believe that his meaning is this: that the laws civil dispose and compel men to *brute acceptance* of "the diversity of passions; in divers men," spoken of at the beginning of chapter 11, and brute acceptance also of "the difference of the knowledge, or opinion each one has of the causes, which produce the effect desired" (p. 63). The effect he speaks of is *felicity*, or the good.

The follies men might believe in are irrelevant to their promises to one another under the covenant. Such follies (fantasies of superstition or even of hygiene, and so forth), may cheerfully *supervene* upon the promises without harm; but the moment they presume to *supersede* the promises, then they become threats to the covenant and invitations to the state of nature to return.

What men pursue is not happiness, but differences in happiness. The commonwealth lets men alone to pursue it, being indifferent to its realization, and therefore to the thing itself. The moral law is unconcerned.

But what the sword of sovereignty enforces is the *hypothesis* of equality and the *fact* of inequality. In between the hypothesis and the fact, men may be at peace.

The tenth law, "against arrogance."

This is Hobbes's law of utopia. It stipulates "*that at the entrance into conditions of peace, no man require to reserve to himself any right, which*

*There is this marginal note on the subject of pride in HMR's 1975 longhand draft: "We agree, then, that the mugger, with his knife, breaches the commandment against *pride*, and brings us, once more, that much nearer to that dread bourne from which it is so difficult to return: the free and equal state of nature."

he is not content should be reserved to every one of the rest. As it is necessary for all men that seek peace, to lay down certain rights of nature; that is to say, not to have liberty to do all they list: so is it necessary for man's life, to retain some; as right to govern their own bodies; enjoy air, water, motion, ways to go from place to place; and all things else, without which a man cannot live, or not live well" (p. 101).

The moral law, which the sword of sovereignty purports to enforce, is indifferent to *utopian ends,* such as felicity, or even the greatest happiness of the greatest number. It is concerned only with *utopian means,* such as bodies, air, water, mobility, and the option of going places. Hobbes's utopia is not a doctrine of last things, but of first things; and these are the only things that count in the commonwealth. To say that of our rights by nature it is necessary, on entering into the covenant, to "retain some," is merely a way of speaking. There is only one right by nature, and that is the right to all, both things and men. One often speaks of the right of *each* to all, and this would be near enough to the meaning, except that in the state of nature, "each" is a courtesy term. Strictly, one has only the right by nature to speak of "all."

The observers of this *tenth law,* Hobbes says, "are those we call *modest*, and the breakers *arrogant* men" (p. 101).

There is, of course, no dialectic of historical development in Hobbes, and no eschatology of classlessness. The problems of "distributive justice" in the Hobbesian commonwealth are not generated out of the "ownership of the means of production," nor do they arise as after-thoughts of revolutionary expropriation (as in "expropriation of the expropriators"), but they are problems of *moral right*. In that imagined or ambivalent intermediate condition between the state of nature and the social contract, the modes of survival appeared as differences of temperament or type, or, as Hobbes put it, "Difference of Manners," and which he had his say about in chapter 11 of *Leviathan*. At that point in our proto-history, both the suppressed intention of retribution and the overweaning presumption that attach to the competitive failures and successes of these types, respectively, had no remedy. In chapter 15, of the eternal laws of nature, they have.

The remedy is the utopian one: the moral law reserves to each contracting party in the commonwealth an equal claim to the patents of personal existence: the autonomy of the individual body, the use of the inalienable individual environment of air, water, warmth, roofing, access to the open or to other spaces, and so forth. After that, the differences in the ends, sometimes called happiness, can multiply to infinity. The eternal fifth law has long since settled the problem of unsociable greed, which is simply the monopolistic tendency, or arrogance, of ends as such.

The moral law now seems to consider that *distributive* justice will arise naturally from the sovereign outlawry of *arrogance*. The covenant is, among other things, a covenant of utopian *modesty*. Modesty here means "moderation" and/or restraint in acquisitiveness.

Hobbes's idiom is, of course, the powerful, rhetorical idiom of a seventeenth-century prose that he has made uniquely his own.

But it will hardly be claimed that in that era of contrary tendencies, neo-medieval, mercantilist, and proto-capitalist, it was the only idiom possible.

With the eleventh law of "equity," or dealing equally, Hobbes leaves the realm of his moral absolutes and returns to the pragmatics of uncertainties. The moral law is not one to neglect them.

The passage from the absolutes of the eighth, ninth, and tenth eternal laws of nature—in a more general way these absolutes of our human limits are figured forth by the third law, of keeping promises, and its successors—to the procedural guidelines of the eleventh through nineteenth laws is a devolution from political *authorship* to civil *action*.

This distinction, made by Hobbes in his next chapter, the sixteenth, between *author* and *actor*, is a distinction largely without a difference. The wavering indiscernibility of the distinction is due to the fact that what Hobbes is arguing is the *locus of responsibility*, and that, while purporting to argue it politically, or so it is generally held, he is really arguing it ontologically; that is, on the plane of the incorrigible inter-connectedness, and reciprocity, of all things that act. So that, in that dissolving sense of responsibility we are surely responsible for our own beheading: we have *authored* it. But the moral law is there to point out that it is not we who raised the axe; we may have authored it, but we have not performed the *act*. The distinction is a political, or *procedural*, one; and the moral law is quite capable of making it. It will insist on doing so.

But once we have understood this unavoidable metaphor—that the moral law both authors the eternal laws of nature, and acts them out—we also understand what is behind the metaphor: *that it is we*, the high contracting parties of the covenant, *who are the authors of the moral law*. The sword given, can be taken away. No doubt, it will then pass into other hands.

The eleventh law seeks to postpone that eventuality as long as possible.

The eleventh law, "equity." This is no longer an absolute, but a calculus of approximations. "Also if *a man be trusted to judge between man and man*, it is a precept of the law of nature, *that he deal equally between them*" (p. 101).

It is now signaled to us that dispensing justice, or performing as a judge between man and man is a procedure of "dealing equally," but earlier, in the third law, we were told that the substance of justice itself is the keeping of promises. Here these aspects of justice come to be connected.

For instance: what concrete and particular promises have we sworn to keep to one another, at that primordial moment when the *third law of nature, or justice,* came into re-instanced being in the Federal Constitution of the United States?

No doubt we swore to treat one another under the hypothesis of *equality*. That is to say, we implicitly promised to treat our slaves as hypothetically equal to ourselves.

(If, however, the explicit language of the Constitution, as for instance in Article I, Section 2, denied that all those covenanted for were also covenanters, that is to say, if it denied that slaves were persons, then the Constitution was not a proper covenant at all, except in the course of its amendment under Articles XIII, XIV, XV, and so forth. What we are talking about here, we must assume, is the Constitution in its Hobbesian ideality, and not the Constitution in its flawed genesis and history.)

The case has then arisen where a radical challenge to the covenant is made in the form of a claim to extradite a runaway slave from the sovereignty of freedom to the soi-disant sovereignty of slavery.

In principle, this profound either/or issue should abide further adjudication by the Union and its designated, sovereign instrumentalities, or strategic political devices, as for instance, the further admission of free states and territories to alter the balance of "absolute power" within sovereignty. For this to happen, the Union must of course remain indissoluble.

The central, critical issue then becomes, was the indissoluble Union the thing covenanted ("the promise made"), as the North claimed, or was the right of interposition and nullification one of the eternal laws of nature, as the South, in effect, claimed?

The question was rendered moot, as the saying goes, by the shot fired at Fort Sumter. The state of nature, thereby re-invoked, is outside of history, a status which it shares with all that is moot. In principle, the required inference is an easy one: *if the South had won, it would have had to restore the Union.*[17] The hedging qualification, "sooner or later," does not alter the principle; or the fact that the questions that would then arise would have to be argued under the eternal laws of nature. "He therefore that is partial in judgment," says the *eleventh law,* of equity, "doth what in him lies, to deter men from the use of judges, and arbitrators; and consequently, against the fundamental law of nature, is the cause of war" (p. 101).

The violation of the eleventh law is called *"acception of persons"*; more familiarly: *favoritism,* or arbitrariness in the treatment of persons.

The moral law is armed with a sword against it, because it leads to war.

The twelfth law, "equal use of things common."

This law is corrective of the utopian principle of the tenth law.

From the whole confluence of preceding premises—for argument's sake they can be taken as one, either the axiom of equality of the ninth law, or the directive to equity of the eleventh law–we conclude, *"that such things as cannot be divided, be enjoyed in common, if it can be; and if the quantity of the thing permit, without stint; otherwise proportionably to the number of them that have right.* For otherwise the distribution is unequal, and contrary to equity" (p. 101).

No doubt, Hobbes had particular indivisibles, and divisibles, in mind, or at the back of his mind: perhaps pasture commons, riparian rights, rights of way that make possible the "going from place to place" of the utopian principle previously laid down, timber rights not already pre-empted by some more eminent domain—or perhaps regardless of such pre-emption; et cetera. Surely he had the sweep of enclosures in mind, since the rightfulness of such enclosures and prevision of the social and economic consequences which they entailed were an overriding concern of the whole Cromwellian period and beyond. But the possible local occasions of his argument do not ever govern the arc of Hobbes's thought, which has to do with eternal laws. What the eternal laws prescribe at this point, when such laws become immanent in temporal-political actuality, is an indefinite apprenticeship in the practice of dividing the indivisible, or distributing access to it.

We credit Hobbes with an indefeasible and quite nominalistic awareness that life under the covenant will be relentlessly confronted with the task of dividing the indivisible. The divisibles will have been appreciably grasped by individual hands by the time men pass from the state of nature into covenant. Whatever is still undivided (forests, unenclosed lands, etc.) will eventually pass under the control of someone or some public body. What is left will go under the contemporary mediocre name of "opportunity," and it is *this* indivisible that the moral law has ultimately to divide. It is "opportunities" that clash (as, for instance, in quota systems that aim to promote or impose "equal opportunity" in education, employment, and so forth) once tangible goods have been brought under some rough-and-ready rule of distributive justice (as in public welfare benefits or free milk to school children).

But what is to become of the twelfth eternal law, for instance, when the dividend of scarcity encounters the divisor of population in a geometric increase? When the question is put this way, it becomes obvious that Malthusian considerations do not subvert the twelfth law. They have merely taken the state of nature as the historical norm, which, of course, the moral law denies.

The moral law's apprenticeship lasts, of course, much longer than the apprenticeship of the guardians in Plato's commonwealth, which was founded, but not covenanted. The moral law's apprenticeship lasts as long as the social contract itself.*

The thirteenth law, "of lot."

This law is the *subjugation of chance to eternal law:* "Some things there be, that can neither be divided, nor enjoyed in common. Then, the law of nature, which prescribeth equity, requireth, *that the entire right; or else, making the use alternate, the first possession, be determined by lot*. For equal distribution, is of the law of nature; and other means of equal distribution cannot be imagined" (p. 101).

The moral law can only perform what it is able to imagine. What it now does is easily imaginable: the randomness of motion is brought within the framework of the covenant. Let the lot err—and what else is chance but error?—and the parameters of the ninth law, of equality, the tenth, of modesty, and the eleventh, of equity itself, are ready to hand to correct the error. The important thing is to get the commonwealth moving. This historical challenge the moral law is prepared to meet.

The fourteenth law, "of primogeniture, and first seizing."

The moral law permits itself a triviality. The triviality, in the form of a gloss on the thirteenth law, offers two instances, presumably paradigmatic, of the subjugation of chance to the covenant: the one, the rule of primogeniture in inheritance; the other, the rule of title, other things being equal, by the first actuality of possessing, or seizure. As in many cases, the triviality reflects a confusion, in this case a confusion between the history of a commonwealth, the English one, and the nature of a covenant. In the history of the English commonwealth, biological chance, or primogeniture, was long regarded as irremediable, until it was discovered that it is easily remedied by being ignored. The moral law has a sense of guilt about biological considerations and sometimes makes self-reversing mistakes about them. The self-reversals may be equally mistaken. The moral law is thus not exempt from the price of triviality.

---

*The lesson plan of this lengthy apprenticeship is made clearer in this paragraph from HMR's 1977 version: "The Malthusian dilemma is actually avoided in the twentieth century by improvement in agricultural productivity. Without being mindful of such benevolent possibilities of social development, Hobbes's considered commitment to distributive equity suggests a strain of optimism in his thought which, if it were not Hobbes, would be almost tantamount to a 'belief in progress,' or at least such progress as will prove necessary."

The fifteenth law, "of mediators."

"It is also a law of nature, *that all men that mediate peace, be allowed safe conduct*. For the law that commandeth peace, as the *end*, commandeth intercession, as the *means;* and to intercession the means is safe conduct" (p. 102).

Is Hobbes here reminding the covenanters of the ancient sacredness of an ambassador's person? That hardly seems apropos, nor, in fact, is it near enough to what the law says.

The law's reference is to "all men that mediate peace." Are there any, then, in the commonwealth who do not, by law of nature, mediate peace? By definition there are none such.

All men, then, are intercessors; and the law of intercession is the instrument whereby the moral law converts the kingdom of absolute self-referring ends, which is by nature, therefore apolitical, into the republic of means *and* ends. Each member of the commonwealth is just such a union.

But note that the imperative of this law falls more upon the *means* than upon the end: "the means is safe conduct."

Hobbes has said that in the commonwealth, our modicum of natural right, though suppressed, or repressed, is unalienable. The adversary relation, so pervasive in the state of nature that it is hardly noticeable, thus becomes a normal disorder of relations between individuals in the social contract. The significant imperative of the fifteenth law is, then, that each covenanter become, one way or another, a *committee of public safety*.

But the safe conduct that the citizen is called upon to promote is not in discharge of a function of the state. The moral law at this point pretends, provisionally, to know nothing of states, but proposes to serve as the protocol of the built-in competitive or adversary relations among fellow subjects. It is when this protocol is grossly violated that the subject–agent of the moral law is authorized to make citizen arrests, if intercession demands, but *not* to make unauthorized usurpation of sub-functions of sovereignty by being an informer or bearer of denunciation. The state waits to intervene when the non-violent "police power" of the citizen, provisionally supersedent of the sufficiently violent police power of the state, will have withdrawn because of evident inadequacy.

The fifteenth law, for all its noble blandness, re-invokes the entire ontological casuistry and self-discipline upon which the social contract is based; cautions us that political conscience, Hobbes's *foro interno,* will not be wholly absorbed into *foro externo,* or social institutions, and thereby depart from us, even in the "peaceable kingdom" of the commonwealth, or especially not there. In this fashion the fifteenth law arms us with the sword of intercession against ourselves. There is enough "terror of punishment" in that to go around.

The sixteenth law, "of submission to arbitrement."

The moral law hastens toward its end. We began with *justice,* and we move conclusively toward *judges,* and the rules of *judging.*

The paradigmatic of judgment is *arbitration.* The rule is, *arbitration* is by law of nature *compulsory.* The judge of first instance, as of the last, is an *arbitrator;* and arbitration is not an option, but an eternal law.

"And because, though men be never so willing to observe these laws,"—whence this "willingness"? is it counter-factual hypothesis, or has the sword of sovereignty induced or conditioned in men, *in foro interno,* a willingness to overcome their overwhelming reluctance by nature?—"there may nevertheless arise questions concerning a man's action; . . . therefore unless the parties to the question, covenant mutually to stand to the sentence of another, they are as far from peace as ever. This other to whose sentence they submit is called an ARBITRATOR. And therefore it is of the law of nature, *that they that are at controversy, submit their right to the judgment of an arbitrator*" (p. 102).

We now have our first inkling of the meaning of *eternal,* an epithet reserved by Hobbes for the laws of nature, and for them alone: that alone is "eternal" which is renewable without stint.

One does not here say "perpetual," since the meaning of perpetual time is by no means clear. For a similar reason one does not say "indefinitely," which suggests the falling arrow of time, and all entropic phenomena, which are hardly renewable.

"Without stint" is Hobbes's expression in the *twelfth law,* having to do with the *equity* of common pasturage and other inexorable arrangements.

Without stint: *without abatement or exception;* not subject to circumstantial manipulation; *without stint:* falling under the rule of *either/or.*

The *eternality* of the eternal laws of nature does not mean that they are not "repealable"; never having been enacted, they are, of course, not subject to repeal. Their eternality signifies a demand for uninterrupted renewal: *either* the covenant is renewed all the time, *or* it has never been in force at all.

The sixteenth law, "of submission to arbitrement," thus enables us to apply Hobbes's social contract to the clarification of legal process. "Submission to arbitrement" imples that in the legal process of the commonwealth, *we confirm our renunciation of our equality by nature,* and *consent to our inequality under the laws civil.* In the first fifteen laws, the effort at conciliation, or the distribution of compromise, has been relentless. But beginning with the sixteenth law, somebody is going to lose. It is inequality that will now be distributed, not equality. Justice now means consenting to losing.

But, of course, the winner in the adversary proceeding of litigation collapses at once, under the moral law, into submission to the eternal laws of *equity*, and the corollaries of such laws, that have accumulated in the governance of the commonwealth up to law sixteen.

Finally: the sixteenth law suggests the relation between the moral law and what is sometimes called positive law, that is, *book* law, whether the "sovereign commands" of book law be written or unwritten.

Positive law walks backward before the moral law, and always submits to it. If the moral law averts its face, positive law responds by capitulation. The meaning of these figures of speech is simply this: positive law, whether written or unwritten, can be repealed, amended, or otherwise revised; the moral law can only be abandoned. With this "terror of punishment" at hand, the moral law does not even need a sword. If we do not know what the moral law is, and therefore cannot reason with one another, then let us litigate with one another, and for such litigation the moral law will provide the rules.

The seventeenth law, "no man is his own judge" (p. 102).

The eighteenth law, "no man to be judge, that has in him a natural cause of partiality" (*ibid.*).

In these two penultimate theses, the moral law proposes various criteria for fullness of performance under the covenant.

It is by no means said to us, judge not, lest ye be judged; but on the contrary, judge one another, but only *as* the other, and also *by* another. And from this follow the criteria of objectivity, disinterestedness, and non-conflict of interest, in the adversary proceedings of the social contract. The notion of a *person* comes obliquely once more into focus.

It now appears that the "naturalness" of a cause of contention arises merely and exclusively from its partiality. If there were a "natural person," apart from the whole commonwealth itself, such a person would be one who has a "natural cause of partiality" in him; and all claimant or self-ostensive natural persons would, under the moral law, stand under suspicion. The moral law has a natural preference for the *feigned* or *artificial* person, that is to say, for the complex of interests that are configurated as the person of the *other*. That complex of interests is also partial, but the partiality is not mine; nor is it directly or necessarily at odds with mine.

Hobbes would no doubt entertain this quasi-Kantian conclusion with great reluctance. But his moral ontology has a spontaneous logic of its own. It is in the deadlock of the adversary relation that *altruism* and the above-the-battle relation are born, in the Hobbesian commonwealth, before which there was neither altruism *nor* egoism, both of which have to be the postures of definable persons; nor judiciousness, which is the gesture of forcibly taking contending persons beyond themselves.

The altruism meant here is the identification not with the adversary as another "natural person" in the suspect sense, but with the ultimate "natural person" that is the commonwealth, and is therefore *entirely* other. The adversary relation that defines itself to reflection at this point of the argument is more like the confrontation of skilled and dedicated gamblers (your "true gambler") than like the confrontation of Roman gladiators. And again more like a gambler than like an athlete, since we wish to abstract from our example the element of superior merit or competence that in principle predetermines the result of a sport competition. The gambler wants to win, of course. But he would rather lose, by hypothesis, than see the rules of gambling abolished or manipulated in his favor. In this sense and for such reasons the luckless adversary wants to win, of course. But more than that he wants the covenant to endure and to continue to reserve a place for him in its reticulated structures of adversity. By the same token he wants a similar place reserved for the other. If he does not entertain the latter want as passionately as the former, that is merely a matter of the variables of temperament.

The commonwealth, born out of the strife of universal self-defense, self-generalizing into universal atrocity, now finds itself shocked into confrontation with an unexpected principle: defend at all costs, but defend the other, that is, the members of the commonwealth in their controlled adversity to each other. The covenanters can only console themselves that at least the principle of *strife* has been conserved.

The nineteenth law, "of witnesses."

The moral law takes leave of the social contract by summoning the covenanters to bear witness, the witness that they bear being inevitably against themselves.

"And in a controversy of *fact*, the judge being to give no more credit to one, than to the other, if there be no other arguments, must give credit to a third; or to a third and fourth; or more: for else the question is undecided, and left to force, contrary to the law of nature" (p. 102).

It is clear that, in principle, the law of nature cannot stop until it has summoned all the contracting parties to bear witness to the *fact* of what has happened. But this is precisely what was at issue in the state of nature. And it was only settled by the moral law, acting through the eternal laws of nature, and their sword.

Hobbes's argument stands, then, to this effect: that government *of* the people, *by* the people, and *for* the moral law, shall not perish from the earth.

Appendix

A more detailed sketch of how this *a priori* happening may be imagined to "happen" is found in HMR's 1973–74 longhand draft:

"Here is a man with a gun in his hand. The man is small in stature, smaller, perhaps than Napoleon . . . . He is just one of those men (or he might be a woman, but let us not seek out ideological and metalinguistic complications, but abide, rather, by the laziness of given language) whom one would automatically describe to the policeman, or the district attorney, as a 'short man. O yes; quite short . . . .'

"We hypothesize his shortness in order to preserve the spirit of Hobbes's radical *egalitarianism by nature*. All men are equally lethal by nature, short or tall. . . . He feels himself to be [omnipotent], and he is. A dream come true. The redemptive potential of sheer power is realized at last: He can kill absolutely, without being killed. There is no death, because only one, forever, is alive. The man with the gun—what an admirable character to have exercised such incredible restraint for so long—notices something. He has noticed it all along, but in the complicated computations of his interior motions it has taken him some time to *notice* that he is noticing. . . . What he notices is that there is a man (or a woman?) over there who has a gun too. And quick as a flash he has notices that there are very many men (and women); and that they all have guns. *Everybody has a gun that looks like his own*.

"The computation of possibilities here is too much for the mind of man. Never mind the 'games theory' at this capital of the intellect or that, this institution or that, War College or Chiefs of Staff, never mind, even, the war in heaven that Milton sang. . . . The human brain has ceased to be a closed system.

"If my finger is on the trigger, where will his finger be? What guarantee have I that I will even know what hit me? I would like to terrorize him, but how can I disguise the fact that I am long since terrorized? . . . I know that his terror is mine, as surely as I know that my redeemer liveth, but how can I know that my terror is his? It is not the same thing. A deception has happened. The reciprocity of motion is not to be relied on. I know that he can trust me, whom else can he trust if not myself?, but can I trust him? A paralysis of incalculability overcomes me. I can only hope that the same paralysis has overcome him. The strength of my fear teaches me that there is some substance to that hope. I notice in him what I wished to avoid in myself. We are gesturing the gun in our hand toward the place of stacking.

"No finality attaches to what is now going on. No finality whatsoever. We can draw back at any moment we choose. I do not know whether he can, but I know that I can. It is already too late for that—for him, and for me. To all intents and purposes I am disarmed. When I am no longer at the ready I know that I am irrevocably non-violent. I can only hope that he is too. Of course he is."

"In this psycho-drama, or something like it, of total mutual distrust, universal disarmament comes about. The word 'universal' simply refers to the whole of the situation that concerns us, whether it be tribal, territorial, insular, or continental. There is no necessity whatsoever that it be global, or cosmic. The global or the cosmic can take care of itself, and it generally does.

"This hesitation dance, this slow shuffle against death, has taken place, so to speak, in despite of ourselves, and all the more inevitably on that account. That is to say, we did not have to intend it; it happened of its own intent. How like a god!

"We have stacked our arms.

"There seemed little else to do.

"Disarmed, . . . we sit there, in the half-way sun and lengthening shadows of our history, and contemplate what has happened to us, what we have done. What we have done is unprecedented and not quite believable: we have surrendered to one another our license to kill. Have we therefore surrendered . . . our natural right? This is not quite so. There is a fine ambiguity in this matter, which merits examination (though not too closely).

"There is a part of our natural right—to kill, and to kill again, at whatever risk—which may be surrendered. It already has been. We look at the immense, very neat pile of stacked arms in the middle of the plaza, and we are forcibly, though not yet forcibly enough, reminded of what has already happened. And there is another part of our natural right which is indefeasible, as they say.

"Let us call this latter part of our natural right: the residual part. This residual natural right of ours has a wonderfully complex function in the rest of our history. It reminds us of where we have been, where we now are, and where we shall not go. It also reminds us of our unanimity, as near as may be.

"We have only to look at the gun that we might like to retrieve, and the merest, most furtive glance is enough to convince us that what *we* might like to retrieve, others would almost just as certainly like to retrieve as well. Almost is as good as certainly here. We had better do something about this.

"There is only one thing to do; appoint a custodian for the stacked arms; a mere watchman, day and night. He might as well be, as watchmen often are, a veteran of the wars, or a former killer or policeman, or whatever. All he has to do is accept, in good faith, as it is said, his job as custodian.

"The transition to covenant is practically accomplished. It was perhaps not really intended, but it was done anyhow. All that remains is to acknowledge what was done. We could not possibly by nature do what we have done, but we have done it. We have established a commonwealth. What is more, painful as it may be, it is a sovereign commonwealth. God save us, one and all.

"He will, too. He has left, to each as his own secret, our natural right. We must keep it well hidden, but everybody knows that it is there: the sovereign above all, he knows. That is why he has been designated: to see that it is kept hidden. So that is a sure and incontestable sign that he knows that it is there, well hidden: our natural right. And if he knows, all know. He knows it in behalf of us all."

PART TWO

Spinoza's Way

Spinoza's way, both the way up and the way down, is there for following in his *Ethic*. This was published posthumously, but it was well thought out before he died. Come to think of it, it is one of the most carefully thought-out pieces of work in the history of such enterprises, having reference to the architectonic of it, the joins and the dovetailings, and the self-understanding of the work as it runs; or, to put it another way, in the constant presence of the whole in the parts.

There are three key propositions in the *Ethic*:

1. *"The object of the idea constituting the human mind is a body, or a certain mode of extension actually existing, and nothing else"** (in Part II, the thirteenth Proposition, and its associated corollaries and lemmas). A lemma is a subsidiary proposition, subjoined to the principal proposition, and used to re-enforce its argument, sometimes merely by showing the concrete, self-manifest implications of the principal proposition. There are seven such lemmas to Proposition 13, and six "postulates" subjoined to the seventh lemma, that further unfold the meaning and application of the entire argument.

2. *"Those ideas are also adequate which follow in the mind from ideas which are adequate in it"* (in the same Part II, the fortieth Proposition, which must inevitably be read in conjunction with the one or two related propositions that precede it and the one or two that come after).

3. *"The human mind cannot be absolutely destroyed with the body, but something of it remains which is eternal"* (in Part V, the twenty-third Proposition).

The first of these three gives Spinoza's notion of "how" one becomes an individual thing in and of God or Substance. There is of course no "how." But "how" is a way of speaking. One could just as well say "why," or "what it means to be an individual," or some similar expression. One either is an individual, since God by nature individuates infinitely and eternally, or one is nothing.

The second of these sets forth the *three* (by a somewhat dragged-out reckoning, conceivably four) "grades of knowledge," according to Spinoza, the third of which is the highest, and in some sense the only one that counts. For, as I shall argue, it is by virtue of the third grade, and only on that account, that the first and second grades of

---

*HMR's references—in this case and generally—are to the W. Hale White 1883 translation of Spinoza's *Ethic*, as revised in 1894 and 1899 by Amelia Hutchinson Stirling, 4th ed. (Oxford: Oxford University Press, 1930). However, where HMR uses "Note" in preference to "Scholium," "emotion" in preference to "affect," and "modification" or "mode" in preference to "affection," he is relying on the James Gutmann edition of the *Ethics* (New York: Hafner Publishing, 1949).

knowledge live and move and have their being, or such validity of being as they do have.

The third of these clearly asserts that there is a "part" of the human mind that does not die with the body, but is eternal. It is, if one likes, Spinoza's quite non-traditional version of "immortality."

(To say "immortality of the soul" here, or, for that matter, "of the body," would be to confuse the issue absolutely.)

Which of these three propositions should one start with in order to go Spinoza's way with reasonable dispatch and with least distraction?

Each has something to commend it as a hitching post and starting point.

The thirteenth Proposition of Part II commends itself to one's venture as a means of quick disabuse of vulgar and languid Spinozism, that we are all god-like, dissolved in god-likeness, and ennobled by it, whether we will or no: catch-the-breath "pantheism," which, conceptualized, emerges as bargain-day mysticism, and contemptible. Anything that promises quick corrective for those particular ills of misunderstanding ought to be welcome.

Over and above this salutary corrective, II, 13 of the *Ethic* tells us why and how we are alone with what we are. This beginning of wisdom might be a good thing to start with.

But the twenty-third Proposition of Part V seems to promise the reader something even better than wisdom: it promises him a relation to "eternity." Perhaps we did not know that we are concerned with eternity, or interested in it. It is, indeed, an unwelcome word, and arouses a certain anger, as if one is being had. But, at worst, V, 23 unreluctantly faces a question that all our lives we have wanted to know the answer to, namely, whether the best we can look forward to is extinction. We have long suspected that we shall never know, but that does not extinguish the question, and we do not quite trust people who refuse to face it.

Our difficulty here is the usual one of being fallen between two stools: on the one hand we do not exactly know what is meant by "extinction" or "nihilation" or some equivalent; and on the other hand the notion of extinction is deeply rooted in our language, and about these matters we have the habit of literalness. The word extinction could not have been invented to no purpose, just to frighten us with; it must mean what it says. But what *does* it mean? The result of these ambivalent fluctuations is anxiety. Is it conceivable that V, 23 might relieve us of our anxiety?[1] That would be worth trying. But a moment's further thought suggests that V, 23 is too good to be yet true: we are not ready for it, and had better wait until we are driven, not merely led, to its conclusion.

II, 40, about knowledge, seems to be something we cannot be fooled by, as we might be by eternity. We know about knowledge. We have been, we think, in our own small way knowledgeable all along. Nobody can let us down about knowledge, least of all Spinoza. Let us start, then, with II, 40 and its surround.

Scholium 2 to II, 40 contains what we are looking for to start with. This Scholium outlines the "kinds" of knowledge as Spinoza at this point conceives them. In part, it reads as follows:

> *Schol.* 2. From what has been already said, it clearly appears that we perceive many things and form universal ideas:
>
> 1. From individual things, represented by the senses to us in a mutilated and confused manner, and without order to the intellect (Corol. Prop. 29, pt. 2). These perceptions I have therefore been in the habit of calling knowledge from vague experience.
>
> 2. From signs; as, for example, when we hear or read certain words, we recollect things and form certain ideas of them similar to them, through which ideas we imagine things (Schol. Prop. 18, pt. 2). These two ways of looking at things I shall hereafter call knowledge of the first kind, opinion or imagination.
>
> 3. From our possessing common notions and adequate ideas of the properties of things (Corol. Prop. 38, Prop. 39, with Corol. and Prop. 40, pt. 2). This I shall call reason and knowledge of the second kind.
>
> Besides these two kinds of knowledge, there is a third, as I shall hereafter show, which we shall call intuitive science. This kind of knowledge advances from an adequate idea of the formal essence of certain attributes of God to the adequate knowledge of the essence of things. All this I will explain by one example.

The beginning of the enumeration is faltering. He lists, to begin with, two different "kinds" of knowledge, and then observes that the just enumerated "two ways of looking at things I shall hereafter call knowledge of the first kind, opinion or imagination." The "two ways" he seems to have in mind are the "mutilated and confused" ways of ordinary sense perception, no doubt as reflected in ordinary language, when we tell each other, or ourselves, by whatever signals, what we have seen or heard, or otherwise sensated, "to the best of our knowledge and belief," but without commitment to the "belief." Until we are ready to act, one way or another, on that belief: then we are committed.

To refer to sense perception, and the ordinary language that goes with it, as "mutilated and confused" seems arbitrary. Ordinarily, we trust our senses well enough, Descartes to the contrary notwithstanding, and do well to trust them. If we are reasonably sensible, we trust them enough to know when to distrust them.

But it is not necessary, and perhaps unwarranted, to take the uncomplimentary characterization—"mutilated and confused"—as an epithet of dismissal. The short, subsequent paragraph, seeking to classify the first *subspecies* of the "first kind" of knowledge, concludes: "These perceptions I have therefore been in the habit of calling knowledge from vague experience." Spinoza is wide open to the question, what other kind of experience is there? What is the alternative to "vagueness" of experience? Does he mean experience that is *not* methodically pursued, under conditions approximating those of laboratory control?

This might sound like Francis Bacon, or William Harvey, but does not sound like Spinoza. It is unlikely that Spinoza intends to lead the reader to "blessedness" by way of the laboratory method. And in any case, what the seventeenth century might have conceived as a "laboratory method" would be vague enough by more recent standards, unless it was the method of magic, or of the alchemists. Their method was quite precise, even by our standards: but was not their "knowledge" precisely "mutilated and confused"?

Let us consider more carefully Spinoza's characterization of the "first kind" of knowledge. I believe that Spinoza, for various historical reasons, has over-stated the separateness of the first kind from the other kinds—an over-statement which is corrected by the further development of his entire argument—and that his over-statement has been compounded by later misunderstandings. These misunderstandings were sometimes natural, historically, and sometimes willful.

1. The contents of the "first kind" of knowledge are thought of as "sense representations" or as "perceptions." I shall take the two labels as interchangeable, since it seems to make no difference which one of them one uses.

2. The objects of the "sense representations" or the "perceptions," or both, are "individual things," and they are sense-represented or perceived in a "mutilated and confused manner . . . without order to the intellect."

3. Subject to a limitation, the product one is now dealing with is a kind of "knowledge." The limitation is indicated when he calls it "knowledge from vague experience." Just how severe is this limitation? Does he mean uncriticized or unexamined experience? If so, how far does the critical examination have to go for the knowledge in question to qualify as habilitated?

4. A distinction has been made (in Proposition 40, Scholium 1) between "individual things" perceived, and therefore known, by us,

subject to appropriate limitation, and "universal ideas," such as Man, Horse, Dog, etc., which we *"form,"* but do not really know at all, since they do not stand for anything that can be perceived, or represented by the senses, however vaguely. These so-called universals are simply the collapse of multiple images into each other, and the consequent loss or abandonment of any original particular identity they must have had.

So far, Spinoza's opening maneuver in the deployment of his epistemology.

Epistemology is the political economy of philosophy, or its dismal science. In Spinoza's time it had not yet reached the fuller development it was to have in British empiricism, Locke, Hume, and Berkeley, and in Kant. But it had been well and dismally launched by Descartes, the point of reference for Spinoza and for most others in the latter half of the seventeenth century, and it is presumably the Cartesian gloom about knowledge which Spinoza is trying to avoid. He is trying to avoid it, but the shadow of it is, I think, responsible for a certain confusion, or triviality, that appears to attend his entry into subject. One feels two things about what he has so far said in his exposition of the "first kind" of knowledge: (*a*) that we have not learned much about theory of knowledge, assuming there is something to be learned; and (*b*) that Spinoza does not consider it a fundamental problem, or at least not the kind of problem that Descartes—and Kant, too, in due course—thought it was; namely, how can we be sure that we know what we know? And so on.

Spinoza's view, clearly enough, is that there is no such problem; and if such an alleged problem is the subject-matter of epistemology, then that science is not a particularly demanding one.

The reason in Spinoza's case is simple enough: *to be is to know.* And, for that matter, there is no *problem* of being; there are simply variations in the presentation of the case of being: to perceive—as Berkeley later pointed out, and as Spinoza assumes as a matter of course, while entertaining a certain distaste for the language of the "being" of substances—is to be; and to feel is of course to be, and therefore to know, as it also is to imagine; and to doubt, if you insist, would also be to be; but what would be the problem of it? The problem of it was, of course, for Descartes, that perhaps the world is merely a great big lie, or a dream, or an audio-visual hallucination; that is to say, maybe the world, and all one's fooling around with it, is the production of a "Great Deceiver," or liar, such as oneself, for instance. And at this point in one's epistemological "scepticism," one gets frightened, and one appeals to an extra-territorial God, by way of one or another of the various onto-, cosmo-, or teleological arguments, or modes of appeal.

If one starts, then, as we have chosen to do, with Spinoza's reflections on the ways of knowing, in II, 40 of the *Ethic* and thereabouts, one discovers that Spinoza is obliquely referring us back to the beginning of things. His mode of referral is to suggest to us that we cannot understand a trivial matter, or why it is trivial, unless we understand something quite important, first of all, and that the importance of it is there all along, if it is anywhere at all.

Spinoza has not failed of his own methodological duty, in his comment on the "first kind" of knowledge in II, 40. If we scrutinize that comment—without prejudice as to what it does *not* wish to say, or what problems it does not wish to become entangled with—we note that it suggests to us what the fundamental concern is, namely: What *is* the "individual thing" that we are going presently to perceive, if we have not already done so; and how are we going to continue to perceive it, or whatever would be the right thing to do at that point, when *other* individual things appear for our knowing perception? In other words: the whole, the parts, and their inter-acquaintance with one another; or ourselves, and the world.

There have always been some differences—petulant, angry, or ostensibly formidable, as the case may be—as to which has the greater urgency: to know ourselves, or to know the world; and which comes first, if there is a first and second in the matter, and how the one leads into the other, and vice versa. Looking back over this long and often agitated history, one has the impression that these differences tend to exaggerate themselves, perhaps for the purpose of being interesting, perhaps for other reasons. But in reviewing the story, however cursorily or synoptically, one tends to come away with the impression that the longest way round the world is the shortest way home to the self, as they say; just as the most direct route to the world is—sometimes—through the self.

But there is one substantial and distinguishing difference in this complex of options for the mind. And that difference has to do with how we consider and characterize the question itself, namely, the question of knowledge. Is that an "epistemological" question? Is it, in other words, a procedural or technical question, sometimes eulogized as a question of method? Are its goals, by the same token, also technical and/or procedural? For instance, the "advancement of learning," or of science, or of technology?

Or is the question *not*, properly, an epistemological question, but some other kind? For example: is the question, properly, a metaphysical one, as they say, or even an ethical one?

Spinoza's place in the history of the problem of knowledge now becomes clearer. The problem for him is not a technical or a methodological one; it is an *ethical* problem. More precisely: it is not a "value" question, as is said nowadays, for that is simply a way of sneaking into technology by the back door; nor a religious question, which is simply a political question misunderstood; nor a "class" question, in the Marxian sense, as has been, in recent times, tiresomely maintained, for "class" is simply self-reduction to sheer sociological abstraction, and thus to Hegel's "bad infinite." And so on. No; the problem of knowledge would be from Spinoza's standpoint, none of these things; it is, rather, a problem of *happiness*. Properly to know is to be happy; that is, blessed.

Since we begin with "vague experience," and usually end up with it, it is important to know how to be blessed—or to achieve blessedness—in the course of vague experience. We have not yet been told, but we have been given a signal.

We advance our question by considering now the "second kind" of knowledge, as earlier described in Part II, Proposition 40, Scholium 2.

"From our possessing common notions and adequate ideas of the properties of things (Corol. Prop. 38, Prop. 39, with Corol. and Prop. 40, pt. 2). This I shall call reason and knowledge of the second kind."

Spinoza has referred us, as is his usage, to earlier and preparatory expositions (or "demonstrations") of the point he is now making. The point he is making is in the first place typically—one is tempted to say paradigmatically—obscured by the imprecision of epistemological language. What, for instance, are "common notions," and what, at this point, are "adequate ideas"? Adequate for what? As for property, we are willing to pass that: it is a property of fire to burn, and that is quite adequate for the purpose of avoidance, among other purposes. Very well. The illustration that has spontaneously offered itself, from everyday fire, is an illustration from "vague experience" and therefore has limited eligibility for extensive inference. Nevertheless, the concreteness of the illustration is epistemologically compelling.

We now know what the case demands: it demands concreteness; and the illustration that Spinoza himself offers—he speaks of a property called *"A"* (there being, in concrete fact, no such property, except in epistemology) and the community of that property with more than one set or group—is not really an illustration but a mental diagram. We remind ourselves that Spinoza was a lens grinder, and that a lens grinder is, in the nature of his practice, both a Pythagorean and a Platonist: that which can only be diagrammed is very proximate to the ultimately real, especially if it is a number, or something like a number. But Spinoza was on the whole quite careful not to draw inferences from his own occupation. He has thus been at pains, in the earlier Proposition 38 of Part II, to which he has referred us, to suggest a clue toward the concreteness which the mind, in this connection, will demand. "Those things which are common to everything, and which are equally in the part and in the whole, can only be adequately conceived."* That is to say: if conceived at all?

It has to be evident that the first and second kinds of knowledge relate, respectively, to different kinds of situation. Knowledge of the first kind—the "vague experience" kind of knowingness—is of Everyman in everyday: let us say, when he crosses the street and has to dodge an oncoming van. If the dialectic of part-and-whole and the methodology of adequate conceiving are at all relevant to this genre of situation, they are relevant to the knowledge that a person's *body* might have acquired in its maturation, since infancy, to "being in the world"; but by the time he is old enough to cross the street alone it is too late for his knowing *mind* to be allowed to have anything to do with it.

On the other hand, there are situations in which even Everyman in everyday is called upon to have a working grasp of part-and-whole argument and to be capable, in a rough and ready way, of putting his part-and-whole knowledge into terms of adequate conceiving: for instance, when Everyman is shopping for some fruit in the supermarket and wants to test a specimen for soundness and ripeness.

(We keep in mind that in Proposition 38 of Part II, which is guiding our present comment, Spinoza has referred to "those things which are common to everything." But we take the liberty of glossing this, hermeneutically, to mean "common to everything *in its kind*." Spinoza cannot possibly mean that all real knowledge is instantly cosmic. We may be reasonably sure that Spinoza would regard this pretension not as knowledge, but as explosive ignorance; or perhaps implosive ignorance; but it would come to the same thing.)

---

*The Demonstration to Proposition 38 of Part II reads as follows: "Let there be something, A, which is common to all bodies, and which is equally in the part of each body and in the whole. I say that A can only be adequately conceived. For the idea of A (Corol. Prop. 7, pt. 2) will necessarily be adequate in God, both in so far as he has the idea of the human body and in so far as He has the idea of its modifications, which (Props. 16, 25, and 27, pt. 2) involve the nature of the human body, and partly also the nature of external bodies; that is to say (Props. 12 and 13, pt. 2), this idea will necessarily be adequate in God in so far as He constitutes the human mind, or in so far as He has ideas which are in the human mind. The mind, therefore (Corol. Prop. 11, pt. 2), necessarily perceives A adequately, both in so far as it perceives itself or its own or any external body; nor can A be conceived in any other manner."

The Corollary reads: "Hence it follows that some ideas or notions exist which are common to all men, for (Lem. 2) all bodies agree in some things, which (Prop. 38, pt. 2) must be adequately, that is to say, clearly and distinctly, perceived by all."

The difference between the situations to which the two kinds of knowledge respectively pertain is now clear: the one situation, that of Everyman in everyday, is one in which reactions have been ritualized by habit, or by phenomenological body language, and in which a pause for adequate conceiving might well be lethal. The situation is typically one in which more than a little knowledge is a dangerous thing.

The situation of knowledge of the second kind is quite different: it is a situation calling for *procedural* knowledge.

The kind of knowledge called for is already evident, in a rudimentary way, in the fruit-shopping situation. It is even more evident in the laboratory situation. That situation may be generalized as the clinical situation. In it, both clinician and subject have discernible epistemological roles. They are both participating in a ripening awareness, as the clinical situation unfolds, of "things which are common to everything, and which are equally in the part and in the whole."

Very well: let us take blood pressure as our paradigmatic concreteness.

Ever since the great William Harvey we have known—as Spinoza of course must have known—that the circulation of the blood, like the orbiting of the planets, is a mechanical instance of part-and-whole behavior, and of the equal distribution of the governing motilities. (No doubt we knew it before Harvey, as well; but there does come a moment for mankind when what mankind knows has to be formalized and made to go public.) Clinician and subject, usually, share this knowledge; each in an idiom that differentiates one Everyman from another. The blood pressure is read from the upper left arm. Clinician and subject both know, without taking any further reading and without articulating their kinds of knowledge, that if the reading were taken from the region of the ankle, or from the anterior region of the instep, it might show some variation from the upper left arm. This would at once be taken, by both clinician and subject, if the latter were brought into the completeness of the picture, as *confirmatory* of the part-and-whole kind of truth, and of the common notions that are anchored in it.

We are now operative—both clinician and subject—on the level of the second kind of knowledge; but we are reasonably far from blessedness.

And we shall be, it would appear, even further removed, as our para-scientific enlightenment proceeds, and as further diagnostic insight reveals to us, standing as we now do on the level of the second kind of knowledge—that metatastic lesions, which seem discoverable, if not already evident—are an even further refinement of part-and-whole circuitry; convincing us, as perhaps nothing else could, of the equal distribution, in part and whole, of the common "notions" pertaining to the matter.

This anguish of the second kind of knowledge might eventually be helpful; but at the moment it isn't.

There is a demurrer that a humane epistemologist might offer at this point in the argument, namely: that in the progress of part-and-whole insights (Proposition 38 of Spinoza's Part II) applied to the grimmer lesions of the human condition, there is a good chance—though it is by no means guaranteed—that ameliorative procedures are discovered that postpone death and relieve suffering. This is the utilitarian demurrer, and it has in its favor all the moral advantages of utilitarianism over fideism. But it would be dangerous, and even debasing, at this point in the argument to start counting advantages, these being factors that can very well take care of themselves. What is significant about any utilitarian thrust brought to bear on the question at this point is that it would only bring us into premature confrontation with Proposition 23 of Spinoza's Part V, the proposition of eternity, it will be recalled, or what to do about the fact that, after a while, we all die. Is it still worth having advantages in the face of the "prospect" of eternity? It might be, of course; it would depend on what they were.

There is no need to force the question prematurely. Let us accept the fact, and try to be content with it, that neither the way to blessedness nor the way to eternity opens from the second kind of knowledge. Nevertheless, Spinoza proposes for it a preferred epistemological status. Why? And how would the preferred epistemological status be a preferred ethical, or existential, status?

The question has managed to answer itself, in the way that the larger redundancies of speculation generally do. The criteria of the second kind of knowledge—"adequate conceiving" and equal distribution in part-and-whole of the decisive factors—have to do with effective procedure. Not only do they constitute the measure of that effectiveness, but they are the *same* as that effectiveness. Put simplistically: a deep breath, properly taken, is the *same* as optimal oxygenation of the vascular system at a given moment; a tennis ball hit in the right way is the *same* as a point scored; or potentially scored; and so on. It is even *necessary* to put the notion simplistically, because by so doing we suggest that Spinoza's progress in knowledge—from, for example, the first to the second kind—*is not necessarily a progress toward more complex and expansive goals*. Rather, it is a progress in clarification and more exact articulation of the relevant procedure in any given situation. The familiar name for procedure clarified and articulated is *action*. The second kind of knowledge is a progress in clarified action, or the capacity for it. It is not necessarily mathematical action, or the technological kind; perhaps on the contrary; perhaps it is the indefinitely multiplex kinds of action subsumed by Spinoza, dismissively, or so it would seem, under "vague experience."

I shall, moreover, argue that the relation of means and ends in Spinoza's thought bears precisely on this point: the conception of action, and of progress in it.

Behind the unhappiness of empiricist epistemology—or, for that matter, behind the Cartesian variety—lies a profound frustration: since we cannot act, let us at least pretend to know; let us ignore, let us even affect to despise, the Aristotelian notion that knowing is the "highest" form of action; it is a mere lyricism of the Macedonian age. By properly despising it, we shall manage to maintain indifference to its obvious, self-verifying converse that clarified and articulated action is the "highest" form of knowing.

Empiricist epistemology, like empiricist ethics, thus expresses itself as a species of *grasping* metaphysics: since we can no longer, with a straight face, use the language of being—it would be a feudal and tasteless embarrassment to do so—let us *hold on* to something; we shall seize the day, grasp at the world—it is all before us, and reach for an end.

The point has to be made with emphasis—even at the risk of caricaturing these other options, such as those arising from uninhibited empiricism—because the epistemological pivot on which Spinoza's thought turns, in moving from the first to the second kind of knowledge, positions us to see the wide horizon toward which the radii of his argument are moving, and from which they have devolved.

The horizon is that of infinite and eternal Substance, known, when it walks abroad, in the cool of the day, as God or Nature. The radii are the acts, metaphysically seen to be infinite and eternal, whereby we live and move and have our being; whereby and wherein we are. These acts, like the Substance which they express, are of course both immanent and transcendent, all at once. The contrast between immanence and transcendence is simply expressive of a provisional halt taken in our unending consideration of the problem: if we come to a halt at this or that point within the provisional bounds of the problem, we speak of immanence, and feel relieved, or enlightened; if we move on to a further halt, "beyond" the bounds of the problem already drawn, we speak of transcendence and feel, perhaps, a proper, sometimes exhilarating, anxiety.

Thus, the words immanence and transcendence are words having to do with the emotional life—which has its own profound importance, as we shall see—but they do not have to do with knowledge, or with its limits; or with the nature of an act, which is definable as *that kind of situation, where the situation is equally in the part and in the whole.*

Therefore the *end* of a durational act—and of course all acts expressed by us are durational acts—is an infinite and eternal end, both immanent and transcendent, and not to be located by starting here or by going there.

Such are the intuitions, premonitory of course, that are released in the mind as we come to terms with the second kind of knowledge, making our peace with the fact that the demands of it do not fall upon specialists, or upon professionals, but upon Everyman. Everyman is a para-scientist, but he is not necessarily headed toward omniscience.

We may as well face the fact that Spinoza is not interested in our knowing everything; and it is not at all clear that in moving from the first to the second kind of knowledge, we have come to know *more;* nor that there is yet *more* to know in passing from the second to the third.

What kind of passage is it?

We return to the second Scholium to Proposition 40 in Part II of the *Ethic*. Once again it reads:

"Besides these two kinds of knowledge, there is a third, as I shall hereafter show, which we shall call intuitive science. This kind of knowing advances from an adequate idea of the formal essence of certain attributes of God to the adequate knowledge of the essence of things. All this I will explain by one example."

The example given has to do with the intuition, or immediate inference, of the fourth proportional in a series when three of the series are given. Thus, given 1, 2, and 3; is not the fourth term immediately known to be 6? That is, once you have understood, and understood once for all, what proportionality is all about.

The implication is that this example is generalizable: all situations have a recognizable inter-connectedness, according to specific principles, of their constitutive elements. Progress to the third kind of knowledge takes the form of increasing insightfulness into the one, or several, basic principles that govern all inter-connectedness. But inter-connectedness as such is an abstraction. Abstraction may or may not belong to knowledge of the first kind—where, presumably, it is the same thing as vagueness—but it cannot belong to the second and third kinds. Knowledge of the second kind is procedural; knowledge of the third kind is not procedural, but *methodological*. That is to say, it is not knowledge at all in the usual, stricter sense, but existence itself. Or, conceivably, it is knowledge only in the sense that existence itself is cognitive.

To speak of existence, or being, as methodological is to make an ethical statement, not an epistemological one. One's mode of being, on the level of the third kind of knowledge, is the method of blessedness. Or, if one prefers, one may use Spinoza's less exalted but equivalent term, and speak of the third kind of knowledge as the method of freedom.

Freedom is exaltation enough for the nominalist instinct, or temperament, which is the instinct and temperament to which Spinoza addresses himself. And in any case, your freedom-loving nominalist does not turn to Spinoza, or to any other philosopher, for edification, but for *increased efficiency in being*. From the standpoint of that criterion, let us look at the third kind of knowledge, and its explicative example, more closely.

Spinoza's examples are, often, among the worst in the literature; and this one, about the fourth proportional, is sufficiently opaque, considering the amount of illumination one is supposed to get from it. If blame has to be apportioned, one should no doubt apportion it between his vocation of lens grinder and his heritage from Descartes. But the example, though cheerless, is not altogether useless.

For example: suppose, in one's ignorance of elementary mathematics, one has trouble figuring out the fourth proportional, though three are conspicuously given, what should one do? The epistemological directive is self-evident: *learn mathematics;* if need be, with a tutor.

At this point, we are confronted by a quite overwhelming inference: *the epistemological imperative of the third kind of knowledge is regressive;* it will, under many easily imaginable circumstances, return us quite simply to the *procedural* modes of knowledge, of the second kind. It is even possible that this regressive thrust does not stop there.

I emphasize the *general* nature of the inference I propose. What it amounts to is this: the third kind of knowledge has no beyond; it has only a *context*.

There are various other ways of putting the matter. In the picturesque, directional language that one is accustomed to use, one would say that we do not go forward from the third kind of knowledge, but only backward, or, thenceforth, roundabout. But this language obviously cannot be taken literally. The only profit in using it is that it strongly suggests the exclusion of two routine errors in the interpretation of Spinoza's doctrine of knowing. One is the self-indulgent "mystical" error that takes the third kind of knowledge as a doctrine of ineffability; the epistemology of the ineffable, as it were. The other error, perhaps a less common one, would be to take the third kind of knowledge as having to do with ultra-sophisticated modes of cognitive manipulation like non-Euclidean geometry. The first error is to be taken cognizance of, and ignored. The second error is hopeless Platonism: at best procedural, and therefore self-limiting in application;

at worst, a reversion to the mystical. Spinoza will not, I think, revert to it, if he can help it.

Our difficulty lies, rather, in Spinoza's example of the intuition of the fourth proportional. We hardly need a theory of knowledge in order to understand that mathematical procedures, even of a quite elementary kind, are not self-communicating, and that if one has difficulty in using them, when occassion calls for their use, one should get oneself a teacher, even if the teacher is only the Socratic slave boy in the *Meno*, with his quite remarkable pre-natal reminiscences.

We need some other kind of example.

Mathematics and medicine are excluded as sources of the exemplary at this point. They are disciplines, as one says, or specialized procedures, though it is sometimes claimed—Plato made the claim early on—that mathematics is paradigmatic for all procedures; but the same claim was in Plato's day, or just before it, made for medicine. The example that we need has to be one that makes the most minimal claim to procedural expertise. In fact, the only expertise that would be here allowable is the expertise of experience, whether "vague" or otherwise. The example we seek has, moreover, to be one in which the inferences arising from a particular cognitive episode, or encounter, have that existentially energizing quality of "immediacy." Finally, the example has to be transferrable to the ethical realm. It might then, and only then, become paradigmatic for method.

We need not search at random. "This kind of knowing," that is, the third kind, "advances from an adequate idea of the formal essence of certain attributes of God to the adequate knowledge of the essence of things." In the neo-medieval idiom which Spinoza, nominalist though he is, seems to be constrained to use, "essence" means what we mean by "actual," or, more precisely, existently actual. It is close enough to what we might mean by "concrete," or unmistakably locatable in specific, for us at least, sensible experience; while "formal" means what we mean by "potential" or possible. I shall assume that the notion of "adequate" does not require translation: adequate is as adequate does.

The general notion thus renders as follows: The third kind of knowing advances from an appropriate idea of the specifiable possibilities of certain attributes of God to the required, or appropriate, knowledge of the concreteness of things.

(One could, perhaps, just as well say "concrete things." But the expression we have used keeps the situation more open.)

There is one element in the quoted sentence that may have a certain initial obscurity, and that is the expression "certain attributes of God." God has infinite attributes, but there are only two that are known to us, and in terms of which we take further cognitive steps:

these are thought and extension. Are these the "certain attributes"? There can be no other. In the working of one or another of the infinite, not-by-us knowable, attributes of God, flowers might very well be responsive to our kind thoughts and loving words about them, but we cannot, in good faith, presume ourselves to have an adequate knowledge of the concreteness of such alleged responsiveness. And, in any case, if there were, *per impossibile,* any methodological inferences from such "knowledge," the inferences could only have to do with ethical method for human beings, not with the life and destiny of flowers.

The "certain attributes" can only refer to the *modal* permutations of the two attributes, each infinite enough, and exhaustive, in its own right. The "formal essence of certain attributes" thus signifies the *possibilities* of these modal permutations. The requirement is reflexive: we can only know those modal possibilities, given a knowledge of certain basic principles to start with, *in terms of the concrete actualities of things.*

We are now ready for an example.

The example we propose is from the notably problematic area of art, and from that sector of the area that has to do with responsiveness to an art object or art situation, rather than with production. The advantages of such an example are: (*a*) The question of expertise is by-passed. Expertise might be relevant for attribution, or for persuasiveness in the realm of criticism, but would have little to do with the *kind of knowledge* that the artist himself would claim. It is just that kind of "knowledge" that the respondent makes a claim to. In this respect, artist and respondent are in the same case: the artist "knows" something that he seeks to bring to expression and is his own audience of the first instance. The respondent is implicitly solicited to recognize, or perhaps to recollect, what the artist purports to have perceived, and thus reproduces, after a fashion, the productive process of the artist. Art production and art responsiveness converge in a shared *experience* as their first and final cause. The *skill* of the artist is both wholly subordinate to and wholly expressed in the experience aimed at. This is what distinguishes it from expertise, which is always separable, in some sense, from the situation, if not from the field, in which it is exercised.

(*b*) Art is disputable, like knowledge itself. There are no rules of art[2]—if there are any, they are wholly trivial—and there are no "self-evident truths." This is why the art example will serve us better than Spinoza's example of the fourth proportional. There can be no disputing the fourth proportional, but dispute about the "artistic truth" (assuming there is such a thing) of, for instance, the *Kreutzer Sonata* belongs to the very nature of *its* case. This makes the *Kreutzer Sonata* more like blessedness, or like the *amor intellectualis dei* that Spinoza speaks of, than the fourth proportional can possibly be. The fourth proportional comes under the rule of contradiction: it either is or is not. The knowledge that one might claim in and from a certain experience of art comes under a *rule of complementarity*. "This too is possible, and this too will pass." It is the difference between Plato in his more rigid moments, and Hegel at his best.

(*c*) Finally, let us say, the case of art, in some deserving instance of it, proposes itself to us as paradigmatic because the ontological problematic of the two "certain attributes"—thought and extension—has a curious literalness of illustration in the phenomenon of art. This is particularly true of the arts of painting, sculpture, music, and dance. It seems to be less true of the verbal "arts," poetry, drama, and the rest. But are they arts? Do they not oscillate between the two poles of medicine (or entertainment) and the form of truth itself, not knowing quite where to come to rest? But painting, sculpture, music, and dancing—these are arts pure and simple; useless, arbitrary though lawful, alien and overwhelming; hostile, intimate, and shameless. And in their instances—*which* is the thought (or the emotion, ideated or otherwise, or the sensation, adequate or inadequate), and *which* is the extension; which the "form" and which the "matter," as the more archaic (and somewhat misleading) version of Spinoza's "two attributes" would put it? Where does the one begin, and the other leave off?

These are precisely the questions that pertain to the two attributes of God or Substance, in Spinoza's *Ethic;* and they constitute what I have called the ontological problematic of the matter, illustrated happily, though not self-verifyingly, in the case of art. If one should urge, as against my proposal, that the illustration in art is not instance or analogue of the ontological problem, but at a best a metaphor for it, the objection has to be taken as self-refuting: who or what stands, with literal feet, outside the metaphor to hold it to account? The objection is a transcendental and Cartesian one: God is the Great Outsider and is irrelevant to Spinoza's ontology.

For in that ontology, the two attributes are wholly distinct, noninterchangeable, without direct recourse to each other—no parapsychology, if you ontologically please, and no "out-of-the-body" experiences—but also *wholly interpenetrant to and with one another,* and *distinguishable from one another only modally,* not substantivally. That is to say, on the second, or derivative level of their being, *not* on the level of one's immediate intuition of God. That is the only level that ontologically counts.

The same is true, whether metaphorically or otherwise, in the case of art. The distinguishing of form and matter, in an art situation, is a gymnastic for certain kinds of criticism—less and less practiced, to be sure—but it has nothing to do with the immediate intuition of the art object.

That intuition is strictly non-procedural, and though it might be eligible to be called "vague," it seems, nevertheless, to operate on the level of *the third kind of knowledge.*

Really?

How so?

Here, for instance, is El Greco's *View of Toledo.*

View of what? What kind of a city is that?

We know, of course, where Iberian Toledo is. It is on a map. It is bordered by the river Tagus. It is 40 miles south of Madrid. We know where that is. There have to be statistics, that could be pieced together from various somewheres about sixteenth-century Toledo; and we could have recourse to those assembled statistics if need be: how many Spaniards there, how many Berbers, how many crypto-Jews and crypto-Arabs, how many surviving Visigoths and/or Arians? How many Cretans?

There must be an internal map, too; something like a town plan. The engineers who helped conquer it for the Aragonese and Castillians, whether patriots or mercenaries, must have had maps, contours, and suchlike, to help them get hold; and after that to build and rebuild for the greater glory and better defense. If there were any point to it, any particular use to knowing, one could work out from such sources the number of houses (approximately), their height, depth, and width, the width of streets; the sense of elevation one might have from the hill, or hills, just out of town; and what kind of trajectory sixteenth-century artillery would have to hope for, sited on the hill outside of town, to clear the sacred spires, or rounded domes before the spires were; and get to the heart of the matter.

All this and more, if need be; though it might seem like a good deal of trouble for nothing better than the second kind of knowledge, and its common notions. Even so, it would remain obscure as to what, if anything, in knowledge so obtained, would be known to be equally in the part and in the whole. Does it simply mean that what we thereby know, we would have to be content with?

It is evident that El Greco's *View* gives us no knowledge that could be either confirmed or disconfirmed by any statistics about sixteenth-century Toledo.

There is a distinction that Bertrand Russell makes between "knowledge by acquaintance" and "knowledge by description."[3]

For argument's sake, I shall provisionally assume that this distinction is roughly conformable to Spinoza's distinction between the second and third kinds of knowledge. Spinoza has added the epistemological-ethical demand that the second kind of knowledge pass, whenever and wherever possible, into the third: and that the acquaintance–knowledge of the third kind shall absorb and retain such advantages as may be justly claimed by the descriptive knowledge of the second kind.

When we see–smell a rose, or taste an apple, we know the rose or the apple by acquaintance. When we attend to the convincing details laid before us about the interior of the atom or of the farther galaxies, we know those entities, respectively, by description.

El Greco's *Toledo*: do we know it by acquaintance, or by description? The question has inadvertently telescoped itself, as in all such cases it tends to do. What Toledo is it that we are supposed to know? El Greco's Toledo? But any traveler's "Toledo" is roughly, broadly, grandly verifiable by the appropriate measurements and set of statistics, greatly gaining in truth and instructiveness, as we well know, from the modifications introduced by verification. But El Greco's Toledo is not amenable to the statistical mode at all. One doubts whether El Greco would have claimed to have been there, if being there means to come-and-go; and if he might claim—or if we might claim on his behalf—that he *saw* it, did he see it by description, or did he see it by acquaintance? Did he tell himself a story, or did he have an experience?

One has to assume, of course, that it was a visual *experience* that he had, *and that in that experience he managed to advance "from an adequate idea of the formal essence of certain attributes of God to the adequate knowledge of the essence of things"* (Scholium 2, to Proposition 40, of Part II).

Being interpreted, this means: that as a painter, or even as a person of ordinary sensibility, he *knows* what light is, light being an exceedingly high-priority mode, or sub-mode, of *motion and rest*—which is a first infinite mode of *extension*—which is one of the two, and only two, attributes of God known to us. It is *as a painter* that the man called El Greco knows the "formal essence," that is, the *possibilities,* of these certain attributes of God. In what way, or by virtue of what organ of knowing, does El Greco know these certain, that is, expressible, possibilities of light? By virtue of his eye, and by virtue of his hand; it is they who know. The rest of him, if there be any rest of him, is absorbed into his eye and hand. Above all, it is his mind, that first infinite mode of the attribute of thought that he owns a piece of, that is absorbed into his eye and hand.

He has seen, then, the possibilities of light. From his eye-and-hand's adequate idea of these possibilities, he *advances to "adequate knowledge of the essence of things."* That is to say, to an adequate knowledge of an actual Toledo. Or to one of the actual Toledos, on this site, by this Tagus, from this perspective, under this sky.

Is that why the city has no full-face presentation, such as no city known to man ever failed to have, but is all, and only all, dismembered *profile* of a city—the dismembered profile wandering to and fro, up and down, between the congealed waters above and the fluid waters below, between the green and the ultra-violet and the infra-red and the black-body of the painter's eye: is that why? But it is said that El Greco was astigmatic; that is, not metaphorically, but ophthalmologically speaking, and that is why it is not only his Toledo, but all his faces, his bodies, and his landscapes have this distortional telescoping into the profile, presented as the one true face of the matter. Is the astigmatic view of things an adequate knowledge of their essence?

It would be as hard, and as foolhardy, categorically to deny this as to defend it. We have to rest with the *possibility* that it is so: with the possibility, that is, that when it comes to seeing things by the third kind of knowledge—that is, when it comes to seeing them by "intuitive science," as one sees the fourth proportional, given three —in *that* cognitive circumstance, the circumstance of art, one has to see the object astigmatically, so to speak. Otherwise there is nothing there to see at all.

One has to remember that it is not God who sees, but we. And that if God sees at all—which would only be a way of speaking; as when one says, God knows; he may know, but he has not learned—it is the "face of the whole universe" that he sees, not being equipped to see anything smaller than that; and if he should try, he could only see it astigmatically.

One is now prepared to generalize, and from the generalization to draw an inference.

(*a*) There is that in the artistic eye-and-hand which always sees astigmatically. Here it is best not to take refuge in the softer substitution of "distortionally" (instead of astigmatically), because there are many ways, apropos to many kinds of situation, of being distortional; but the artist, situated as he is in his fatal field of vision, chooses one of them.

(*b*) The object of the artistic vision will always and necessarily be, so to speak, an astigmatic object, *because the artist performs the object of his vision*. Repeat: he does not "create" it, which, whatever else it might mean could mean nothing, epistemologically; but he *performs* it. If we put our problem of artistic "statement" into the idiom of linguistic analysis—say, the language of "sentences"—then we say that artistic statement is a "*performative utterance,*" or a series of them.[4]

(*c*) The peculiarities-*cum*-absurdities of artistic statement—El Greco being a particularly happy example of them—have a precise epistemological explanation. They are due to the fundamental commitment of artistic statement, which is *to express "formal essences" as if they were "essences of things"*; or, in other words, *potentialities or possibilities as if they were actualities*.

This is what El Greco has done with the empirical dilemma of the alleged full-face presentation of things in the normal encounter with them. He *performs* it differently, as it "really" is; he has to. So does Cézanne in the perfectly stabilized teetering instabilities of his still lifes: they will stay that way forever in accord with his knowledge of the third kind. So does Duchamp, when his cubistic meta–*Woman Descends the Stairs,* flung into their appropriate space by knowledge of the third kind. So, perhaps, has Bruegel done, when his *Icarus* fell for him, between the castle and the ploughman, into the sea.

(*d*) We sum up our generalizations in this inference: if artistic knowledge has been correctly taken as paradigmatic, then we say that *all instances of knowledge of the third kind are instances of performative knowledge*.

Performative knowledge, or "intuitive science," will fall somewhere in between knowledge-by-acquaintance and knowledge-by-description. It is knowledge by self-description and, unlike the taste of the apple or the smell of the rose, by non-durational acquaintance. The "truth" of the experience of a work of art arises, naturally, from encounter with the work, but it does not depend on the maintenance of that encounter, or the memory of it. That truth passes into one's structure, *as a thing done*.

The "intellectual love of God" of which Spinoza speaks will have this in common with the experience of art: it, too, is not "had" but *performed*.

The difference between art and life, as it is called, can be put quite simply: in everyday experience we dare not take potentialities for actualities, as art does; we would do so at our peril. In this sense, art remains, and is content to remain, hypothetical, though it is hypothesis performed. Art is by no means "divine," or god-like; for God is not a bohemian, the bohemian being one who lives the life of hypothesis; art is, in fact, hardly "creative," in the traditional and sentimental sense. Rather, art is the attempt to be ethical without the penalties of an ethic. It is, therefore, paradigmatic for the third kind of knowledge, but *only* paradigmatic.

We have considered Spinoza's doctrine of knowledge as a mode of entry into the *Ethic*, and we have taken it, I believe, as far as it will go. If it will go no further, it is because Spinoza's epistemology, such as it is, will not take us that far. Spinoza as philosopher is condemned to use the language of cognitive self-elevation. So he speaks of first, second, third, and possibly fourth (as between the first and the second), kinds of knowledge; but it is only epistemology, not human development, that can conceivably be frozen on the level of the first kind.

Human development, for Spinoza, is radically and concretely ethical development. This is inclusive of our development as knowers, but that type of development is not specifically dependent on our acclimatization in the positive sciences.

The general implication for the positive sciences, from Spinoza's doctrine of knowledge, would be to this effect: The positive sciences, as knowledge of the second kind, are beckoned forward by quite heroic possibilities for human amelioration and expansion. Many of these possibilities have been notably explored since the seventeenth century, and one assumes that the exploration is by no means exhausted. But, both in principle and on the evidence, there comes a point in the development of the positive sciences when they tend to harden into mere technologies, or else to be counter-productive in that the unintended side-effects overwhelm the intended goals.

This tendency, which is a cliché of culture observation in our own time, was not yet clamoring to be defined in the seventeenth century. Nevertheless, Spinoza's refusal to follow the Baconian-Cartesian path—"knowledge is power," and mechanism is the soul of power—of itself signifies that the positive sciences have, for Spinoza, no eschatological role to play in human development. More than that, the positive sciences, as a knowledge of the second kind, are themselves in need of habilitation: the second kind of knowledge must pass into, or be informed by, knowledge of the third kind; and knowledge of the third kind is no longer knowledge in the usual sense, but a certain way of being and acting in the world.

The backward and forward echoes of this notion are recognizable; they go backward to Plato, and forward to many contemporaries.[5] What is distinctive in Spinoza's version is the refusal of myth, as in Plato and mysticism, and the refusal of illusion, as in materialism and utopianism.

Very well. When we have disencumbered ourselves of epistemological myth and illusion, what is left for us as the goal, near or ultimate, of cognition? If not a second chance for the soul, and if not the indefeasible technological redemption of the human condition, then what? Is knowledge its own reward, and shall we call that blessedness, not expecting God to love us in return for our knowingness, since we would not know what to do with it if he did?

This would be an aestheticization, so to speak, of the doctrine of knowledge, and it is, I believe, quite far from Spinoza's intention. It would be, moreover, a misunderstanding of knowledge of the third kind, and, therefore, of the dynamic of knowing as such.

Let us briefly sum up the doctrine of knowledge thus far, and then raise the question of its goal.

There are, basically, two kinds of knowledge for Spinoza: (1) procedural knowledge and (2) the knowledge he calls "intuitive science."

Procedural knowledge has a forward thrust. Its goals are transcendent; they lie beyond the procedure; the purpose of biochemical research, for example, being the increase of human health, or the prolongation of life, or, contrariwise, the simplification of dying—"death with dignity," as it is called, or euthanasia.

"Intuitive science," on the other hand, *has a backward thrust*. It is, so to speak, retro-scendent. Its *terminus ad quem* is that area of quasi-knowledge which Spinoza has called "knowledge of the first kind." It is not so much derived from "vague experience" as it is that experience itself. It is toward that realm that "intuitive science," once acquired, will move. There is no other place, and no other direction, for it to go. Along the way, it will no doubt inform with its intensified and clarified vision the many-colored and far-ranging procedures of knowledge of the second kind. But it will not stop there, and could not, unless our goal is the pseudo-Cartesian-Comtean one of a positivist-technological organization and management of human life. Such a management would, of course, have to cover art and play as well.

Spinoza's "intuitive science" is not programmatic in that sense, nor in any technical sense at all. Its program is that *radiant transformation of "vague experience" which he calls human freedom*. Everything else —and, on the whole, "everything else" is what we have—is human bondage. Human freedom is not part of that eternity which is our last end, *but eternity is a part of our human freedom*.

In short: the goal of cognition for Spinoza is human freedom. We must now turn to an examination of that.*

There is a metaphoric correspondence between Spinoza's notion of freedom and the (Christian) theological notion of "before the fall." Spinoza says that "if men were born free, they would form no conception of good and evil so long as they were free" (Part IV, Proposition 68). Is this tantamount to saying that the condition called freedom would be the same as the mythically imputed state of innocence, before they, he and she, ate of the fruit of the tree?

---

*The discussion of art has left us with the finding that knowledge of the third kind is performative. Here, knowledge resides in the very action, not in some goal beyond the action. The action HMR has in view does not require (though it may include) technical training. It is, however, highly skilled in another sense, and may require another kind of training, or sensitization.

There would be several things wrong with a conformation of metaphor along such lines.

The first and most obvious thing wrong with it is that Spinoza's freedom is not a state or condition, not even, essentially, a political condition, but a form of human action.

The second thing wrong with it is that the cheerful theological metaphor of Adamic and Eve-esque innocence before the fall is a metaphor in bad faith. They weren't all that innocent, and knowledgeable theology—that is, theology that does not insist on being simplistic and devious—knows it. Nobody who gave name (and with it, determinate being) to the animals of Eden—which Adam, be it remembered, had done long before the confrontation with the serpent —could lay plausible claim to innocence. The imputation of innocence is merely a devious way of quite correctly insinuating that Adam and Eve before the fall were shameless, and that history begins with the discovery and experience of shame.

The third thing wrong with it is that Spinoza's free man will die, like any other, whereas the theological myth purports to equate innocence with deathlessness; or so a sufficiently trivial hermeneutic of the text will maintain. To put the matter bluntly, Spinoza's "deathlessness" could happen to a man only after he had died, not before.

Spinoza's remark is not, I believe, casual or careless—I find it difficult to impute either the casual or the careless to Spinoza's atomic sentences—but it has to be read with the qualifier that self-evidently belongs to the text, and has been spelled out in the Scholium to the Demonstration. The Scholium reads: "It is clear . . . that the hypothesis of this proposition is false." The Proposition should therefore read: "if men, *per impossibile,* were born free, etcetera."

Concede, then, that the qualifier of the Scholium is an essential part of the statement. Conceding it simply throws into higher relief the argument of the predicate: *that to be without knowledge of good and evil is part of the ultimate ideal of freedom.*

What does this mean? The rhetoric of it is overwhelming: if it does not mean the innocence of ontological myth, then it ought to mean something even better than innocence; and only such a meaning could justify the rhetoric. We retreat before the power of the rhetoric to consider, briefly, what has been invested in that power.

1. It is well known, to the point of being self-certifying, that in Spinoza's doctrine God or Nature or Substance has no concern with good and evil. God is not a worrier, and the laws of Nature (it is not allowable in Spinoza's case to complete the familiar formula with, for example, ". . . and Nature's God") are not God's worry-beads. Let us put it even more bluntly: God has no conscience, not even that sort of "holy conscience" that might have satisfied Kant; and, more

bluntly still, He is not providential, neither particularly nor generally, neither deistically nor (God saving us all in our foxholes) as a nightcap Presence.

2. God is without contradictions, and therefore without conflicts, not even those whose solution is eschatologically guaranteed, but postponable. Under God, or in God, there is no "problem of evil," that is to say, the question how could a good God have created such a disgustingly bad world does not arise, *because God is not good*! This is heartbreaking, but we are thereby relieved of some excruciating dilemmas. For example: the enervating Cartesian dilemma of having to decide whether God is demonic or Cartesian, whether he is a liar, or merely inconsistent and mysterious; given, that is, to *double entendre*. Once we decide, or submit to understanding, that God is not good, we are also spared the burden of doing something with Bradley's paradox, that the world is the best of all possible worlds, everything in it being an unmitigated evil. One has long ago understood the moral superiority of Bradley's paradox to Leibniz's demoralizing proof that the world is simply the best of all possible worlds; but Leibniz's proof can be easily ignored, whereas Bradley's paradox is a responsibility.

3. We meet that responsibility only by understanding that there are no *possible* worlds. Only in art are there possible worlds, not in God.

4. What, then, is freedom?

We remind ourselves that we are asking about *human* freedom. God's freedom is quite infinite; it consists in whatever is going on, and what will go on.

Human freedom is quite finite: that is to say, we are altogether *determined*.

Do we, then, escape from the trap of traditional paradoxes and/or obscurities simply to come to rest in a brutal paradox of Spinoza's own: we are altogether determined, but free?

Yes, conceivably. But the paradox is a brutal one only under the brutal spell of misunderstanding. And the primary misunderstanding, in this connection, has to do with the notion of *determination*.

5. Let us therefore examine the meaning, more particularly Spinoza's meaning, of determination. It may be that our circuitousness here may prove to be the shorter distance between knowledge and freedom.

(*a*). We discover that the first meaning of determination is *individuation*, as in Spinoza's famous formula in his Fiftieth Letter: "determination is negation." (The formula is given an approximate paraphrase in the *Ethic*, Part I, Proposition 8, Scholium 1.)

The meaning is evident, and has little or nothing to do with the gothic, or pseudo-gothic, mythicization of negation–negativity–

nothingness in recent writers like Heidegger, Sartre, and the others. Spinoza's meaning is a perfectly ordinary-language meaning: the primary identifying process of the notion and being of "me" is "*not* you," "*not* her," "*not* him," "*not* them," "*not* us," and so on. Plato said it. That said and done, one can then go in search of one's identity, if there is anything left to search for.

If, for example, we say, in all humility, that God is self-determining, what we meaningfully say is that God is *self-individuating*. Eternally so. We, on the other hand, however that we are in God, are *not quite* so *self*-individuating as all that.

(*b*). It follows from the meaning of determination-as-individuation that a further meaning is *advance*.

One may, if one likes, prefix the expression "creative" to the notion of advance, as with an echo, slightly disturbing, of Whitehead. Nothing much is thereby gained, and something is lost, as something is always lost when we are prematurely enticed by the lyrical while we are about the sober business of a concept. Creativity on the serious level belongs to God, in his role of *natura naturans*, or Nature Naturing. Not that it is invidious to speak of creativity on the human level—Spinoza's God is not really, or not usually, a jealous God—but that, precisely noted, human creativity, as in the arts or the inventions, is a form of knowledge, or a contribution to the ethical, even if the contribution is self-canceling.

The meaning of determination-as-advance is best brought out by Hegel, whose meaning is inclusive of Spinoza's (and by no means unaware of its kinship-class) but has features of its own. Hegel's negation-negated, etc., simply means *going ahead* (there being no other place, whether for *Geist* or its Absolute, to go). In a neo-Hegelian metaphor that comes to mind: determination-as-advance is the one small step of the Absolute that might turn out to be history's regrettable giantism. But we should not moralize prematurely.

One is more comfortable with Spinoza's version, or implied version, of determination-as-advance because it exempts us from theodicy. Hegel's "history" has to be justified, even if it turns out that it does-it-itself. But Spinoza's God does not have to be justified at all. We must love him, but he will not love us in return, even if we should ask for that love, as we should not. He simply *advances*. Infinitely. *And as he advances, he infinitely individuates.*

This is what is *creative* about our determination. Our determination is a mode, under God, of advancing individuation.

As we advance, that is to say, endure, we further individuate ourselves and, from the original core of individuation given us in God, we individuate with respect to *others*. That is to say, we act and are acted upon; we determine and are determined.

(*c*). The traditional term for these features of existence is *causality*. And that is the next meaning of Spinoza's determination: we are imputed absolutely to *causal existence;* we cause and are caused, in God.

Consider: *being caused* is an absolute condition of *causing*. (God too—if we have recourse once more to the totality of metaphor—is *being caused;* but he is caused by himself; so that we do not learn much about *our* causal situation by the contemplation, rapt or otherwise, of *Substantial* causality. Indeed, the best thing, on the whole, to do about Substance, once you have determined that it is there, is to ignore it. It might, in turn, be indifferent to you, but there is no ontological chance whatsoever that it will ignore you.) Could there be subject without object, or, contrariwise? The purpose of Substance—or, so to speak, God's linguistic purpose—is to keep us in mind that existence is without benefit of *inertness;* just as there are no two substances, so there are no effects without causative power. To *be* is to cause, and thus to hold membership in an infinite order of determination. The voting power of a particular membership is not easily calculable: "for want of a nail . . . the kingdom was lost," and so on.

In the infinite order of determination, the only calculation that can be quantified is the ethical one. Only *freedom* can call the priorities in the causal order. If men were born free, they would have no idea of good and evil, but they would indeed have knowledge of causal priorities and would act accordingly; their knowledge, that is, their self-adequation in the order of insight, and their action, in the circumstance and meaning of freedom, being one and the same.*

Freedom and determination are thus not merely correlative, as the saying goes, but are one and the same.

We specify this as follows: freedom is, so to speak, resistance to determination. But determination itself, and as such, is resistance to determination, for the purpose, in redundancy, of determining. There would be no folly whatsoever in speaking of God's freedom, infinite enough, for example, as consisting, among other things, of an infinite spectrum of *resistances* to the infinite individuating determinations which God, in creating, is and has made.

Our interpretation of Spinoza is thus, at the same time, a gloss on Scripture and its cryptologic concern with knowledge-of-good-

---

*Put with less brevity, HMR can be understood as follows: If men, *per impossibile,* were born free, they would have no idea of good and evil. But, given that inevitably they would become aware of causal priorities—which is to say that they would recognize their essential *un*freedom—the human move toward ethical self-empowerment (knowledge of good and evil) would have to follow. Ethical self-empowerment is freedom insofar as it makes any difference, humanly. It is the freedom that we *do* have—not by birth—but by a certain kind of effort.

and-evil, and related matters. The situation in the Garden is introduced to us as a situation that lacks determination; which is to say that it is without resistances, or individuation, and by the same token without freedom. The animals are individuated, having names, for even to belong to a species is to be in some measure individuated, by habitat, diet, and natural, biological weaponry; but Adam has no name—Earth-Man is not a name—and has no species. Eve has something more of a name—for Life-Type, or Life-Person, approximates a name.

It must be—and doubtless has been—a matter of gnosiological and heresiarchical speculation as to who introduced resistance into the Garden. Was it God himself, in discontent with ontological non-resistance, or Adam, who hides behind one tree or another at crucial moments of the dialogue, or the serpent, or was it Eve, as John Milton suggests in the grand, serio-comic near-seduction scene,[6] where the creature–creatrix, who purports herself to be sleeping (or so John Milton thought), lets the fallen angel know what eros can be and do, when God has had a hand in shaping it?

We do not know, and perhaps will never know.

But it is conceivable that the cryptic myth has at this point touched the nerve of the issue more precisely, even, than Spinoza has.[7] If the fruit-of-the-tree-of-knowledge-of-good-and-evil is reserved for the teeth of the gods, or God, it is a scandal, an ontological offense. It is precisely human fruit, even though misnamed, because human beings know *responsibility,* and God does not.

In a quite different, and quite relentless, idiom Spinoza's argument is to the same effect: to be "born free" is a dialectical Pickwickianism. What it means is to be *unborn,* that is, speaking abstractly, to be *undetermined,* or *merely* self-determined; and, therefore, either wholly absorbed into Substance, or to exist quite apart from it, and immune to its infinite determination, which is absurd.

Spinoza's argument, like the crypticism of Scripture, de-ontologizes good-and-evil; but he does it more bluntly, and more radically, because he wishes to expel the rubrics of good-and-evil from the language of freedom, and of morals.

One need not be convinced, as I am not, that this is altogether a good idea. But it is a price that Spinoza is evidently prepared to pay in order to ground his ethic absolutely on the bedrock of *human responsibility for one's own determination.**

---

*To sum up, theologically: Human beings never have had the sort of freedom that has been equated with innocence. God has it. Human beings do not. Human freedom is therefore intrinsically concerned with good and evil. "Action"—in the sense earlier prefigured (but not instantiated) by art—both embodies and directs this concern.

The word "responsibility" would be an uncomfortable word in the context of Spinoza's thought. I do not know whether the word would have a legitimate status in purportedly faithful rendering of a significant term in Spinoza's Latin and/or Dutch text. Nor does it matter. What we are dealing with here is the problematic of convergent tendencies in the history of moral ideas. That history is more like a geölogical scenario than like the saga of the strife of concepts. When the tendencies are not convergent, then they are stratified one upon another, and thus spiritually cognate to one another, when they are not igneously fused to one another, yet discernible to inspection, in the heat of historical action.

"Responsibility" is a notion from the complex vocabulary of transcendence. The tradition of ethical transcendence is partly theological, partly Kantian–neo-Kantian, partly simplistic, from common sense. It means, to begin with, answerability, or punishability—whether "guilty" or no, for one does not have to be guilty in order to be punishable; and then the notion gets confused and productive of confusion when the bar of answerability undergoes levitation to a transcendental, "actual" realm, or thaumaturgic translation into a highly noumenal conscience, that operates by excruciation.

The word "responsibility" is thus in bad odor. It becomes more respectable when it undergoes a political distillation, as in Hobbes. We are responsible for the commonwealth, and for everything, or nearly everything, in it, because we did it and are it.

But Spinoza's accent is less civic than Hobbes's, possibly because his civic situation is less neurotic than England's was in the seventeenth century; though, of course, Holland had its paranoid moments too, but they tended to be channeled off into the relatively stable circuits of Protestant orthodoxy; stable, perhaps, because tending toward the catatonic, and thus self-arresting.

Spinoza's civic reflections are segregated off into two treatises, the *Tractatus Theologicus Politicus* and the *Tractatus Politicus*. Both are no doubt, and have been, of sufficient interest to historians and specialists, but from the standpoint of ethics, ontology, and dialectic they seem like poor relations of the *Ethic*. The one treatise, the *Theologicus*, is a contribution to the sophisticated hermeneutic of Scripture; it is angry and somewhat bitter, but the subject is a bitter one, and Spinoza had a bitter experience, which helped to make his theological touch, when he probed, more brutal than it should have been, or perhaps need have been.

The other treatise, the *Tractatus Politicus*, seems altogether shadowed by something else, perhaps by Hobbes's blinding light on the subject, and emerges from that shadow with evident self-inhibition. It seems to emerge in the direction of what we have come to think of as the liberal idea,[8] or the democratic one; but the needle giving that direction is exceedingly tremulous in the seventeenth century, even in Holland.

Thus, Spinoza has himself, in effect, told us what his text requires of us: and it is not exactly *political* responsibility, and political guilt, toward our parthenogenetic commonwealth, and social contract; but responsibility toward ourselves, and our duration.

This is the last full measure of responsibility, and its bitter cup. We would prefer to be responsible to anybody, or anything, rather than ourselves. We do not quite know, we are not prepared or to begin with willing to know, quite what it means. And in fact the notion is not a self-evident one.

The bounding parameters of the notion in Spinoza are *conatus* and *adequation*. These govern the way our determination passes into our freedom—without losing its character (by way of mystery and miracle) as determination—and help to celebrate and make possible our self-maintenance, in duration and, more than that, as an eternal *individual* in God.*

Various aspects of the problem thus come together in Spinoza's notion of the individual. Let us therefore return to that, and begin with it.

Our clues are Propositions 11 to 13 of Part II.

"I exist in that I think as a body."

I have thus paraphrased the complex argument that culminates in Proposition 11, but is rooted in several preceding propositions. Proposition 11 reads as follows: "The first thing which forms the actual being of the human mind is nothing else than the idea of an individual thing actually existing."

"Nothing else" is a polemical phrase. The polemic has to be against Descartes and his mischief-making *cogito*. Who says *cogito ergo sum* is under summons to answer the question: "you are thinking of *what*?" The respondent dare not, of course, answer, "I am thinking of thought." That might be blasphemy, since in Aristotelian myth, and its medieval successors, God is supposed to be doing that. Or if not blasphemy, which is to say impertinence, it might well be nonsense.

If one manipulates this nonsense with sufficient relentlessness,

---

*Regress to imaginary primeval innocence, and transcendence toward imaginary future realms (political or noumenal) have both been ruled out. Ethics consequently resolves into the practice of proper self-maintenance. The individual, in all his or her relevantly important facets, must be properly maintained. The discussion below will turn on the question of the kind of individuality *we* have, as opposed to the kind God has. If we know that, we will also know what the relevantly important facets of our individuality are—that have to be maintained.

one lands in transcendent incoherence: that is, with two (or more) substances, and a Prestigidator in the wings.

One has traveled this dead end before. One pulls back sharply. One knows, by now, that God or Nature or Substance exists, since even nonsense exists, and that he is necessarily one; that is, coherent. If one has to begin with incoherence, one would do better not to begin.

Is God an individual?[9]

The question, presumably inevitable, has certain tiresome associations from which it should be separated.

On the one hand, it suggests the older, more mythic question: is God a person? Is he, for instance, even *one* person, let alone three, or three-in-one? This question is mythic because, if taken serio-literally, it simply leads to a melodrama of question-counter-question that remain pictorial: they have no answer; they are not even questions. Is the devil a person? Is an amoeba a person? Is a fetus a person? Is a vegetable-person a person? Is a molecule a person? Or a chromosome or a gene? Is Justice, with or without a blindfold, a person? No, of course not; that's a metaphor, a figure of speech. Then, what's a person? What the law says a person is, that's a person. But the law, except the law canonical, does not say God is a person. And so on.

A person, perhaps, is an individual that has personality? Oh, of course! Then what would an infinite personality be, or be like?

From these abusive and regressive questions one tends to forget that God or Nature or Substance is *infinite*. Once reminded that that is so, one is no doubt willing to revise the question; is God, then, an *infinite* individual? Yes, of course. But what of it? To say that he is an infinite individual is simply to say that there can be only one God. It does not tell us what an individual is. God himself, so to speak, tells us what that is. And he tells us that by inviting—nay, compelling—attention to what his nature, or, as is sometimes said, his being is: *God* or *Substance* or *Nature is an infinite action*.

We know two things about that infinite action: it is extended, and it is thoughtful, or has the character of minding. It is quite correct to speak of the mind of God, though one should not try to put it, ghost-like, into any machine. It is already there, in *any* machine, though not, be it observed, in a cosmic machine, for the simple reason that there is no cosmic machine.

In what sense can we speak of that Infinite Action—for the present purpose we capitalize the words, as the Thomists and neo-Thomists might capitalize their favorable notion of God as "Pure" Act, in disregard of the interesting problematic as to what an "impure" Act might be—as being *an* individual? Would there be any difference between the notion of the infinite action *constituting* an infinite individual, and the notion of such action being the action *of* such an individual?

To the several connected questions we have just raised, the following answers seem apropos:

(*a*). As to the last question: there can be no meaningful difference between the two ways of expressing the notion of God's uniqueness and individuality, if individuality is one of the characters that his notion properly enjoys. The reason for the absence of a difference is this: God has no qualities apart from his action. It is in this sense that he is "pure," and in this sense that he is one Substance. His infinite action might, then, very well be infinite individuality.

(*b*). Is it individual?

What precisely is our question? Are we in pursuit of the indivisible monad—confident that having found it we would find it invested with supremacy? Are we in search of God's thumbprint, its whorls, etc.? What images of grotesqueness shall attach to, or be excluded from, God's putative individuality?

When the seriousness of myth has had its say, we are forced back upon a more ultimate seriousness. The only ultimate thing we can mean by individuality is: coherence, consistency, indefeasible identifiability (therefore the mythic thumbprint). One might say, rather, self-identifiability, as one sometimes says self-verifying.

Does the notion of God in Spinoza's *Ethic* satisfy these requirements? Is he an individual?

As to the first two, the answer has to be self-evidently yes. By definition, or by essence. God-Nature-or-Substance has to be infinitely coherent and infinitely consistent or he is not infinitely God-Nature-or-Substance. Not at all.

As to the third requirement: this is an old Platonic (as also Kantian) requirement of all such cases, which there is no getting around. That by which we identify everything else is self-identifying, or else we can identify nothing. What is meant by self-identifying, in this connection, is simply constant, incontrovertible presence. God-Nature-or-Substance being always there—or here—is naturally self-identifying, seeing that it is *uniquely* always here or there.

I do not see what more we can demand of God. He is an individual. An infinite one. But it is not important.

God's individuality, just as such, is unimportant. (His personality might be important, if he had one, but it is not evident that he has.) What is important is the way that individuality infinitely works. It works by infinite and/or eternal *determination*. Eternal in this connection means, so far as we are concerned, *incessant*. It also means un-begun; but that is important only in another connection, which we have not yet arrived at.

It is the infinite determination of that infinite individual that God is, which is important for us. It is what is responsible or accounts for the individuality that *we* have. That is where we find ourselves: condemned to an individuality that is absolute enough in its own kind.

We are confronted, then, with a state of affairs as follows:

1. God is an infinite individual, individuating infinitely, and infinitely determining and determinate.

One may as well avoid the traditional expression, "self-determinate," and the variations on it. Such expressions tend to suggest that God has a self. Does God have a self? We do not know. Selfhood may or may not belong among the *unknown* infinite attributes of Substance, but it is hard to see what Substance could do with it that it is not already doing with the two known attributes of extension and thought.

2. From the foregoing character of God a certain specificity of metaphor necessarily follows. For instance, it would be inappropriate and misleading to invoke the metaphor of emanation, whether explosive emanation or the suffusive, capillary, and osmotic kind, to image forth, or render account of, God's infinite, inexhausting, and inexhaustible creativity. Why would such metaphors—some of them in traditional actual use and some of them a standing temptation to be used—be inappropriate? Because there is an entropic rule of thought governing such metaphors: explosive creativity must explode in a burst of *random motion* (and if eventually, why not now?); *or else offer itself as simply another miracle-and-mystery for the day's thought*. Malebranche's "occasionalism" does not disguise the miracle-and-mystery of it; on the contrary, it simply dramatizes *and* mechanizes it. To complete the argument: any metaphor of explosiveness tends to produce in our thought—a thought necessarily and very properly conditioned by "knowledge of the second kind"—a conceptual-image of a world product, *natura naturata*, we say, that is inconsistent with our defined and defining notion of God. An infinite, determining, and individuating God cannot ("will not") produce a world, a "cosmos," or whatever, of *random motion;* not even if sustained by the hope that it will right itself.* There will be no Second Coming for Substance.

Therefore, the explosionary-emanationist type of metaphor is excluded.

---

*Here HMR holds that the doctrine of emanation, because it includes the notion of a world that arises by progressively distancing itself from God, will by the same token include the notion of a world of progressively diminishing causal (that is, divine) efficacy. Finally (at its outermost boundaries), such a world must become a world of random motion.

On the whole, our rule of specificity of metaphor has an exclusionary force, rather than otherwise. It does not matter, it seems to me, which metaphor we use, provided we avoid the use of *certain* ones. Let us think of God, if we must, as a weaver, or an infinite player of the game of cat's-cradle, or, more exhaustingly, as an infinite musician given to infinite syncopation and infinite ragtime, or, better, as your typical eighteenth-century meta-mathematician, deistically inclined, and altogether knowledgeable in non-Euclicidean, meta-Riemannian mathematics, etc.

The main thing is that the metaphor be consistent with the *definiendum* it seeks to explain.

3. Hence it follows that the finite individuals, whom the infinite God has creatively individuated, must, under the attributes, be like him.

This is Spinoza's *imitatio dei*. It is not really a matter of choice, but of determination and *understanding*.

This means that our finite individuality—trivial as it may be—is both causative and determined, and indefeasibly coherent, under God. Spinoza's activistic word for that coherence is *conatus*.

Conatus is our persistent individuality in God. We maintain it in and through God, as he, in accordance with his infinite nature has endowed us and himself with it, in the first place; and if there is an overtone of effortfulness, or even strain, in the notion of conatus, as if it performs against odds, that overtone quite properly belongs, for the odds are infinite; and they obtain, so to speak, against God himself. That is to say, *individuation is an unlimited career of resistance.*

On God's level, the unlimited is the infinite; but on our own durational level, the unlimited, or the refusal of self-abandonment, is the best that we can do.* It is, in fact, the only thing we can do. But we can do it more or less *adequately*. If more-or-less and adequate-inadequate have a quantitative echo, which seems incompatible with "higher" considerations, as if trying-a-little-harder could bring one closer to God, that is because we now speak on the level of knowledge of the second kind, where procedural quantifications have importance. And we speak now also on the level of knowledge of the first kind, or *vague experience,* where the difference between quantity and quality is an indiscernibility. And that indiscernibility is precisely true

*God, as the boundless source of individuation, becomes—in us—the refusal, on ethical grounds, to allow ourselves passively to be trespassed against, and the human refusal to give up on ourselves. This intrinsic refusal cannot be merely stubborn or outraged. Its rights and momentum must be understood by us. Also, we must be "up to it" (adequate to the occasion) emotionally. The discussion of these convergent human requirements continues below.

on the level of knowledge of the third kind: *it is precisely for Spinoza's "intuitive science" that quantity and quality are one and the same.*

To put the matter strongly: the ultimate verification of an actuarial statistic, for example, is not its "accuracy" (if it were "inaccurate," it would not be a statistic), but its *adequacy*. Adequate for what? What kind of adequacy? The adequacy of Spinoza is an *ethical adequacy*. A certain rhetorical advantage might lie in conceiving this as "adequacy for freedom," but Spinoza's argument is, I believe, a caution, in part, against allowing the notion of freedom to become a dialectical intoxicant, as in Hegel, or a source of moral bemusement, as in Kant. Freedom is a tragic matter—at least it is so, I believe, in Spinoza—and men are not born free. Nor will they, I think, become free when they die, or become unborn; they will merely become eternal.

We are not, then, to think ourselves and the world in terms of good-and-evil—we cannot help doing so, and will no doubt continue to do so, despite Spinoza's somber demurrer to the practice—but rather to think ourselves and it in terms of *adequation* and *understanding*. The two notions are much the same: adequation is conatus at work; understanding is conatus in a contemplative moment; but contemplativeness is a forced figure; there is anguish in it, at least as much, as in the pursuit of adequacy.

Our argument aims to zero in on the defining characteristics, and sub-characteristics, of human individuality. Before coinciding with that target, we pause to ask: which of the categories that have been deployed, and are yet to be deployed, are the primary metaphors for the existential action—the career of individual human conatus—that Spinoza seeks to describe and advance by his argument, and which are the secondary sub-metaphors of the case? Here is what we have to choose from: conatus, emotion, adequate/adequation, idea, understanding. Anything else? Shall we not spin out the list to include the inevitable psychological (psychomatic) terms, such as desire/aversion (aversion being negative desire), love/hate, fear/hope, et cetera? Shall we include freedom? Or intellectual love?

The answer has to be no. That answer is dictated by the dialectical moment in which we now stand.

We are considering human individuality as an action, or moment, of ontological conformation with the supreme, effortless effort of individuation expressed by God-Nature-Substance in, and as, his very being.* In the usual metaphor of such argument, we are therefore constrained to derive, as it were, human individuality from God's individuating-individualhood, but we are *not* constrained, in fact we

---

*In a condensed way this voices the theme of all the arguments to this point.

are interdicted, to derive human *freedom,* such as it is, or human *love,* such as that is, from God's freedom, or God's love, such as that may be. In fact, though we are bespoken by our *ethical* conatus to love God, and prevented by our structure from really and truly hating him, it is ethically empty and absurd to expect him to love us in return.

The relation between God and man in Spinoza is a quite special one, and notoriously misunderstood. *That relation is both profoundly interpenetrant, and asymmetrical.*

For example:

There is no conceivable circumstance, or sense, in which God's action can be thought to have undergone, or to be undergoing, any sort of diminution, or fall into passivity, or suffering. But the human situation is quite different. *We are a finite sub-mode of the first infinite mode of the attribute of extension, namely, motion and rest.* There is no rest for God. There is not literally any for human beings either, since rest is simply an unexpected form of motion; but there can very well be a diminution of human power of action. Under what circumstances? When we are bound, or imprisoned? But this is trivial, to the point of offensiveness. We do not need a metaphor of freedom to advise us that jails are contra-indicated for gracious living. Hobbes, as political ontologist, has said a sufficient word on this subject: freedom is power, or ability. *Spinoza's notion of action is a sub-category of ethical conatus.* Human beings act, and are adequately self-individuating, when, being in the order of determination, they move and are moved, according to such portion of knowledge of the third kind as they are able to attain to, thereby rising, in an ethical ascent, to the intellectual love of God.

We sum this up in a single formula: the notion of human individuality, in Spinoza, is an *ethical* notion. God being free and indifferent to good and evil, the human being, from the moment of his finite, durational, modal manifestation, turns his back on God and seeks a freedom which is no longer God's, and never was. The human individual is now confronted with a quite exalted developmental opportunity: he will be indifferent to God's freedom, and will love God in despite of God.

We now have an answer to our earlier question: which is the primary metaphor for this stage of our argument? The primary metaphor is *adequation of an emotion.*

This metaphor, more forcibly than any other, keeps us in mind of the difference between man and God. Whether or no God has personality, or personhood, it is inconceivable that he should have temperament, and by the same token inadmissible that he should have feelings, or emotions. The case does not change if we substitute the more abstract-sounding term "affects," which has been offered and used as a preferred translation of Spinoza's term for the phenomena. God might "affect" himself, as he could not conceivably feel for himself, but then the term "affect" no longer means what it ought to mean. It has to mean the human structure, as a *mobile* of body and mind, moving between an *inadequate* understanding of its place in the order of determination and an *adequate idea* of that place. To have an adequate idea of that place is a considerable achievement. It is sometimes called blessedness, or the intellectual love of God; and might as well be called freedom. It is not under any circumstances to be confused with resignation, whether in the Stoic-pagan or Stoic-Christian version of that ambivalent virtue, so charged with bitterness and helplessness.

The *adequation of an emotion* seems to be the most intense form of action that Spinoza is able to name. That adequation can only be accomplished through, or by, *another and higher emotion,* that is to say, by what Spinoza calls an *idea*. An idea is the mind acting. There is no other form of action known to God or man. But the mind's action, on the human level—we need not for the moment concern ourselves with what was even too grand for Job, namely, the mind of God—is only expressed and known to us through the *objectification* of the action in the human body (the body being nothing else than the object of the idea that the human mind is). Another way of saying this is that the mind, when it acts (and by definition when it does not act, it is nothing), acts *extensively,* and only so; there being no other way to act. What of God? But of course he acts extensively too; and only so; and in the first place; it is one of his attributes. Does he then have a body? Why would he need that? He has, and is, *natura naturata;* and just this side of that far horizon there is (as Spinoza calls it) the "face of the whole universe" to remind us that God does not need a body, and cannot have one, *because he is not human*.

In sum: Spinoza's term *emotion* (in whatever translation of itself the term comes to us) is not a psychological term, but a term for the basic form of *peculiarly human action*. As if to say, in describing a human action, *he performed an emotion*. We do not speak that way, because we do not, and need not, speak in metaphors. But, perhaps, we *are* a metaphor: a metaphor for a sub-modality of the first infinite mode of motion-and-rest, maintained in its integrity, like any other act of God's primordial and infinite creativity, by a self-stabilizing ratio of self-quantification, that persists and is recognizable, in God's infinite commitment to individuation, no matter how many times, and in what devious ways, the molecular tissues of our bodies renew themselves, in perpetual self-displacement, every seven years, or seven times seven.

Man has turned his back on God, but God has cooperated with that ontological gesture by endowing man, so to speak, with a peculiarly human form of conatus, or *eternal action*, called the adequation of emotions. This is what I have called the ethical conatus, and, so far as I can see, it is the only conatus that the human being has. The rest of it, or of him or her, is not necessarily entropic—ontologic entropy is what one cannot make any sense of—but it is certainly self-reductive to a sub-state of non-affairs, the cosmic dust of existence, that cannot even be counted in angstrom units; or would not be worth the count. Entropy might even be improvement on such a condition.

What we have proposed is that the individuation of the human being, in and under God, is an *ethical individuation*. His track or spoor in the so-called cosmos is an ethical spoor. And the primordial and eternal act of creation that has individuated him becomes, when that act passes into the eternal custody of the individual thus individuated, a primordial ethical act.* This act is constitutive of man. Shall we assume, with Spinoza, that the action-called-man is maintained in its individual integrity by a dynamic of internal eurhythmics, or moving identity of ratio (as in Spinoza's fond metaphor of the fourth proportional), that will persist in being recognizable and identifiable through all the superficial changes of biology and circumstance? We have to assume that the individuality of man is an *eternal* individuality, even though *he* does not last very long; that is to say, he belongs to the durational order, and has a high and soon mortality rate. Shall we, in other words, take *literally* Spinoza's attempt to read human individuality, in its claimed persistence, as a quantifiable corollary of the physics of the attribute of extension, in its modal operations and declinations?†

We can, if we like, be as literal as Pythagoras may have been, or as Plato, in his own Pythagorean longings; or as literal as the ineffable mathematics of quantum mechanics, which, for all we know to the contrary, might propose that the life style of a human individual be predictable within a precise range from the mathematics of his genes. That is to say, given that, for example, the probative evidence of the individuating thumbprint is lost to us, owing to the amputation of

*It is the individual's taking custody of himself that is the primordial ethical act, not God's creation of him.

†The quality of our individuality having been discerned, in its distinctness from God's individuality, the next question can be confronted. How long does our special kind of individuality—the "action-called-man," the performing of appropriate emotion—how long does that last? Does it endure through all the circumstances of life? Under what circumstances does it fail? When we die, does the action-called-man also die?

the hands, we might—in fact we must—still take an electromagnetic reading of the original extensive act that constitutes the person's body and individualhood, regardless of diet and disguise.

One has only to remind oneself that these absurdities of science fiction, taken as speculative possibilities, arise as a by-product or side-effect of excessive strain placed upon the (procedural) knowledge of the second kind.

I do not see any possibility of empirical demonstration, or confirmation, of persistent individuality. I shall assume that Spinoza did not see any such possibility either, and was not interested in guaranteeing it. I take it for granted that the argument he sketches for us (in Lemmas IV to VII, Part II, Proposition 13)[10] is sketched from the vantage point of such knowledge of the third kind or intuitive science as he believed himself to have attained.

These four lemmas (IV to VII, Part II, Proposition 13), reproduced here without their amplifying or supportive demonstrations, scholia, etc., read as follows:

> Lemma IV. *If a certain number of bodies be separated from the body or individual which is composed of a number of bodies, and if their place be supplied by the same number of other bodies of the same nature, the individual will retain the nature which it had before without any change of form.*
>
> Lemma V. *If the parts composing an individual become greater or less proportionately, so that they preserve towards one another the same kind of motion and rest, the individual will also retain the nature which it had before without any change of form.*
>
> Lemma VI. *If any number of bodies composing an individual are compelled to divert into one direction the motion they previously had in another, but are nevertheless able to continue and reciprocally communicate their motions in the same manner as before, the individual will then retain its nature without any change of form.*
>
> Lemma VII. *The individual thus composed will, moreover, retain its nature whether it move as a whole or be at rest, or whether it move in this or that direction, provided that each part retain its own motion and communicate it as before to the rest.*

Just as extension itself is the primitive axiom without which the world could neither be argued nor perceived, so the begotten modalities of extension, and their self-maintaining harmonics of individuation, are a primitive sub-axiom without which human conatus cannot be apprehended. Why do we have the conatus to endure? Why not rather the conatus to languish and die? Might not the death wish be the primordial project? Why not? Why not the "sublime" and illiterate merger with the conglomerate called pantheism?

It is evident that Spinoza has answered these questions before he began.

Human individuality is an *adequated emotion*, or an idea. It naturally, and inevitably, objectifies in the extensive posture of the human body. The "body language" that one sometimes speaks of is the language of conatus. It is a conatus *to be*.

But this futurism of human conatus has nothing to do with any myth of progress, or with any of the various eschatologies of positivism—such as *ewigstreben* and a "republic of ends" technologically realized. The "intellectual love of God" has no future. The on-goingness of human conatus has to do not with that form of investment called "hope," nor even with belief in things unseen (for there is nothing unseen to knowledge of the third kind), nor with cutting one's losses, for that matter. It has to do with *the nature, or essence, of an action*. And with the indefeasible *unity of an action*. And with an action's *eternal now*.

When does an action begin? The action of raising one's arm, for example. And when does it end? When does determination begin, and where does it end? Which part of the action of raising one's arm is the *real* action? The electrical impulse in the neuron? The orbital jump of the electron that is "responsible" for the impulse? Or the pantomime of an arm *raised*, for astigmatic contemplation, and response? Is the real action the clenched fist at the end of that arm, or the impact of that fist when, by conatus, it descends? The *real* action is in God? Nonsense. God is *of*, not in, *all* the real actions; and all of them are real. Therefore, he is not in any one of them.

The locus of the real action can only be adjudicated by human conatus; and this will be an ethical decision. What did I mean when I raised my arm? Did I mean anything? Granted that I am not to be burdened with precising a meaning that I do not yet know, and perhaps am afraid to know, nevertheless, I am not allowed to take refuge in the posture that I did not mean *anything*. Who or what does not allow me? My body does not allow me: the object of the idea that my mind is, that does not allow me.

On the level of human conatus, there is no such thing as reflex action.

This need not plunge us into anxiety, and I assume that it will not. For on the level of human conatus many, if not all, decisions were primordially made, as the saying goes. And were therefore made in an eternal now. Spinoza's eternal now does not lie beyond the knowledge of the third kind, but before it and below it, in the area of "vague experience," where the action is.*

From the Note to the Demonstration of Proposition 23 in Part V of the *Ethic*:

> This idea which expresses the essence of the body under the form of eternity is . . . a certain mode of thought which pertains to the essence of the mind, and is necessarily eternal. It is impossible, nevertheless, that we should recollect that we existed before the body because there are no traces of any such existence in the body, and also because eternity cannot be defined by time or have any relationship to it. Nevertheless, we feel and know by experience that we are eternal . . . .
>
> Although, therefore, we do not recollect that we existed before the body, we feel that our mind, in so far as it involves the essence of the body under the form of eternity, is eternal, and that this existence of the mind cannot be limited by time nor manifested through duration.

The Proposition, which has been demonstrated, and then glossed, reads as follows: "The human mind cannot be absolutely destroyed with the body, but something of it remains which is eternal."

The impulse to image forth the Proposition and its demonstrative glosses is both irresistible and doomed. Let us for once, then, refuse to yield to the irresistible, and finally eschew any attempt to speculate about the sensible form of the mind's eternity. The "something" of the mind, for example, which remains, is it a "part" of the mind, or something other than a part? Since it is obvious that the body, which is the object of the idea that we call the human mind, has to be inseparable from its idea, what sort of destruction is predicated of the body, to which destruction the mind, or "something" of it, is guaranteed an eternal immunity? Being dissolved, as it must be in death, into its molecular parts, does the body nevertheless *survive* as a particular ratio of extensive "parts," held-eternally-together by the mind's eternal character as a self-objectifying idea? What does it mean for a "ratio" to survive? Would Spinoza care to speak, quasi-Platonically (at least for the Plato of the *Timaeus*), of the survival of something-like-a-ratio? What is it to be something-like-a-ratio?

---

*Again and again it will be suggested that, although the eternity of human individuality is expressed within our action, it is not traceable, inductively, beyond that dread bourne from which no traveler, etc.

It is evident that to pursue such questions would be an exercise in seeing how near one might come to myth, while evading it. It is further evident that we are not talking about survival at all, but about something like being-under-the-form-of-eternity. If one has that form, or quality, or quantity of existence, one does not continue to have it, as one might continue to climb uphill even when one is tired, or continue to have the fatigue of such a climb after the climb is over; one simply has what one has. One might indeed refuse to acknowledge that one has what one has. But this would be to form oneself in the image of a fence, or receiver of stolen goods, who necessarily denies that he has what he has. Until it comes to disposing of the goods. For that brief instant of duration the fence, let us say, suddenly ceases to "hate God." We knew all along that "no man can hate God"; but it is entirely feasible to try. In the same way we can try not to be eternal. It is a disgusting effort, aesthetico-ethically, but of course it has been made.

Am I saying that we are, in Spinoza's argument, eternal in spite of ourselves? Yes, of course. But I am also saying that, in Spinoza's argument in the *Ethic, there is no great merit in being merely eternal.*

All said and done, there is nothing much to eternity: it is merely the praise-word, by tradition, for the indefeasible *now* of action; that *fact* of our existence that it has neither beginning nor end. Is there really nothing that has beginning or end? Of course, there is. *Effects,* for example, being the durational, or pictorial, sectioning of an action, viewed from the "wrong" or counter-productive end of it—they have beginning and end. There was a durational moment when such effects were *not;* that is, not yet, or yet to be; and there is a durational moment when they *are;* that is, have been, and are no longer. The same thing, though contrariwise, may be said of *causes;* or, at least, of the *secondary* causes, which are all that we are concerned with on the durational level. Causes are thus the sectioning of an action, viewed from the "right" or productive end of it.

We may be sure of one thing: in Spinoza's argument there is no ontological difference between ends and means; they are both the wrappings of the *eternal now of an act.* If men were "born free," *they would have no conception of ends and means.* But men are not born free. (If they were born free, they would not be men.) There is therefore an *ethical* difference.

We are being told, by the argument, that there is a continuous red thread of eternity, so to speak, running through the durational (and thus counter-eternal) fabric of our lives. We have been given an epistemological clue as to how to recognize our *own* (or, in Heidegger's gothic idiom, our "ownmost") eternity. The eternity of God-Nature-Substance is of no particular consequence *to us;* though, of course, as the starting point of all being, and of reflection on it, it is of utmost consequence to its own totalizing expression in the "face of the whole universe," and therefore to us when it becomes appropriate to be concerned with our own situation as a part of that "face." For instance, in that high-pitched Kantian moment when we consider the "starry heavens above" in their alleged equipoise with the "moral law within."

But most of the time the thing that matters to us is our own eternity, not God's, nor his large-scale astrophysical modalities.

The recognition clue that has been given us is, of course, the knowledge of the third kind. "Intuitive science."

We now know that this knowledge is *ethical* knowledge.

That is to say: (*a*) Its only avenues of application are in the procedural operations of knowledge of the second kind, and in the exponential complexities, many of them regressive and counter-productive, of the life of "vague experience." Both these kinds of knowledge are specifically, that is, necessarily, *ethical,* in that they are human. (Contrariwise: animals, for example, are "born free"; there is nothing in their experience that could be called "vague," even when they are kittenish or playful, and they evidently have "no conception of good and evil.")

(*b*) "Intuitive science" is properly called *ethical* knowledge, because it is that knowledge by which, and which alone, we recognize human individuality.

The "recognition" of human individuality is the eternal awareness of the idiosyncratic character of a human actor, or of his eternal agency.[11]

If we express this—as we have had to do—in the somewhat dessicated formalisms of Spinoza's Part II, Proposition 13,* we say: that the recognition of idiosyncratic eternal agency is the eternal persistence (or simply, existence) of a given sub-modality of the first infinite mode of extension, motion, and rest.

The givenness of that sub-modality is what we may call, for lack of a better term, the persistence of a ratio. The one advantage, and perhaps a sufficient one, of these quasi-mathematical metaphors is that they make absolute the uniqueness in question. The unextended ratio—say 3/4—is a mere universal, and could be anywhere or nowhere; or could be only formally, that is, potentially, and thus concretely and empirically not at all. But conceive that same ratio as extended (as in music), and it can only be, given God's inimicality to nothingness, eternally here or there.

---

*The Proposition is given at the opening of this essay.

If the human act, or uniqueness of an agency, has eternal persistence, it can only have that by being eternally subject to *recognition*. For the attribute of thought does not withdraw from the world, to abide the outcome of the systole and diastole of extension in the world. "Intuitive science" is Spinoza's name for the program of eternal recognition of eternal things. This eternal recognition is, necessarily, in and of the order of determination. While recognizing, we are being recognized; while identifying, we are being identified. Identification, like mis-identification, intrudes upon our uniqueness, while sometimes, for a vanishing moment, corroborating it. *In the infinite order of determination, to recognize is to act, while being acted upon.*

The criteria by which we identify, recognize, and act—that is, the criteria by which we *adequate* our existence (or the "emotion" of it) in the world—are now *ethical* criteria. That is, altogether "unfree," and necessarily infected through and through by "conceptions of good and evil." The conatus of our eternal persistence in the face of these "conceptions of good and evil"—that is, of advantage and disadvantage in the "eternal disguise" of being—is what we have no choice but to call an *ethical* conatus. The ethical, for Spinoza, is not a "category" subjoined, or adjoined, to human existence, but is that existence itself.

Then, what is it that "cannot be absolutely destroyed with the body," but of which "something . . . remains which is eternal"?

But he has made it clear: it is the "human mind" of which he is speaking.

Perhaps it is clear, but it has to be made explicit. The "human mind" cannot "remain" to its proper eternity unless the "human body," which is the object of that idea called the human mind, participates in that remainder. We are not laying down, so to speak, a condition *sine qua non* for the mind's remaining; we merely state the irreducible meaning of any claim, in Spinoza's idiom, that the mind remains. Not "if that," but *in that* the mind remains, the body remains. For "in God . . . there necessarily exists an idea which expresses the essence of this or that human body under the form of eternity" (Proposition 22, Part V).

The "essence" of this or that human body? All it means, in Spinoza's language, is the *unique specificity* of this or that human body: the unique specificity of a given object of this or that finite human mind. "Essence," it will be said, and has been, does not prejudice the question of existence.

It does not? What kind of "question of existence" is not being prejudiced by a language of "essences"?

Let it be said at once that we are not going back on this neo-scholastic road that leads straight to the dialectic of "nothingness," its problems, mysteries, and confusions.

We already know what kinds of existence Spinoza is talking about, and we, for the moment, in his name. He is talking about two kinds: *durational* existence, the one we more or less get used to, and *eternal* existence, the one that does not require, and hardly allows of, any getting used to. We already know that either kind of existence is individuated absolutely, and that the individuations are not *summed*, not even in God; or if summed, are summed infinitely; and the rhetoric of "infinity" does not help us in this connection, for we are dealing with matters that belong to knowledge of the third kind, and infinity is merely a procedural device for the mathematical operations of the second kind of knowledge. Our individuated ethical conatus is not infinite, but merely eternal.

Let us review the matter once more. The durational human body is an *ethical body*. We put this in the Kantian metaphor: it is a "good will" made flesh, and a born loser. It will not carry its acquired conceptions of "good and evil" into its eternity, just as it did not derive them *from* the eternity which, in its own essence (that is, in its own specificity), it has always had. Where, then, do they come from, these conceptions of good and evil?

Our dilemma is now clear. We want God to be responsible for us, and as providential as he has time for. We want eternity to have duration. We want "it" to have a sense-datum beginning and a sense-datum end. We want knowledge to stop at the second kind; and, if necessary, not to be knowledge at all. We want a five-year plan for eternity, and the controls on it to be of the strictest possible kind. We do not believe that we are going to die, but we do indeed believe that we are going to be resurrected. In short, we are willing to settle for living forever.

We break the horns of this irrational, passional dilemma by returning to knowledge of the third kind.

Our ethical bodies, and their acquired appropriate conceptions of good and evil, do not come from anywhere. They certainly do not "come from" God, any more than El Greco's astigmatic vision of this or that human, Iberian saint, or city comes from God; though no doubt it is sufficiently in and of God, like everything else. It would surely never have occurred to El Greco—at least not in his metaphysical moments—to ask where his astigmatic vision came from. *He knew that he came from it*. At least, as a painter that would be where he came from. Similarly: our ethical bodies come from our highly individuated self-insertion into the human order of infinite determination. Animals, microbes, and crystalline structures have not performed this mode of self-insertion (though some doubts are sometimes esoterically expressed about crystals): *which is to say they do not have ethical bodies;* or, more precisely, *that they do not have bodies at all*. They may very well have souls.*

Having abandoned the question, where do our ethical bodies come from, we are left with the question, where do they go? Where do they go when? When we die, of course.

This question is easy: *they will go wherever the social contract is*. If there is one on Mars, or in outer space, or in the kingdom of heaven, that's where our ethical bodies, when we die, will go. We do not need a new metaphor for this insight of "intuitive science"; we have one. The "eternal *a priori*" of the *moral law* and its durational (or "historical") expression in the social contract, is metaphor enough.

And by virtue of the same metaphor we now know the answer to an abandoned question: where we, as ethical bodies, came from. We came from the place we are going to: the social contract as *a priori* of history.

We insert this back into Spinoza's idiom.

We have become, in the course of our human duration, agencies of ethical causality. We cannot attribute such causality, in any sequential sense, to God. God has no sequences, and he has no history. To make such attribution would be to reduce God's Substantiality, and thus to blaspheme. Job, it will be recalled, refused to do that. We should do no less. It is thus not *hybris* but a proper piety if we say that ethical causality originates with human existence. God is not competitive and has made no claim to a monopoly of creative origination. If an objective inspection of eternity should disclose that its "eternal now" is *ethically contaminated*, that contamination must be taken as the human contribution to eternity. There is no reason to assume that eternity is ontologically sterile.

But we have noted that in the dimension called "eternity" we are without benefit or handicap of "conceptions of good and evil." What shall it profit us, then, our "ethical contribution to eternity," if that contribution is beyond good and evil?

Once more, regrettably, we are seeking to pass from the order of duration to the order of eternity as if it were a matter of going from one room to another, or one "mansion" to another, in the same house. We are seeking, regrettably, to subvert the conception of eternity as an eternal now. The tools of that subversion are two ingrained habits of empirical thought: the one quasi-Darwinian, or evolutionary; the

---

*The very fact that—like other natural things—we cannot float free of our bodies, but—unlike them—also are *accountable* in and for our bodies, puts us in a different position from anything else in nature. One should be wary of trying to "spiritualize" one's way out of this position.

other, entropic. They go together: in a pre-Socratic colloquialism, "the way up and the way down are one and the same."

These unhappy questions present themselves as follows: does not the "social contract"—the organization chart for the ethical bodies we have been dealing with—have a historical origin, and by the same token can it not cease to be? We have already seen the answer to this question: it is no. The question erupts once more because it thinks it sees an opening in the landscape of eternity, with nobody looking. But that same landscape was behind one, before the question was asked. The sun also rises, the sun also sets; and so does the social contract. But the notions of rising and setting "depend" on the sun, and not vice versa;[12] and the same is true of the fortunes, good or ill, of political history; they depend on the social contract, and not vice versa.

So we then ask: what good does it do us to mythicize (if that is what we were doing) about the laying up of ethical treasure, by strictly human depositors, in heaven, if we, in our tenacious, progenitive future, cannot draw on that account for our future durational benefit? In other words, are we insured against entropy? And when we arrive at our future, will we even be allowed to draw on the account at all? Does the "cultural heritage" really include ethical improvement, increased control of good-and-evil? What about absolute evil? It happened yesterday, did it not, even if it was not born yesterday; and who is to say that it will go away tomorrow?

If something of our "ethical bodies" is not absolutely destroyed with the body, but remains . . . , and is eternal, does this eternal remainder constitute a capital for human history; and if not, why not? What good is eternity?

The two questions: what good is eternity, and what good is the social contract, are one and the same.

The two questions are one and the same, because they are being asked about one and the same logical (and therefore ontological) substance. Eternity and the social contract are, as it were, two "attributes" of one substance.*

There is a sector of the metaphysical order which is creatively originated in and by the human order. That order is, of course, in and of God; as all else is as well. But just as *natura naturans* is immune to the curve of entropy—though it might very well absorb some chapters of entropy into its own history—so it does not intervene in the human order at a point in time. Providentiality would be a work of calculated supererogation, because God was always everywhere there; where

---

*Human eternity is meant here.

the act and the agency were. He would presumably be there in the ultimate heat death, too, because it would require a certain effort, an expenditure of extensive conatus, to stay dead. On the level of the second kind of knowledge, we fossilize eternity in the primeval mud. Necessarily so. Eternity does not mind. By the same necessity, if so minded, we locate the emergence of political structure, or form, some aeons after the first strut of proto-man, in his inauguration of post-arboreal history. But the social contract does not locate in this serio-comic literalness of evolutionary theory. The grooming "dialectic" of the tailed primate family does not impose itself on our scientific faith as an early form of the social contract.* It would be a "fallacy of misplaced concreteness" to seek the origin of eternity at a point in time.

Let us take a moment to differentiate aspects of the conception we are dealing with. There is the eternity of God, and there is the eternity of the human order. There is no doubt the eternity of the crystalline order, too, but we are not called upon to account, by a methodology of the occult, for the detailed workings of those infinite attributes of God that we have no knowledge of. We are only required to account for the metaphysical status of the *ethical bodies* that the argument has led us to take note of. We know that they are individuated, and we know that they are eternal, because any other way of accounting for them leads to the breakdown of God. We must conclude that their eternity is specifically human. Because to invest God with man's ethical conatus is to foist upon him a burden that he cannot carry. God wants nothing to do with the problem of evil. I am speaking, of course, of Spinoza's God. He has left it, *and everything else,* to the individuated order of determination. That order is by definition an infinite order. But within that infinite order there is an infinite series of finite orders. One of them is the human order.

The career of the human order is identical with and expressive of ethical conatus. This ethical conatus is human history. Human history has no goal other than eternity. This is to say that human history has no goal other than to endure as history. The first infinite mode of historical conatus is the *social contract*. The social contract stands to human eternity as extension stands to thought. Within the body of human history there arises the phenomenon of *evil*. Evil may very well be the one absolute we know, *but it is an absolute in and of the social contract*. And the answer to evil has to be an answer within the social

---

*HMR's 1973–74 longhand draft of "Hobbes's Secret" notes: "Animals do not have to come out of the state of nature because they are never in it, in the *human sense* of being in it. . . . Here is the other aspect of the reason: animals do not, would not, cannot *stack arms*."

contract. If there is a social contract on Mars, one looks there for the answer to the "problem of evil"; if there is one in heaven, one looks for the answer there. But this would be merely a mixed metaphor: to look for unknowable infinite attributes in order to know them. The social contract is eternity within human history, and all its answers, like its questions, are there.

This leaves us without heaven and hell; but how much heaven and hell can we afford?

We can probably afford more of hell; at least one is inclined to think so. But even in hell, if we could arrange one, there would be a problem of justice, and the over-riding question whether that quality can be dispensed without some admixture of mercy; and this calls at once for a social contract in hell. So that we would be no further along. The generations of hell would be seeking eternity within their own determinate order.

We recapitulate:

The individuated human agent of an eternal action remains as an eternal agent after the body is destroyed.

So far as we know that agent is *human,* in the strict sense, only during the life of the body.

What we necessarily mean by the "strict sense" is the *remembered* sense. The human agent *remembers* its own agency only during the life of the body.

We may define memory as the first *finite* mode of the first infinite mode that the social contract is. This means that memory, as a sub-mode of the human body, is by nature *individuated*. Memory is an individual, sub-extensive relation to the social contract. There is no social contract after death, and no memory. There is also, in life, no collective memory, and no racial one.*

Where there is no memory, there is no anticipation, and no expectations, great or small. In this life, we may, or may not, expect great things of God. But in eternity, loving God, we do not expect him to love us in return. It is enough for us that he loves himself with an infinite eternal love.

The ethical conatus, through which the social contract expresses itself in our individual lives, necessarily expresses itself through particular ethical *intentions*. These intentions are, of course, our concep-

---

*Personal identity is in large part a construct of memory. Memory (as such a power to construct persons) does not persist beyond death. Therefore, after death, the individual does not maintain the specific commitments and attachments that the social contract worked to safeguard and sanction in durational life. In this sense, the social contract—insofar as it worked to protect one *personally*—does not survive death. Nevertheless, it will be argued below, the eternity manifested in human action is unaffected by death. The social contract reflected in that eternity is likewise unaffected.

tions of good and evil. There is no reason for particular intentions, so conceptualized, to survive the death of the body, and the consequent withdrawal of the social contract from the extensive diorama of an individual human history. Once more: there is no social contract after death, and therefore no conceptions of good and evil.

What we are saying is that if the sun were to be "extinguished," the length of the cadmium line would still be "there"; somewhere. If our conceptions of good and evil come to be rendered null, in the death of the body, the "face of the whole universe," that part of *natura naturata* that we are concerned with, would still be indefeasibly contaminated with *value*. That is the human contribution, so to speak, acting in obedience to its own order of determined-self-determination, to *natura naturans*.

Irrepressibly, we of course now ask for epiphany, or for assurance thereof. How, and where, does Substance, sick with value in its eternal now, locate itself in our human life?

Where else but on the level of knowledge of the first kind, in the realm of "vague experience"?

We have seen that this realm of "vague experience" is, in fact, the horizon toward which the third kind of knowing moves. If, for purpose of analysis, we order this moving in a series of moments, we find: first, that we have arrived at this horizon of our being, "freed," so to speak, of value. Being "freed," as it were, of ethical intentionality, our ordinary experience, enlightened into its original, eternal "innocence," is through and through *corrupt*. "All men are liars," the ancient saying has it;[13] and the ancient saying is dutifully echoed, with embellishment and improvement, by Calvin, by Freud, and by other students of the state of nature in man.

It is not difficult to quantify the ancient saying, rendering it more descriptive: all men are liars, *and* truth-tellers, *when it suits them*, and *killers, and* overflowing with the milk of human kindness, when they kill. This has been called the state of nature. But it may also instructively be thought of as the *order of infinite determination* become manifest, and expressed, so far as that is conceivable, in the quite finite order of "vague" human experience.

Human experience, when it puts the substance of itself into categories, has construed this presence of infinite determination in the warp of human finiteness in two ways: on the one hand, it speaks of "chance"; this is the way the infinite has been apologetically handled for cognitive purposes. On the other hand, it allows for *art;* and for the unpredictability—purposefulness without purpose, as Kant said, the spontaneity and resistance to programming, and meta-cognitive character of the syndrome of aesthetic performance.

But neither art nor "chance" would enable human conatus, engulfed in the infinite of "vague experience," to endure. The reason is that both art and "chance" are derivative, as categories always are, and not themselves ordering operations of the first instance.

The ordering operation, so to speak, of the first instance, is the *social contract*.

The social contract—this extensive incursion of "eternity" into human existence—is what begins to make sense out of our otherwise infinitely enlightened "vague experience." Given the social contract, *and its eternal laws of nature,* we then have art, enabling us to see and experience, astigmatically, what otherwise only God sees and thinks; we also then have "chance," or a methodology of reflection, whereby we outwit infinite determination by acceding to it according to rule, in actuarial protocol, in gamesmanship, and in wagering. Neither art, nor the etiquette of chance, would make any sense unless the social contract were there. The mind makes no sense without the body, even in eternity.*

We may read the situation as follows:

On the level of human conatus the social contract and the order of infinite determination are in *eternal* dialectic. Or confrontation. Out of this dialectic arises what Spinoza calls *human freedom;* or, more precisely, the career of the *free man*.

Spinoza's doctrine of the free man is given in Part IV, Propositions 67 to 73, inclusive. These are the very last Propositions of Part IV, which Spinoza has entitled "Of Human Bondage." The morphology of the text suggests Spinoza's profound belief that human bondage, viewed under the proper aspect of eternity, is self-corrective. But the notion of the self-corrigibility of things is simply an implication of the infinite order of determination in God. It is not a doctrine of metaphysical *laissez faire,* nor is it a doctrine of "progress." It is an expression, rather, of the ontological status of what we have called ethical conatus.

In a Note to the Demonstration of Proposition 66 of Part IV, Spinoza introduces his doctrine of the free man as follows:

> If what has been said here [i.e., in the Proposition and Demonstration to which the Note is appended] be compared with

---

*Only the fact that we have bodies compels us to meet scarcity and fear, conflict and rule making—and finally the requirements of fairness. Thus human action, spot-lit as it is by the requirements of fairness, or the social contract, *must be bodily action*. Neither art nor tactics are exempt from the general, contractual requirements of human action. It follows that, if this definitive aspect of our action is to survive and be eternal, *something* of our bodies must also survive and be eternal.

> what has been demonstrated about the strength of the passions in the first eighteen Props., pt. 4, and in Note, Prop. 18, pt. 4, it will easily be seen in what consists the difference between a man who is led by emotion or opinion alone and one who is led by reason. The former, whether he wills it or not, does those things of which he is entirely ignorant, but the latter does the will of no one but himself, and does those things only which he knows are of greatest importance in life, and which he therefore desires above all things. I call the former, therefore, a slave, and the latter free.

A certain puzzlement arises from scrutiny of these seven propositions toward the end of Part IV, Spinoza's "few words," as he says, "concerning the character of the free man and his manner of life." The seven propositions audit in the mind as follows:

Proposition 67: the free man does not think of death.

Proposition 68: those who are born free—which is nobody—have no notion of good and evil, provided they stay free. The Demonstration points out that the hypothesis is counter-factual, and also impossible. It has two and only two instantiations: God himself, in his proximate causality to man, and the proto-human couple in the Garden of Eden, before the fall. —It is not clear what dialectical use Spinoza is making of this image, since it must be taken that he does not believe there was any such couple, at the time and place alleged. His own gloss, in the Note to the Demonstration, suggests (*a*) an undeveloped theory in Spinoza's mind that notions of good and evil arise from a "zoomorphic" fallacy, that is, a mistaken notion in the mind of Adam that *animal emotions,* were an acceptable model for his own emotional life; (*b*) that when patriarchal man, and his successors, came to be touched by successive moments of grace, they oriented toward a purified conception of authentic human nature. Led, then, by the "idea of God, which alone can make a man free," man comes "to desire for other men the good he desires for himself." That this development actually takes place, or should take place, Spinoza says he has already demonstrated (in Proposition 37, Part IV).

I am going to assume that my own gloss on Spinoza, in the form of my argument concerning man's relation to eternity through the social contract, bears on Spinoza's esoteric allusions in the Note to Proposition 68 of Part IV. The social contract, of course, both in its eternity and in history, is the ontological-political (if political it has to become) expression of the indefeasible, universal community of individuated human nature, and of the fact that man by nature—once he is "freed" to that nature—is given over to desiring for others the good he desires for himself. This good can, of course, be a quite unexpected good, and Spinoza's delineation of such a good is not exactly routine: being absolutely centered in the individual and his particular profit, and, at the same time, hopelessly enmeshed in the infinite order of determination, and co-determination, of the goods of others.

It is evident that there can be neither biological, nor Benthamite, nor actuarial-historical verification of such a hypothesis. We have sought, with Spinoza, such other types of verification as are apropos.

Proposition 69: avoidance of danger, even flight, may be a virtue.

What Spinoza means by virtue is increase of human power, or conservation of such power as one may have; and conservation would, in the nature of the case, be increase, so far as the durational order is concerned; for in that order power is subject to—that is, expresses itself—in the modal variables of motion and rest; it would be meaningless for power to stay "just the same."

This Proposition is one of the more puzzling ones in the cluster of enunciations concerning the "free man and his manner of life." The free man's life style, or formed ethos, one might say.

In the first place: what is the argument directed against? Is it against the heroic ideal? Whose "heroic ideal"? Hegel's? Carlyle's? That of the Achaeans in front of Troy, or of the Trojans? Henry's, in Shakespeare's *Henry V*, on the field of Agincourt? And so on. But the heroic ideal in its classic, or mythi-poetic form, has never assumed the opposite of this proposition, or its contrary: that danger, for instance, is never, under any circumstances, to be avoided.

Is the argument directed against some form of neo-feudal romanticism, or against a resurrected version of it in our time, as for instance in Ortega y Gasset's exalted ethical homily that to live dangerously is to live well?

Does the argument echo a cliché of strategics, that retreat, or the feint of it, may be the best gambit toward "power"?

Is the argument reminiscent of some episode in Spinoza's own life, as for instance when he would have taken to the street before his own house, and discouraged a lynching mob there empowered, in the case of the De Witt brothers? But in that episode, Spinoza's performance was antithesis to the present thesis: he did not avoid danger, as he might have, but risked his life, or tried to. Why? In conformity, one assumes, to his own ethical conatus, which in that moment had no regard for the present thesis, or regarded it as inapplicable.

Merely to raise the foregoing questions suggests two things about Proposition 69: (*a*) there is some lost topicality here, either personal or historical; (*b*) the thought being rendered, perhaps because it is incompletely rendered—and this incompleteness would by no means be the same as Spinoza's lapidary-geometric style, emerges as tending toward the trivial.

In our dealing with Spinoza this is an occasion for astonishment, and concern.

Spinoza's intention here seems esoteric to the point of elusiveness. A Stoic triviality does not seem apropos to Spinoza's context of human freedom. Perhaps the argument has become momentarily inattentive to the fact that it must be guided, through and through, by an *eternal* social contract. Or perhaps it is rushing beyond that, toward the direct love of God, and blessedness, in Part V, "Of Human Freedom."*

Proposition 70: "The free man who lives amongst those who are ignorant strives as much as possible to avoid their favors."

There can be little doubt that here we stand on biographical ground.

If Spinoza failed to regard himself as a free man, as human freedom goes, then he was badly mistaken. And he lived, as all men do, amidst much ignorance. Even in seventeenth-century Holland.

But the argument is a generalization. It suggests (*a*) that the social contract that Spinoza, to all intents and purposes, will presently name—in Proposition 73, is not descriptive of a utopia, and its treacheries, fantasies, and deceptions, but of ethical action and relation, for which the State, as it happens, is a preferred occasion; (*b*) in utopia itself, *per impossibile*, only those who live according to reason will be free; the rest, by the social contract, will have given their ignorance over to authority. This too, perhaps, is a utopian assumption. In any case, Spinoza will not be tempted to misplace the concreteness of anthropomorphic freedom. He is still interested in God, and the freedom possible in him. We remind ourselves that this arises from knowledge of the third kind. Armed with such knowledge, we have less need of favor than we might otherwise have.

We must go with our knowledge of Spinoza's life, such as it is: he was offered favor by those in high place, and declined it. But was the prince elector who offered him the university chair that he declined, was he, too, among the ignorant? "Was Saul also among the prophets?" Spinoza's life does not necessarily support his generalizations, but here and there it instantiates one or another of them.

Proposition 71: "None but those who are free are very grateful to one another."

The Demonstration is as complex as the Proposition is simplis-

*Presumably, the motivating presence of the eternal social contract—even in acts of necessitated flight—would be a fit subject for a more sober and extended appraisal than Spinoza has given it here.

tic, and startling. The Demonstration invokes the following considerations, which have already been argued (in preceding propositions of Part IV): the notion of individual profit (individual good) as the goal of individual life; the commonalty of human nature in individual lives; freedom and friendship as the common recognition of commonalty of nature; interaction of profit seeking as the product of this recognition; such profit sharing is properly called living in accordance with reason; it is significantly useful to call it so, that is, by its right name, because to call it reason reminds us of where we stand in the moving grid of knowledge. It also reminds us of how we make our most advantageous contribution to the infinite order of co-determination. Finally, as net product of all these considerations, stands the Proposition: gratefulness is one of the two, and only two, virtues (of a traditional catalogue) singled out by Spinoza in his synoptic "few words concerning the character of the free man and his manner of life."

The other one is honorableness, as opposed to deceitfulness.

Thus: the ethical conatus, which is the peculiarly human form of self-insertion in the order of determination, takes the name of a virtue called gratefulness. Gratefulness may be understood as that self-insertion itself. As a virtue it is nothing more than an emotion, at the highest exponent of the metaphysical power that an emotion is. Of course, a really powerful emotion is an act of *self*-understanding, and of Substance–Nature–God.

Thus is the nature of God linked up with a psychology of the emotions—routine, and even banal, as such a psychology has to be, it is the only eventful part of epistemology, for Spinoza—and, in due course, linked up with the conatus of the political order, viewed from the inverted telescope of eternity.

But we are not yet in view of blessedness, though we are on the way.

Proposition 72: "A free man never acts deceitfully, but always honorably."

The Demonstration invokes the appropriate preceding propositions to show the incompatibility between being-guided-by-reason, which is class-inclusive of being-more-or-less-free, and practicing deceit. To attempt to establish consistency between being-guided-by-reason and deceitfulness is an exercise in the logically absurd.

The substance of the argument is familiar from its later Kantian equivalent: a purportedly ethical maxim is ethical insofar as it can be universalized. The test case is much the same for both Spinoza and Kant: namely, suppose one's life is at stake? The answer that both give is much the same: not even then; the allegedly exceptional case cannot be used to *prove* the rule; it does not enter within the purview of the rule; there is no method known to reason by which the *ad hoc* can be universalized.

The argument has been criticized; classically, by John Stuart Mill, and by many others. One cannot even be sure that Hegel would subscribe to the argument in its Kantian innocence, or blandness.

Before we take note of the formidable metaphysical problem of truth (what is it?, etc.), pulsating within this argument, let us note: that the test case is usually understated, and therefore misleading. It is not when one's *own* life is at stake that the maxim is tested, but when it is the life of *another*. Philosophers must know this, of course, as well as prisoners of a terror, facing torture by the terror, to reveal the names of others. In that circumstance, the outcome is not usually decided by the recollection of the maxim.

Nevertheless, even when mindful of the grimness of the test case (and Spinoza, as well as Kant, must surely be so mindful), the ethical maximalist might still argue, with significance, that (*a*) one *does* what one manages to do, under the worst, as under the best, of circumstances; and is answerable for it; (*b*) but one is still unauthorized to make a *principle* out of one's doing; the principle is *a priori* to any possible doing, or even to any instantiation of itself; and it is the *principle* that all possible doings are answerable to, and not vice versa.

At this point the argument becomes highly abstract, and begins to take on an aura of irrelevance.

Spinoza's Note to the Demonstration of Proposition 72, and the following Proposition 73, distinctly suggest that Spinoza is aware of the real issue here. The Note says, "if reason gives such counsel," the counsel to lie, "she gives it to all men, and reason therefore generally counsels men to make no agreements for uniting their strength and possessing laws in common except deceitfully, that is to say, to have in reality no common laws, which is absurd."

I detect irony and impatience in Spinoza's note. The reason has to be that the true nature of the case is exigent in his mind: it is not maxims he is talking about, nor even a Categorical Imperative, crowned in ontological beauty as such an Imperative is, but the *social contract*. "Common laws, etc." The social contract might be destroyed, but it cannot be constructed out of mechanisms of self-destruct.

You will do what you think you have to do, under the peculiarities of your circumstances, but the *social contract*, and it alone, will invoke the *a priori* maxim to which you are answerable. It and it alone will decide whether your case was a "true," that is, confirmatory, exception to a non-subvertible rule. That is, for instance, to an "eternal law of nature," armed with a sword.

It will make that decision retrospectively, that is to say, after your doing; what other timing for a decision is conceivable?

This deciding after the fact is what we mean by an "eternal law of nature." We mean that eternal laws of nature are absolutely *nominalistic* in their impact on human existence. Before the doing, there is no deed, and no decision on its ethical status. The Good Will is not a deed, and therefore not a determinant in the universal order of determination.

But eternity is there, all the same; it is there in the circumstance that the question has arisen at all; as it must; given the fact—as by now we take it to be—that human actions are expressions of a set, or sets, of infinite modalities that are already, so to speak, tainted by a modality, ethical in essence, that has erupted in and from specifically human conatus.

Epistemologically, this specifically human conatus attains definition on the level of knowledge of the third kind. But its locus, or empirical provenience, is in the vagueness of "vague experience." Neither *natura naturans* itself, nor animal life, nor the life of crystals, enjoys such specifically human vagueness. This vagueness is simply the social contract *in foro interno;* preparing to arm itself either with art, or with a sword; or with both.

"A free man never *acts* deceitfully, etc." We are reminded by the verb that the human individual is a particular mode of action, given over, by his eternal derivation from the social contract, to *adequation* in the infinite order of determination. The adequation appropriate to his status in that order is ethical adequation. If I *say* that today is Tuesday when I *know* that today is Wednesday, then (*a*) either I am talking in a certain form of code, which gamesmanship may be trivial, playful, or solemn-serious; or (*b*) I am engaged in conspiracy, and what I am really advancing, or seeking to advance, by my "saying" is a conspiratorial cause of one sort or another. In either case, I have not really *said* anything, in the simple literal sense: I have merely acted deceitfully. The consequences might be either merely trivial, or entertaining, or dead serious; or, unexpectedly, a combination of these results.

My intended self-advancement in the order of determination may very well have misfired.

If I do not *know* that today is Wednesday and have therefore said that it is Tuesday—here, again, what have I said, and whom have I deceived? If I live in community, under the social contract, I will quickly be enlightened; if, on the other hand, I am alone on the desert island and, for some reason or other, it is important for me to know which day of the week it is, then, indeed, I am in a sad case; I must rethink the problem; why do I have to know, and if I cannot know, then what it is I have to do in order to re-devise a calendar suitable to my abandoned condition?

It is worth considering whether problems of contradiction cannot be seen as (*a*) problems of sensory deprivation or mischance, or (*b*) loss of community, or (*c*) moral conflict. All three cases would be challenges to *adequation*. "The world is whatever is the case." What, indeed, *is* the case? I do not find a case, from a Spinozistic point of view, that does not come under the social contract, or the peculiar form of conatus that the human being is. "The order and connection of ideas is the same as the order and connection of things." It is not metaphysically possible to brainwash the world, even if one is content to start with a single member of it.*

Proposition 73: "A man who is guided by reason is freer in a State where he lives according to the common laws than he is in solitude, where he obeys himself alone."

We have arrived at that moment in the argument where each demonstration has the character of a coda, bringing thought, already developed, to a formal close; and in doing so, the formality of it becomes inevitable, and casual. We have already seen this, the argument says; let us put our seeing under the high intensity of a conspectus, all at once, of our axioms, definitions, lemmas, notes, and proofs. We shall not again have the opportunity, or need it.

Therefore, once more, a variant definition of the invariant of freedom. Insofar as a man "endeavours to preserve his being in accordance with the bidding of reason, that is to say (Schol. Prop. 66, pt. 4), in so far as he endeavours to live in freedom . . ."

That is to say. Freedom is mere self-preservation; generalized, it is mere conatus; *but*, it is conatus in accordance with reason; and reason, we have at a certain cost learned, is ethical reason, which sounds even better, since it has been said more often, than ethical conatus; and ethical reason derives from (or is the same as) knowledge of the third kind; and knowledge of the third kind is a mere luminosity, astigmatic or otherwise, of the presence of the social contract in the order of human determination.

We are better guided by reason when our reason is a political reason. But we have long known that. *That is to say*. Art and "vague experience," too, are sub-realms of the social contract.

Very well. But we shall not be convinced this way. These metaphors of our existence have now served their purpose; and what we wish now to be confronted with is what is not metaphorical at all; or if metaphorical it has to be, let it be the primary metaphor, or the primitive axiom of all metaphorical systems. What is that, for Spinoza, and for us? Self-evidently, it cannot be any conceivable state; Hegel

---

*The rational emotions of gratefulness and non-deceitfulness describe the virtuous character of human action. Both emotions actively *acknowledge* human inter-dependence—"the infinite order of co-determination." They invoke and reinstate the social contract as the meaningful response to inter-dependence.

could conceive one, but Spinoza cannot. Even Kant permitted himself an undernourished flirtation with what he somewhat tremulously thought of as a "world republic" of peace; and Plato, for his eternal part, permitted himself the luxury of despair. Spinoza, for his part, will not rest with any of these positions. The *Ethic* is meta-political; or if political it is the politics of eternity; and eternity is political only by courtesy.*

Our question has to be: what is the primary locus of the kind of social contract that I have imputed to Spinoza as the guiding hypothesis of his metaphysical ethics?

I am raising this question with particular and exclusive reference to the *Ethic*. We have already noted that the two works of Spinoza which have a formal bearing upon the categorial question of "social contract"—the *Tractatus Theologico-Politicus* and the *Tractatus Politicus*—have, from the standpoint of my present argument, practically no bearing at all. They deal with questions of history, of "political dogmatics"—as in the constitutionalism and strategies of Scripture, and with the problematics and ambiguities of government. These issues, like the simple annals of the poor, have their own dignity and sometimes urgency; but they have nothing to do—neither history, nor dogma, nor government—with the case of the social contract in its present sense; the sense, as I have argued, of the *Ethic*; the general case of the human aspect of eternity.

The locus of the eternal social contract in the Ethic is the human body.

So far as I can see, the human body is *not,* in any aspect of Spinoza's argument, what is sometimes offered up to speculation as a "microcosm." The reason is twofold: (*a*) properly speaking there is no "cosmos" in Spinoza's dialectic; God has no crystal ball which he looks at from time to time; and *natura naturata* is neither the epilogue to astronomy, nor its detritus; (*b*) if, counter-factually, there were a cosmos, the human body would not be interested in it. *It is, indeed, concerned, as it must be, with the infinite order of determination;* but that order is meta-cosmic, and supersedent of any and every possible cosmos.

The human body is the primary locus of the social contract because it is that unique modality of infinite individuation *where infinite co-determination takes on an ethical quality*. It does so because it, the

---

*There is an inner gesture of courtesy, between individuals, by which it may be said that eternity is brought into the politics of human experience. If the courtesy is not to be a put-on, one has to slow down for it. It takes a bit of time. In that time there is the recognition that we die, that we had better mean what we say and do, and that we cannot control each other. All this "recognition" is precisely propaedeutic to the social contract.

human body, is the primary object of human *understanding*. It would be correct to say that it is the *sole* such object, if one could say it while rigorously excluding "microcosmic" illusions. As the primary object of understanding, the "final cause" of the human body is *human freedom*.

As in most applications of the Aristotelian locution of causes, final causes express themselves as efficient causes. The human body thus reminds us that *extensive modalities* are synergic with thought—in the infinite individuation, and the infinite self-love of God—that *natura naturans* is properly about.

The human body is, then, equally with mind, the executor of freedom, and of its conative actions.

Inasmuch as these actions are now, at this stage of our conspectus of the matter, contaminated with freedom, or ethically tinctured through and through, we ascribe to the human body that role, hallowed by language, of being first among equals. *"He who possesses a body fit for many things possesses a mind of which the greater part is eternal"* (Part V, Proposition 39).

And thus the Demonstration:

> He who possesses a body fitted for doing many things is least of all agitated by those emotions which are evil (Prop. 38, pt. 4), that is to say (Prop. 30, pt. 4), by emotions which are contrary to our nature, and therefore (Prop. 10, pt. 5) he possesses the power of arranging and connecting the modifications of the body according to the order of the intellect, and consequently (Prop. 14, pt. 5) of causing all the modifications of the body to be related to the idea of God (Prop. 15, pt. 5); in consequence of which he is affected with a love to God, which (Prop. 16, pt. 5) must occupy or form the greatest part of his mind, and therefore (Prop. 33, pt. 5) he possesses a mind of which the greatest part is eternal.

At the risk of being simplistic one must say bluntly what this does *not* mean: the optimal "fitness" of the body here invoked does not, because it cannot, mean the athleticism of a possibly Greek, or Graeco-Roman, ideal. Even though Spinoza, a little later on, uses the stereotype "sound mind in a sound body" to make a related point,[14] I do not know how one would go about imputing to Spinoza's thought the trivialities of merely "physical" fitness as the basis for anything. From which kind of knowledge would such fitness derive, and what would be the gymnastic regimen for its descent into "vague experience," or into art?

And as for the simple ideal of good health, there was of course no reason for Spinoza to be opposed to it, since he did not have it, and had an early death, like many of his contemporaries, from lack of it; but it will hardly be argued that we have in Spinoza's conception of the body a proto-argument for a theology of "science and health."

What, then, is the "fittedness" of the body that seems to be here invoked as the *necessary and sufficient cause* for the love of God, and the mind's eternity?

I propose that by the "fittedness" of the body is meant *the fullness of the body's entry, or activation, into the eternal social contract*. It would be just as well, perhaps, for many purposes, to say "the human being's entry, etc." But we are now considering the human being as a *mere eternal mode of extension;* not an infinite mode, but an eternal one; that is to say, as wholly given to himself and to us in and through his body. For that, and that alone, is what is given to *us;* that and that alone is the agency of co-determination that we know of, on the ethical plane where, unexpectedly, we find ourselves. If there is such a thing as Kant's "Good Will," it is of course the human body, and nothing other. More precisely, the so-called Good Will simply celebrates the body's failure.

If we examine the foregoing proposal from the ground up, we see that what is meant in the first place is the body's *infinite relatedness.*[15] This is not an achievement; it is a mere fact in God. Given that we have arrived at, and departed from, the knowledge of the third kind, we may act, *contributively,* with the power of that fact, more than we were able to act before.

It now becomes a fact to be maintained, since human eternity is not entirely self-maintaining, and certainly not self-maintaining in spite of itself.

How is human eternity maintained? The significance of the question "how" in this connection is "*by what*?" The agency for the maintenance of *human* eternity has to be the social contract. What we necessarily mean by the "maintenance" of human eternity is the conservation of its—"eternity's"—operative presence in our durational existence; that is to say, in that segment of God's empirical order where "we feel and know *by experience*" that we are eternal. We do not guess at our eternity; we do not deduce it; we "feel and know" it by direct acquaintance, by immediate inference, and with the inevitability of such knowledge of the third kind as we have inevitably achieved, if we have achieved any knowledge at all.

It is the human body that enacts the social contract, by and through its existence as a human body; and in so doing enacts that "essence" of itself, in God, that will partner the mind's own eternity; for the extensive objectivity of the mind cannot be shed, or abandoned, when the mind, at death, leaves the durational body, eternally.

We have been told that it is a "*part*" of the mind that does not die with body, and so on.

The inference has to be, then, that there is a part of the mind that *dies* with the body, etc.[16]

What part of the mind, and what kind of part-mind, can that be?

It can only be the body's *own* mind: if the expression has not become too threadbare for use, one says the "*body*-mind."

When we speak of the body's *own mind*, we affirm, or re-affirm, (1) the indissoluble and distinct consubstantiality of extension and thought in God, and of their modalities and sub-modalities in God; (2) the uniqueness and distinctiveness of these modal structures and sub-structures; (3) the differentiated powers of action expressed in these modal individuals; (4) the finite *inequality* of such powers; (5) the eternal conservation of such inequalities.

Precisely in that dimension of eternal conservation is where the thing called "value," or that unfree appreciation of good-and-evil, arises.

And when we speak of the body's-own-mind, we concede, with proper good cheer, that *that* part of the mind does, indeed, die with the body. "The mind can imagine nothing, nor can it recollect anything that is past, except while the body exists" (Part V, Proposition 21). Spinoza has thus defined for us the body's-own-mind: it is that part of the durational skeleton, muscular and tendon system; vascular, glandular, and neurological network; and micro-organic overpopulation of the human body that *remembers, imagines,* and the rest. That *part of the mind* does, indeed, die with the death of the body.

We remember very well when we have been ill, or otherwise traumatized: and of course the very amnesia with which we console ourselves is a form of such remembering. And it is a truth of reason that we will forget such experiences when we die; because the organ that remembers them will have died with the body.

The body-without-a-past is of course the body dead. But the mind, with its appropriate deathless object, that remains after the death of the body is not amnesiac. It has not forgotten, because it has no need to remember. The body's legacy to the mind, in eternity, is the social contract. The social contract, then, like the mind itself in eternity, "knows neither before nor after," and has never known whatever there is to know of "before and after." For historicity never defined the social contract,* nor circumscribed its provenance; and by

*It is, rather, the social contract that gives to history such discernible form as it has.

the same token death does not define the human body, but ethical conatus does.

The body's duration is a certain individuated power of ethical persistence. This power is a finite mode of *natura naturans,* expressed through the attribute of extension. Whence, however, has *natura naturans* acquired this appreciation of good-and-evil, so obviously incompatible with its infinity and with its perfect freedom? It has not "acquired" it; or, if indeed there is an aspect of ethical accession to itself in God's eternal state, "from now on," then God could have "acquired" this appreciation only from the eternal aspect of human existence. We would not wish to suggest, here, the inversion of a grim theological platitude: that God, for instance, in order, perhaps, to avoid incarnation, "makes himself in the image of man." That would be carrying the intrigue of transcendence too far. What is suggested, rather, is that *in* the infinite order of co-determination the ethical conatus of the human body, which is to say the eternal social contract, is not only self-revealed in the infinite diorama of *natura naturata,* but is also *eternally self-insertive in natura naturans*. The cosmic humility of man, proffered by Kant and by astronomers, is rejected of God, except insofar as he can use it.

What good would memory and/or imagination be in the face of such concrete responsibilities?*

Historically speaking, man has already, and inevitably, responded to these awesome solicitations in his "vague experience," or his knowledge of the first kind.

That is where it all happens.

And it is to that highly selective area of *natura naturata* that our hard-won knowledge of the third kind now directs us for concluding inferences and observations. The empirical order, where we begin as well as inevitably end, is from the standpoint of Substance, *self-selective*. Many modes of Substance are called; perhaps all of them; but few are chosen; and those that are chosen must be significantly self-elected; or else the infinite order of determined–co-determination would have undergone diremption; and Substance would confront itself as being more than one; which is absurd; and grotesque.

---

*In sum: the "bodily-action-called-man" is significantly itself only as ethicized action. This is what is eternal about us, and intrinsically unkillable. And it is so —despite the falling away of memory and imagination in death—because man's self-ethicization reaches to high heaven (i.e., affects and is incorporated within God's originating action). This does not mean that man becomes consciously cosmic. That interpretation is rejected below. Rather, it would seem to mean that God becomes "human"—not via incarnation—but by taking the influence of what is best in ourselves. By our "concrete responsibilities" is meant that ultimate and ongoing influence.

The self-insertion of human conatus in *natura naturans,* of which we spoke, is of course an *eternal* self-insertion; it has no date or calendar; though it will acquire all that and more—clocks and minutes too—when it expresses itself on the durational order as *history*. The cosmos has no history—it has only a quite bloodless, or perhaps shadowy, eternity—but the social contract has. The social contract has a certain interest in cosmos; because, for one thing, it is, conveniently, the receptacle where *disvalue* goes. It is not quite clear in Plato's *Timaeus* whether the grand "Receptacle" offered there is offered as the *source* of disvalue (a soothing word for "evil," having the false promise of freedom in it), or merely, it so happened, its collaborator. But if offered as a source, it will not do; because it would require the social contract to extend itself so as to comprehend the cosmos. And the social contract rejects that opportunity; by virtue of the same self-assertive rule whereby the social contract wholly assumes responsibility for itself—will share that responsibility with nothing cosmic—and is content, in the end, to be thought of and known as responsibility itself. Even in astrological playfulness the stars are sheepish about assuming responsibility. There is no cosmic, let alone astronomical, name for that.

The last, perhaps unhappy, question for the social contract is, then, the "problem of evil"; but that question, or problem, need not be answered, because the problem of evil is the social contract itself.*

Let us say, without reluctance, that the "problem of evil" has to be a cluster of pseudo-questions, and one actual question; and that the "problem" consists in sifting the actual question from the pseudo-ones. Among the pseudo-ones is the question "why," which is more or less the same as the question "when"; both these pseudo-questions tending to have the same answer, such as "then and there," or before-and-after-the-Fall, or thereabouts; or, *when* "God so loved the world, that . . ."; or, with utmost sophistication, in the course of Perfection's search for its own identity, that is to say, self-realization as the best among the possibles, or, as an admirable work-of-art, of which, in its admirableness, one could-not-would-not change a single shadow of its infinite, divine chiaroscuro, or a single finite groove of its cross-hatching. Leibniz's metaphysical work-of-art has an admirable and attractive sadness in it; but it has nothing to do with anything. God is not "Perfect" in Leibniz's sense; or in any other sense that might

*Since it cannot be supposed that our influence *on God* could be negative (i.e., could diminish Him), the discussion must now concern itself with the eternal consequences of human action when it is evil. Where does the *evil* "bodily-action-called-man" go when it dies? Does it make any difference—to God or to the rest of us—from the standpoint of eternity?

signify "Complete," or "Self-satisfied," or *fait accompli*, or Above-the-battle and therefore quite Benign. Substance, too, for Spinoza, is of course perfect; but all perfection means in Spinoza's dialectic is *infinite*, which is always self-manifest and self-verifying; and all that Spinoza's perfection requires of us is to speak of something else, such as the love of God, or blessedness, or the understanding and fittedness of one's body; or proper pride; and all these are matters of the social contract; which God will have nothing to do with; having eternally left it to other hands.

So much for the pseudo-questions: their venerable ancestry in the remotest antiquity of theology, both orthodox and gnostic, and mythology, and stories, may be taken for granted, and ignored.

The actual question is the following:

We have argued that the eternal social contract is expressed, durationally, in the character of the human body, and in that durational complex of body relations that we call history.

What, then, is the status, in the face of the eternal social contract, of the thing called *evil*?

We remind ourselves, first, of the necessary and sufficient definition of evil: evil is injury to the durational human body. Absolute injury is absolute evil, etc.

Our actual question, then, as to the status of such evil, is a question that answers itself: actual evil is injury to the eternal social contract; absolute evil is metaphysical subversion of the social contract. This means that by appropriate injury to the human body, the doer of evil aims to withdraw, eternally, from the ethical conatus of human existence, and to become infinite; that is, to abdicate the co-determination already eternally achieved by human existence and to become *mere infinite determination;* that is, to become *free*, or, *per impossibile*, Substance itself.

Traditional metaphor is quite familiar with the syndrome: it speaks of *hybris*, or of trying to be God.

Determined—that is, intended—injury to the human body is trying to be God; that is, it is absolute evil.

Subordinate questions at once raise themselves: such as, what of punishment, or claim of therapy, or, paradigmatically, *capital* punishment?*

Let us first isolate the self-answering aspect of such questions: there are, indeed, circumstances under which the eternal social contract has no choice but to try to be God. That is, unless the ethical

---

*These are cases where the body is or may be injured, and yet we *do not* think of them as cases of evil.

conatus of human existence is to be allowed to collapse altogether, subversion of the eternal social contract has to be suppressed; lest anybody or anything become God; and there would be no God. The test here has to be: *clear and present danger to the human body*. Whose human body? Any human body. The knowledge of God is the knowledge of any human body; it might happen to be our own. We happen to be everybody, merely individuated; and it has nothing to do with our eternal minds.

Questions that have been self-answered manage to leave others for answering. For instance: shall the social contract forgive itself when it puts a man to death?

Let it; or let it not forgive itself; it will eternally not matter; only the human body will matter. It has long gone without saying that anything and everything the eternal social contract does, it does at its eternal peril; and the peril here is that it will cease to be what it is; that is, that the social contract will cease to be.

Granted, then, that the social contract is not sky-based utopia, and is, indeed, as far removed from such mythological conditions—whether called classlessness, or kingdom of God (on earth; where else?), or "beyond history," or whatever and wherever—as eternity is from "immortality"; and granted, then, that the social contract persists, eternally, *vis à vis* the perpetual co-determination of subversion; but granted, also, that the social contract will, in the nature of the case, continue to be as long as human individuation continues to filibrate within *natura naturans*, and out of it; such questions as the following then arise for the social contract as a diorama of history, and of the physics and "metaphysics" of history:

Does evil persist, durationally, as stubbornly as the good; only somewhat more so? If so, what is its fate as evil, both physically and otherwise? Is evil progressive, even though the good is not? What would such a triumph of evil amount to? We have already seen the answer to that, and have discounted it as having no particular dialectical status: the moral entropy, which the extirpation of the social contract would amount to, does not seem to be a serious metaphysical threat. Such entropy would, in the long run, have to co-determine God himself, notwithstanding that God, in his freedom, is self-exempted from knowledge of good and evil; and entropic Substance does not seem to be a notion that the ordinary language of the mind can handle.

But we are committed to finding as much coherence in our history as we can; and if we cannot find it in the simple physics of history, then we shall have to supplement that physics with other kinds of metaphor, such as a law of "compensation," for instance; or tales of reincarnation; and so on. Do they help any? That is, do they help to make the future prospects of the social contract coherent with its eternity?

Not particularly. Of the two standard options* just mentioned—compensation and reincarnation—the fantasy of reincarnation, especially with the promise of degeneration in it, seems more instructive than the oscillatory pseudo-physics of compensation. What is pseudo about it is its attempt to make the self-restrictive investigatory knowledge of the second kind a meta-knowledge or a moral knowledge of the third kind. So that Foucault's pendulum, altogether sufficient to establish the rotation of the earth upon its axis, becomes, obscurely, the model for the psycho-physics of yin-and-yang, or "eternal recurrence," and so on. We prove very little when we make ontology yawn.

Compensation is a metaphor for the retributive rules of the social contract; but outside of the social contract, what goes up need not by any means come down.

The instructiveness of the myth–metaphor of reincarnation lies in its greater closeness to the eternal dialectic of the human body. The human body is both the achievement, so to speak, of the eternal social contract, epistemologically the evidence for it, and in its determined action the expression of it.† Positive evil, that is, highly motivated subversion of the social contract, thus defines itself as the *purposive attempt to cease to be a human body*. The great evil-doers of human history do not seem to have visibly, empirically, succeeded in that effort, at least not so far as we can tell, since the vivid little metaphor of Nebuchadnezzar eating grass is not susceptible of concrete historical substitution. The social contract will, of course, always be busy trying to put these great evil-doers out to pasture; but it does not always succeed *in their lifetime;* and that is the matter we are now concerned with: what happens to the deathless, eternal mind, and its eternal body-object, of the evil-doers, when they die?

Must we know?

Well, of course we have to know; our knowledge of the third kind will presumably tell us when to stop.

For the sake of coherence, we have to assume this much, at least, of continuity between the ethical conatus of human existence in its durational aspect, and the farther being of the mind after the death of the body. If one tries, as best one can, to divest oneself of social-contractual determinations in one's lifetime—that is to say, to live against reason, practicing cruelty and other forms of evil—there is

---

*These are two standard options for handling the specific question of the *evil-doer's* fate after death, or in eternity. They are not treated here as handles on the more general question of human welfare in eternity.

†This is one of the central points of the whole essay.

no reason to assume that one might not partly succeed; or more than partly. "*Under the aspect of eternity,*" one might succeed in becoming a *non-human* body.

"No man can hate God" (Part V, Proposition 18). But a life-long effort at doing just that might have some partial effectiveness: the body's *rites de passage* into accompaniment of the mind's eternity may succeed, from life-long practice, in being counter-productive.

More than this, it seems, we cannot know, and need not ask: the *infinite attributes* of God, which of course he has, are not very interesting. We would be none the wiser—since the science fiction of knowledge of the second kind cannot give us wisdom—if it should happily turn out that the great evil-doers of our evil histories became fungoid growths; unless the proof of that should be offered us by Hieronymus Bosch the Elder, and his like; and the proofs offered us, in such art and other "vague experience," are of course substantive contributions and accessions to the eternal social contract.

There is, of course, no contradiction between the human being's conative commitment to *indefinite* duration and the evil-doer's *project,* in the nature of his case, to "eternal suicide" in God. Nor is there any contradiction between the self-abusive, hedonic, and addictive glutton's intention to live happily ever after, and his body's project to die —quick or slow—an over-dosed, a diabetic, or a cancerous death. *The body is not committed, in God, to an indefinite duration;* on the contrary. It is committed, only, to contributive conatus to the social contract. It has freedom, so to speak, within the infinite order of determination, to refuse that commitment. The body has little or no option as to how, or when, it will die; or if it has such options, the mind knows of them only "occultly"; that is to say, in an order of experience that is not merely "vague," but shadowy: in dream, in the premonitory images of self-abortive, and self-suppressed, art, in a mimicry or caricature of the knowledge of the third kind, while pretending that such knowledge, if it exists, and whatever its claims to a nuclear role in ethical conatus, is in all probability subordinate to knowledge of the *fourth, fifth,* or *nth* . . . kind; that is to say, to *gnostic* illumination, in all its breathlessness.

There may well be, of course, cases to the contrary: that is to say, a case or two, or more, when under the guidance of "intuitive science," wholly absorbed into the body's limited modalities, within the infinite order of determination, a person's body might choose, within the limits of choice, the occasion of its ethical death; and because the choice is "only" the body's choice, without the mind's intention, as intentions go, the ethical character of the choice, and its contributive weight in the social contract, remains obscure, or esoteric. There was no reason, for instance, for Lincoln to have ignored the ample ominousness of the warnings he received not to go to Ford's Theater on that Good Friday evening of April 14, 1865. There was no reason, even, for him altogether to ignore his gothic dream about an awful grief in the White House, that he had had not long before. Mrs. Lincoln's sad unstable greed for the theater that particular evening was not enough reason for Lincoln's purposive, and ambivalent, obliviousness.[17]

One might argue that Lincoln's body had *chosen* this particular moment, or one that might be near enough—and it turned out, in the infinite order of determination, that this was near enough—in order to enact in its durational history that "last full measure of devotion" of which the body, and its mind, had found itself speaking, some time ago, in the cemetery at Gettysburg. Or if not Gettysburg, then perhaps the Second Inaugural; with its slow, subliminal doom-beat about historical debts, unforgiven, and their reimbursement.

One might argue that in this particular case, Lincoln's body knew, and made a choice, which his sociable mind could hardly afford to talk about.

I will not argue that these images, concerning the *possible* conative mechanisms at work, in a particular case, on Friday evening, April 14, 1865, in Washington, D.C., are self-certifyingly Spinozistic, according to the *Ethic*. Hardly. I propose these images mainly to suggest how far removed Spinoza's conception of body has to be from Descartes' conception. They seem hardly to belong to the same order of determination; though, of course, under the aspect of eternity, they must. And I propose them also to suggest, from the opposite end of the appropriate dialectic, how the ethical body might conceivably *choose* the mode and moment of its co-determination, within the infinite order. The Lincoln image is an easy one, though not too easy; for no image of possible self-insertions of human duration into the eternal social contract can be all that easy; any such image must remain a trouble, and problematic, to the mind. But the Lincoln image is still an easy one, *because it entered history*. History may be painful, but it is relatively easy.

In what sense, then, does the evil of evil-doers enter history? If it was possible for Lincoln to do it—at least in the sense that the *image* of that entry has a verifiable history in the moral art of Lincoln's country—in what sense does the evil of evil-doers find entry into history?

The entry of evil into durational history seems to be an *undifferentiated* entry. The profound *monotony* of historical evil seems to be capable of achieving "exceptionality"—that is, a self-differentiated character—only by quantitative means: a *huge mass of evil*, as in effective, or nearly effective genocide, or the same achievement by any other name, seems to have the status of a spot of darker pigmentation on the face of history. Otherwise, there does not seem to be much difference, worth taking note of, between one evil-doer, and his evil, and another. In this respect, evil has the monotony of pornography, and may claim to be the pornography of history.

The dialectic we are concerned with offers a reason for this: members of the social contract—that is to say, of the human order—*are individuated modalities in God*. The "remaining" of the mind after the death of the body is Spinoza's assertion of the eternal indefeasibility of that individuation. Our argument now suggests that the durational history of the "free man," that is, of the person freely entered into co-determination of the human order, is contributive to and enhancing of, that eternal individuation, or of the eternal mode of action which an individual is. Evil is the self-erosion of action; and the evil-doer thus ceases, in principle, to be an individual. In principle, in this case, is the same as eternally.*

Are we now, in effect, re-arguing a venerable Platonic metaphor: that evil, when it is real enough, is simple *non-being*?

Not exactly. The notion of non-being—whatever elusive provenance it may have in the Parmenidean border-territories of Plato's thought—is hardly a clear and distinct idea, even for Plato, and doesn't gain in intelligibility when it becomes a material cause for the God of theology to use when he performs the miracle of creation. I argue that so far as Spinoza is concerned, there is nothing in Substance that can metaphysically cease to be; and that this way of putting it, required by our language, does not make nothing into a something. These, I believe, are not concepts, however hard one may try, but more like failed puns.

There is no way by which the evil-doer can cease to be—much as he might welcome it when he comes, if ever, to his "awakening." With regard to this conceptual hallucination of non-being, Spinoza's thought speaks the most ordinary of all possible ordinary languages. His thought merely asks, "ceases to be *what*?" So transposed, the question of the evil-doer's ontological fate has some clear and dismal possibilities of answer. The evil-doer has already begun, in his durational phase, to cease to be a *human* body. Perhaps the infinite stress of the infinite order of determination confronts us all with that ominous possibility from our birth. Our conatus, that is, our career of durational co-determination, necessarily consists, in tragic measure,

---

*The evil-doer is engaged in self-suicide, first in history and finally—out of habit, if nothing else—in eternity. This simply follows from the fact that to do evil is to cause one's body to cease to be a human body. By contrast, Lincoln's ethical (if unconscious) action, in causing-his-body-to-die durationally, had quite the opposite significance. That is, it illustrated "the last full measure of devotion."

of *resistance,* in God, to the infinite order of determination. That resistance, which is the active "emotion" of understanding itself, may be greater or less, depending, in its turn, on a quite infinite number of things.

We have seen, in close conformity with Spinoza's usage, what the free man's optimal fate might be in eternity: he necessarily maintains his coherence as an individual in God, that is, in *natura naturans;* some part of the eternal action which this individual now eternally expresses must necessarily be action "tainted," so to speak, by the eternal social contract which had the metaphysical, but irreversible, misfortune of entering into durational history. Take the taint away from it, as the metaphysics of radical purification or salvation would seek to do, and that individual loses the coherence essential to the very concept of himself; and Substance becomes a history of tiredness; ultimately of self-exhaustion.*

So far, no element of myth—no matter how inevitably metaphorical our idiom in this connection—has entered the conception. We can, if so minded, *impute* myth to this conceptual moment; but we have already been put on notice that the dialectic of eternity is *asymmetrical.* There is, indeed, a certain expression of eternity, to be understood by knowledge of the third kind, in the lion and the lamb and their mutually indifferent lying down together in, for instance, the landscapes of Henri Rousseau, *le Douanier;* but *though eternity be in the lion and the lamb, the lamb and the lion are not in eternity;* nor even, according to Spinoza, the memory of them.

We are content then with what, being free, we shall eternally have: it would be quite graceless to insist that it be imaginatively packaged even *there.*

Our question, then, as to the fate of the evil-doer in eternity permits of the following answer: his fate is the fate of *deliquescent individuation.* The evil-doer has launched himself on that career in his durational evil. He cannot carry that evil with him into eternity (that is, after the death of the body); since in eternity, we are given to infer, there is no "knowledge of good or evil"; but the evil-doer can, indeed must, carry his durational incoherence with him; and since, in eternity, there can be no absolute incoherence in God, the evil-doer must necessarily resolve into the strictly neutral coherence of entities eternally outside the social contract; there being many such, to infinity.

---

*The consequential character of the individual's action continues—if need be, in world after world. HMR's point here is that it is *never* ultimately dissolved in God. And where there are consequential actions, there are the bearers of those actions, or responsible agents: hence, individuals. Necessarily, the *same* individuals who performed the actions.

This is what gives the metaphor of reincarnation, at least in some aspects of it, a certain relevance to the argument of an eternal social contract. But reincarnation, if it exists, is only one way: the conception does not admit of a passage back from the non-human to the human order. There is no need of such a passage from the viewpoint of the ethical conatus. That strain of *natura naturans,* having once and eternally undergone the self-insertion into Substance which is its eternal "history," has now the infinite order of *co-determination* to draw upon; and from the standpoint of the evil-doing entity's fate in its eternal deliquescence, that entity has eternally more than it deserves; it no longer has the opportunity to *try* to hate God.*

We have no doubt carried these metaphors as far as they allow. They have had this result: we now know the *limits* of eternity, that is, of human eternity; which is the only variety of it that we are allowed, in the nature of the case, to be concerned with.

The eternity we are concerned with, conceptually delivered to us by the *Ethic,* is, after its fashion, like the physical space of neo-relativity physics: *curved;* that is, infinite, but, alas, closed. So the eternity of the *Ethic* returns us, in due course, to our "blessed" selves; there being nowhere else, under the aspect of eternity, to go.

Our concluding theme, then, is blessedness.

We find ourselves unfree: and it is precisely there that our blessedness lies.

Our unfreedom signifies that our primordial and indefeasible individuation as a modality in God has a specific and unique determination: namely, our human body. The quest for "life on other planets" is thus a profoundly frivolous quest—as everybody no doubt knows —because, by definition, there is life on all the planets. And on all the meta- and infra-planets too; since extension and thought are all there is, anywhere; and "life"—which is an ambiguous term, as all terms are when constrainedly used as deriving from knowledge of the second kind—is not a biological notion but a lost and unhappy metaphysical one, so that our proper quest, if we must have one, is not for "life on other planets" but for *a human body on another planet*. And this quest, if it were possible, would be self-fulfilling, because if there were a human body on another planet, we would already know of it, even if not in confrontation with it.

When, in our well-developed knowledge of the cartoonist kind,

*It has earlier been observed (p. 148) that there must be mercy even in hell—since there, too, the social contract (with its provisions for pardon) would have to obtain. If this observation were granted, then it would follow that it is better to be in hell, and suffer there in one's self-chastised humanity, than to lose that humanity altogether. It is the latter process that is here being described as irreversible.

we figure forth the "living beings" on other planets as having carrot-spiked heads, etc., etc., we are celebrating an answer that we know: there are no human bodies on other planets, because the social contract has not got there, and the bodies or non-bodies that might be there are in any case non-human.

All such entertainments, harmless enough in their own right, are moments of respite from blessedness.

There is an unfortunate confusion, moreover—or at least a possible one, which is worth dispelling—of blessedness with the ecstatic. Blessedness is of the body fully thought through; the ecstatic is of the exhausted imagination: the body collapsed into its own negative infinite; the entropic emotion of helplessness. This is sometimes called, in certain kinds of organization chart of the ecstatic, "union with the divine"; or sometimes conceived, in variations of the same type of chart, as exponential explosions of the erotic. But the erotic at its best —and, of course, it has a best—is simply displaced, or prematurely localized, blessedness; seeking to relocate itself in the old familiar way of repetition.

Nor should the notion of blessedness be prematurely given over to the exalted.

One starts, for instance, with Jane Austen's no doubt accidental version of blessedness in one of her titles: "sense and sensibility"; as perhaps also in the principal texture of her work. There is no doubt a deficiency of the erotic, in its current sense, in this writer's "comedies of manners"; but there is a quite a bit of the knowledge of Substance, as expressed in the fringes or in the woof of the social contract; and that writer, or her heroines, must have known the body, and thus the world. This of course is knowledge of the third kind, and has to be blessedness itself.

The fittedness of sensibility for many things is of course a fair start on the adequation of sensibility toward the higher emotion of sense; or perhaps idea; and the idea of property, or endowment, with which the human body, male or female, is much concerned in the writings of Jane Austen—that idea is an emotion which the social contract is eternally concerned to adequate. For all we know, it may never do so. Political science is not likely to experience the self-insertion into *natura naturans* which the human conatus, by definition, has achieved; but the *historical* human body has already adequated the idea of property: in its dress, in its decorativeness, in its art, in its mumbling or in its singing speech, in its gesture; and perhaps in its suffering. But that is not quite adequate yet; unless we apply to the proposed blessedness of suffering an adequation borrowed from the rhetoric of Marxism: from each a suffering according to capacity; to each a suffering according to need.

We remind ourselves of the simplest of all Spinozistic formulas:

adequation of a human emotion consists in its controlled and directed passage from its status as a passion—which is a negative exponent of human capacity to act—to a status as idea, which is a form of knowledge and of power.

Blessedness is Spinoza's lyrical word for the optimal achievement of understanding and therefore of capacity to act.

But the capacity to act is not a second-order consequence of understanding; it is that understanding itself.

We have been told this lesson, by the text and by its exposition, but it is a lesson hard to retain, and even harder to believe, when retained.

If I come, at long last, to understand the Pythagorean theorem, like the lad in the *Meno*, in what significant sense does my laborious adequation of my initial bewilderment constitute an *action*? Of course it is an unhappy labor *performed*. But now that I have performed it, and have broken through to an *understanding* of the operational adequacy and perfect rationality of incommensurables—in what sense is my hard-won and new-found mathematical complacency an increase in my power of action, and an advance toward the mind's eternity?

Given that I am not proposed to be a geometer, a surveyor, an astronomer, the answer is: *in no sense*.

But this enlightenment by the Pythagorean theorem is only knowledge of the second kind: it can only affect some *program* or other for the human body—let us say, the program of all positivists, past and present—or, so to speak, the future human body; it does not affect the present body; or the body itself.

Let us concede that there may be exceptions to the generalization just made: there are people who have experienced blessedness —that is to say, the *intellectual love of God*—on the discovery of certain basic mathematical truths. In that case, blessed are the bodies of the geometers, for they are the meek, and theirs . . . etc.

But Spinoza himself did not quite believe this, and has intimated as much in one of his Letters;[18] and whether he believed it or no, the defect of mathematical knowledge as the starting point for blessedness is easy to name: *mathematics is not vague enough*.

Nor, for that matter, is the poet's well-known "blade of grass."

We have to search, in the over-determination of our "vague experience," for an experience altogether *present in the body* to start with.

There is such an experience, altogether familiar to human conatus: it is the experience of bodily *pain*.* I call this experience "vague"

---

*If blessedness involves—emotionally and intellectually—active self-localization in one's body, and is of such a kind that Jane Austen may be said to have a better grip on it than, say, Saint Teresa, then the next task will be to find an illustrative moment of such self-localization that is *sufficiently concrete*. This turns because it is the one human experience which is (*a*) incomparable, in the sense that it does not lend itself to comparison with anything else, but only with itself; and is therefore (*b*) ineffable. It is thus the one human experience in which the "mechanisms" of infinity, so to speak, have a kind of *immediacy* of presence to human modality which no other aspect of human experience can show.

By the mechanisms of infinity, and their immediacy, I wish to suggest (*a*) the manifestation, or expression, of infinite determination; in which the *infinite individuations* of such determination have the unseizably paradoxical character of being both intensely and unbearably *localized*—as in toothache, or as in torture applied to the genitals—and at the same time being *nowhere at all;* so that one wishes for nothing except to go away from *it*, and there is no place to go: this is the definition of infinity; there is no hiding place from it. Infinity, like God himself, whose attribute infinity is, has no *dasein*. (*b*) In this exposure to, or confrontation with, the immediacy of the infinite, human ethical conatus generally appears ready and willing to surrender its eternity; as if that were possible.

This apparent readiness to surrender eternity has an ominous import. In the willingness to die rather than to continue to bear such pain, there is more than a willingness to surrender one's body. The pain-bearing human being has a natural belief in the "essence of the body," that is to say, in the persistence of the metaphysical body in God, after its durational death, and a *natural disbelief* in the assurance given us that that eternally persistent body in God *will have no memory*. Or if not an absolute disbelief, at least a compromising scepticism. The pain-bearing body, at that moment of "infinite" pain, would prefer not to take a chance. In wishing to die, it is ready and willing to die metaphysically. This is to surrender one's human eternity: to *dissolve* into the infinity of God is to surrender ethical conatus; for that has meaning only as the eternal self-insertion of ethical individuation into *natura naturans*, or the infinite determining being of God.

Of such a character is the distressing "vagueness" of bodily pain. Where is the blessedness of that, or the opportunity for it?

The question of courage, whether "moral" or "physical," is not central to this matter. The reason: the essential *neutrality* of the virtue called courage; it is equally at the service of ethos and anti-ethos; its loyalty or commitment is to the *polis*, which might equally well

---

out to be harder than it looks. Many phases of experience are too abstract or too fragmentary to provide a proper illustration. Hence the turn now toward the experience of pain, which is neither abstract nor fragmentary. The trouble with pain, however, will be that its concreteness is so overwhelming as to put our humanity in jeopardy. That discussion is pursued below.

be the City of God or the City of Man or the City Anti-Both. And the *polis* is a historical abstraction in God; not individuated by *natura naturans* but by *natura naturata*—as when we say, or think, there are many solar systems, and many suns to send them orbiting—ours is but one among many. At which point there is nothing at all to stop one from saying: the many, truly taken, are but one; and some day we shall figure out how the many work as one; the yin-and-yang of density and expansion giving us, according to exact physico-mathematical laws, one-half "the face of the whole universe," the missing half being merely Substance itself.*

Courage is thus a constitutional virtue, not an ethical one; in the somewhat archaic language that has had great influence, it belongs to "positive" rather than "natural" law. The law of nature will always forbid cruelty; positive law, or civic duty, has merely to define cruelty out of sight and mind, and infamy may uninhibitedly obtain. Infamy may thus be not merely a side-effect of courage, but courage itself in the nominalism of politics. The Aristotelian distinctions between rashness or foolhardiness on the one hand and true courage on the other, are but clinical quibbles; taking the temperature of an act, before or after.

These resolute confusions arise from the blurring of the distinction between the *polis,* or the state, and the social contract. The beautiful metaphor that Socrates intends in the *Crito,* concerning the City in Heaven and its Laws in Heaven which cast their divine shadow on a man and his foot-chafing iron chains, should not be taken pedantically: what is writ in heaven is not the city, but the social contract: from it all constitutions, known and unknown, derive, but the contract itself has no constitution, and does not obtain one from the Convention and its sentences.

To die for one's country is altogether proper, and has, historically, a high incidence of necessity to it; but it is not sweet; and the blessedness of it would have to be argued in each case from non-political premises.

Our question, then, has not moved from its starting point: in the crucial instance of the body's "presence to itself," which is pain, where shall one locate the possibility of blessedness?

---

*Abstraction is thus a step in the direction of effacement of the situation one was considering: here, the situation of courage as one proposed antidote to bodily pain. The problem now is that courageous stoicism in the face of bodily pain may readily transmute into insensibility in the face of political cruelty. Such insensibility was clearly *not* the kind of concreteness that HMR was looking for, when he settled on pain as the experience that might illustrate bodily concreteness. It would be preferable to take pain without antidotes than to be hardened to it—and to much else in the social order besides.

Spinoza's argument here—if one disregards the exalted rhetoric which is more to be imputed to some of his loving commentators than to Spinoza himself—has a directness, even bluntness, which bears comparison with some of the traditional metaphors that have been circulated in this connection. We do not, according to Spinoza, praise God from whom all blessings flow: the praising him is the blessing itself; the praising him is loving him; and the loving him is having an adequate idea of him; and this is only possible from an adequate idea, or understanding, of one's body; which arises from knowledge of the third kind, and so forth. "He prayeth best, who loveth best"; no doubt; and if love is the substance of our relation to God, and of the same substance as his relation to himself, then the modalities of that love are all one: they are called understanding.

Nor do we say, as traditionally we do, "thy will be done"; for God has no will apart from his own infinite ideas; and, though we cannot aspire to the ecumenics of infinity, whatever ideas we have are in God and of God, being merely modalities of his well-known attributes; and since finite ideas, unlike infinite ones, have a location, the location of our ideas is *our body*.

It would be quite wrong to say God is in our body—the fallacy, and an offensive one, of simple metaphysical conversion—but our understanding of our body, *and of its pain*, is a mode of God's infinite love of himself.

We may quite briefly pause at this point to ask: is the body's *understanding* of its own pain—this, in Spinoza's form of nominalism, is the only meaning of the body's presence-to-itself—a finite mode? Or, like motion-and-rest with respect to the attribute of extension, is it a *first infinite mode* of God's infinite self-love?

I shall assume that this question has no dogmatic answer; and that the answer to the question, if it has one, can do no more than annotate the meaning of the difference between finite and infinite in Spinoza's argument. This may be briefly done, and sufficiently so for our present concern: *finite* refers us to human limits, of perception, apprehension, formulation, imagination, and *action*. Action is the decisive term, since it includes the others. *Infinite* refers us to what is beyond human limits. One thing is excluded from infinite action, namely, imagination. All things are present to God; therefore he does not imagine anything, but merely infinitely knows by his attribute of thought. But the infinite and the finite, though hardly co-extensive, are entirely interpenetrant with one another.

Thus, motion-and-rest, though a mere mode of an infinite attribute, is a quite infinite mode, because the forms of possible metamorphosis in *natura naturata* are beyond the limits of construal; that is to say, they have no finality, but we nevertheless are constrained to impose periodicity upon them. God will not recognize such periodicity (a refusal to acknowledge this is what gives cosmologies their inalienable aspect of triviality), but he will provisionally abide by it. For God not to honor the co-determination that inserts itself not only in *natura naturans* but also in *natura naturata* would be incompatible with the honor of God. This metaphor will serve for transit and return to our present problem: the order of love and the order of pain; that is to say, the order of *infinite* and the order of *finite* emotions, that have nowhere to go but toward the infinite.

Infinite Substance suffers no pain, but it does have emotions; there being none higher than the ones it has.

What we are challenged to argue is that there is *no* love *that passeth understanding*. If God's idea of our bodily pain is *part of the infinite love with which he loves himself,* we are challenged to "participate," modally, in that love. The presence in the argument of such a challenge clearly suggests that the finite and the infinite have all the possibilities of association, if not contact, in human experience that they could conceivably use. The point is: can human experience meet this challenge of the argument? In the moment of bodily pain can the human body love God with an intellectual love?

And supposing it could? That is to say, what difference would it make, for the pain and for the body of it?

For the pain: the improbable difference to be conatively expected is abatement. Improbable, but perhaps not impossible. By entire attention to the perspective of the infinite causality of one's pain, and to the details of that perspective—relentlessly omitting nothing of one's own co-determination in the durational past and present, and relentlessly excluding all "ethical," pseudo-conative intentionality, so that one is as nearly as one can get quite one with nature, by such attentiveness it is conceivable that one's pain, if not absolutely abated, is at least transformed into the sufferable.

Such transformation might be aided by the discovery, in the course of attentiveness, that sufferableness is merely the norm of durational existence: since even pleasure, in any degree, and especially in its highest, is merely sufferable. The saint attentive to the "martyring" of his flesh, or the natural scientist attentive to the terminal ravages of cell-formation in his own body, may conceivably be managing the transformation of suffering into the sufferable. Would such transformation be tantamount to blessedness? Can the understanding of one's body, in the moment of pain, achieve an extensiveness of range, and thereby an intensity and "height" of intellectualized emotion that would enable one, without posturing strain, to consider it, that is to say, to experience it, as *intellectual love of God*? That is to say, as the greatest joy?

Reluctantly one concludes that blessedness stops short of the threshold of pain: the intellectual love of God can make little or no difference to it. An ethic of pain would have to content itself with such propositions and stratagems as might derive from knowledge of the second kind. An ameliorative ethic of pain—such as J. S. Mill's, for example—would at best be merely instrumental. The acceptance of despair that is in it, the hopeless willingness to settle for infinitesimally small gains, provided there be widely distributed eligibility to enjoy them, this posture has its own clear coherence with the eternal social contract; and, no doubt, might in some eternity or other legitimately claim responsibility for varieties of ethical self-insertion into the infinite spectrum of *natura naturans*. But this would be eternity's business; where the prospect of blessedness does not arise; since blessedness there is all one; and there is no memory of when blessedness was not.

One need not quibble with amelioration for principle's sake. An ethic of amelioration is self-justifying; and there is a point of view from which the eternal social contract might be taken as Substance itself in an ameliorative mood. The flaw, however, in such over-interpretation would be at once obvious: the moods of Substance, so to speak, are infinite; and if one wishes to draw inferences for human freedom—or for blessedness—from the welcome history of amelioration, one must be prepared to do the same for the history of *side-effects* too; and the argument that what side-effects need is more-of-the-same will not do; for the reason that infinite regress will not do; it is abhorrent to knowledge of the third kind, and to freedom too.

We renounce, therefore, any illusion of conative salvation from a pedagogic program of self-hypnosis-at-will, or from any ready-to-hand technique of auto-induced selective sensory deprivation; or from the promise of bliss by oral or by vascular or by pulmonary merger with dosages of the infinite. We renounce, in short, the illusions that an ethic of positive evil might offer, whether in the form of the effort to achieve *indetermination* by commensality with the infinite (through drugs) or in the form of effort to levitate to the godhead by self-mortification.

The *Ethic* directs us toward the understanding of the body as the method of progress toward the intellectual love of God. Given that we meet the conditions of adequation, that understanding is the love itself.

Some inferences and related questions now offer themselves:

An adequated understanding of the body necessarily enlarges the object of that understanding to encompass not only the *durational* body but also *the body under the aspect of its eternity*. This means an understanding of the body's essence: that is, as an extensive object of an idea in God.

Would this relieve pain when we have it, let alone allow or enable that pain to "sublate" into blessedness?

The question is ambiguous. By "relief" of pain does one mean the extirpation of it from a given moment of the durational order? But this would be asking for the exemption of given moments of duration from the order of determination; which is absurd.

Relief of pain, or from it, must therefore mean the utilization of pain, or of some element in it, not as a *means* of progress toward a "greater perfection"—which would be moralism's cliché—but as that progress itself.

It then becomes more accurate to say not the "utilization" of pain, as if pain were external to individuation, but rather the *discovery* in pain, so far as possible, of an overlooked element of perfection itself.

Provisionally, let us call such an element by the name of *suffering*.

(Spinoza, of course, uses that word in the sense of impotence, or diminution of the power to act. But the demands of Spinoza's usage are not absolute. A *refusal* to act—or "be"—along certain lines, in order more effectively to act or be along others, would be accretion of power, not loss of it.)

But the self-incremental, or progressively adequate understanding of the body's essence, that might arise from knowledge of the third kind, would transform the character of the *suffering* that lies in pain, and is often beholden to it. Pain is not the same as suffering; nor is suffering necessarily pain. But the suffering that lies in pain arises from an *eternal capacity, eternally individuated*. Pain is not a capacity, but suffering is: that is to say, pain is not a power, but suffering is; or might well be. Suffering is "of" the essence of the body's individuation; or, it is the essence of that individuation itself. So conceived, suffering is distinguishable, and perhaps separable from pain; and, speaking metaphorically, may well be the means whereby we transcend pain.

That, of course, will not prevent us from *feeling* pain, when the painful happens to us, or is applied; but that is not quite yet (nor yet again) the question.

Strictly speaking, we cannot transcend pain: that is, we cannot, while continuing to feel the pain, go beyond it, and while carrying it with us make it into an element of its opposite, for instance, pleasure; and literally experience something like pleasure–pain, or pain–pleasure. If we manage to do that, or think we have managed, in all likelihood it was not pain that was felt in the first place, but simply ordinary sensation, more delicately nuanced than might be customary; as if the determinate order of ordinary sensation, in, for instance, "vague experience," had been broken up spectroscopically, and re-fused into its ordinary "vagueness," but not quite completely so. To insist otherwise is to ignore the true character of pain; which is almost, as it were, "extra-sensory."

Pain is a threat to the being of sensation; as it is a threat, however remote, however delicately or subtly made, to the very being of the body. Uninterrupted application of pain, it is reliably reported, leads to the disappearance of sensation altogether, or to loss of consciousness, or to death itself; and presumably the mere *threat* of such pain, if sufficiently believable, might have the same consequences.

The explanation is simple enough: the application of pain has to be quite local, and usually is; or is felt to be so, which comes to much the same thing; as in the torment called "pressing," applied in the older law courts, when the respondent chose to stand mute; the whole body of the offender being then subjected to the pressure of great weight, as if to press testimony out of his contumacious muteness. This pain, too, is no doubt felt locally; since if truly felt diffusely and distributively it could be no other than the comfortable discomfort of a very hot steam bath, russian or turkish.

The acute toothache is thus traditionally, and truly, the paradigm of pain; and the tongue compulsively caressing the toothache is by no means committed to transcending the pain; since it does not believe that can happen. Transcendence, of course, requires belief, as the start of adequation.

To complete the foregoing explanation: the absolute localization of pain, so far as the human body permits of it, is essential, so to speak, to the painfulness of pain because of our relation, in and through our bodies, to the infinite order of determination. Very simply: our bodies are the insistence of the ethical conatus by which we have come into being in our co-determinative role in that infinite order; to that extent our durational bodies are a mode of *resistance* to the infinite order. The application of pain is thus, so to speak, an "application" of the infinite order at a single point of entry; there being no other way to invite the infinite order to take over, since it has been there all the time, and in its infinite existence has gotten on reasonably well with our finite, and resistant, existence. Death, of course, is simply invasion by the infinite order at all possible points of entry. The *licht metaphysik* of the medievals, and of a neo-medieval like Descartes, ignored certain instructive implications of the optimism of light: when the sun's ray are focused in a burning glass, they kill.

In sum: pain cannot be truly transcended: it can be deadened, if the circumstances and resources permit; or endured; and it can be *suffered*.

We are therefore required to consider, if but briefly, the difference between "suffering" and "pain."

We distinguish, first, between the notion of "suffering" that we propose to offer and the notion of "pity" as traditionally advanced.*

Pity I define as false pain. Let us consider it as pretended, or faked, ethical stigmata.

Spinoza's characterization of the "emotions" at the beginning of the *Ethic*, Part III, in a running catalogue of proposals and propositions, which he calls "Definition of the Emotions," and again toward the end of the *Ethic*, Part III, suffers from the same erector-set ingenuousness that derives, for nearly all seventeenth-century thinkers, from the unhappy Cartesian spastics on the subject. Descartes' *Passions of the Soul* is sometimes a miracle of suggestiveness, particularly in its initiating sortie that *"admiration,"* or wonder, is the first passion, but much of it reads like a testamentary last word from the bureaucratic death of insight. None of us since, without exception, has escaped the dubious influence of that testament, even if we were not present at the reading.

Spinoza, I believe, has done his best to escape it, but he is not always sure; nor can we be.

Spinoza's situation, in dealing with a first-class traditional virtue like pity, is that he is also, however unwillingly, dealing with one of the *middot*—"measures," attributes or parameters—of God: mercy, or metaphysical softness, is the left hand of God, in traditional and rabbinic theology, as justice is his right hand.

Therefore, Spinoza's disparagement of this traditional virtue (given and suggested in the *Ethic*, Part III, Propositions 22 and 28 and their surrounding context) has not only the force of an unexpectedly strong side-critique of traditional blandness and/or sentimentality about ethical temperament, but also delivers a *metaphysical thrust* which is not to be ignored. God does not pity; therefore, etc. This is the hard face of Spinoza's ethics. But that face is turned upon the human situation with understanding. It is this understanding which permits us to entertain great expectations of our individual ethical duration.

Spinoza's disparagement, expressed or implied, of pity has to

---

*Pain—though sufficiently local and concrete—cannot be made an example of Spinozistic bodily concreteness by combining it with biofeedback or other techniques designed to decrease its force. There is nothing wrong in principle with such techniques. But they would not allow pain to be illustrative for HMR's purposes, since it would then cease to *be* pain. Pain can be illustrative of Spinozistic concreteness only insofar as it sublates into suffering, while not *thereby* ceasing to be itself. Suffering has now to be distinguished from the ersatz suffering of pity.

do with pity's necessary involvement in the bad faith of "imaginings" about somebody whom we like or whom we feel to be "like ourselves," and whom we "imagine," or think we know to be undergoing pain.

It is at once obvious that the virtuous notion of pity is involved in regressive ambiguities beyond repair.

For instance: When Spinoza, in the *Ethic,* uses the word "imagine," or "imagination," he is tending to refer to something—an entity of relation or a process of the mind as to the state of its body—whose status is fundamentally ambiguous.[19] The fundamental ambiguity of imagining something, or the having of something in one's "imagination," lies in the fact that imagining something always raises the question: does the something imagined actually "exist"? That is to say, is it *so*? And if it is *so,* that is to say, if it once *was* so, is that sometime experience, relation, emotion, modality of inter-determination, etc., now *present* to the body, and its mind? Or is it now, necessarily and in the nature of the case, *absent* from the body and "its" present, and therefore "present" only to the mind, as memory, as image, as *misunderstanding,* and the like?

I assume that Spinoza is aware of these ambiguities, but does not see them as open to clarification in their own terms. The reason is that the claim imagination makes is necessarily an unclarified claim in which the framework of durational qualities is taken as ultimate. "I remember . . . I have a very good memory, and what I remember was really so . . . I have never had this illness, and do not now have it, but I *know* exactly what the symptoms are according to knowledge of the second kind, and can describe exactly what the patient is *feeling* . . . I witness this public execution of the malefactor in question, and *though I do not enjoy the spectacle,* or the smell of it, which is indeed far worse than the smell of bread burning, *for some reason I cannot quite tear myself away*. I suppose I stand here, or continue to dwell on it in *imagination,* after the (repulsive) affair is over, and I have actually left the scene of it, because it is (was) my *duty* as a member of the commonwealth, and perhaps as a fellow-human-being, to have been there. I further do my duty by *pitying* this malefactor. And in token of my *pity* I say to him, and to *myself,* 'there but for the grace of God (thank God!) go I (thank God!) . . .'

"To prove matters to you I will, (*a*) cite the fact that I have dropped a coin in the charity-box on my way home from execution square (*Place de la Concorde,* it is now called; for all these events were yesterday and long ago; that is to say, no longer *now*); and (*b*) make the claim that I have exactly—or more or less exactly—the same virtuous emotion of *pity* in me when I bring the bed-pan to the bedridden and the moribund; and I do not know how else, and with what further proofs I can prove to you that the *pity* I feel is pitifully real; that is, *very* real; no matter what I feel."

To which Spinoza's answer might very well be: you do not feel it; for the reason that the emotion you claim to feel does not exist. What is there to *feel,* since you do not feel, and *cannot* feel the other subject's *pain. To claim to feel the other's pain would be to deny the infinite individuation of Substance, and the infinite continuity of individuation in the modalities of Substance;* and thus, in effect, to interpose an absurd claim of "counter-Substance."

To the imaginative, but false, claims of pity, the knowledge of the third kind might continue to respond as follows.

When the pitying subject shall have *adequated* the degenerative and regressive emotions which in the pretended act of pity he is cultivating, he would no doubt find that his pretended "empathy" or "identification" with the body of the other is only possible as *an act of understanding of the body of the other in God.*

This may be difficult and rare; but however difficult and rare it is not, after all, so uncommon: it is called the *understanding* of suffering; it is suffering itself, adequated. It is not inconceivable that this suffering could be experienced, and is to be experienced, in one's own case.

We do not mean to propose that suffering is the same as blessedness. It is something less than that that we are called upon to argue. We have only to make conceivable that there is a conative element in the mind's relation to the body's pain that is akin to the highest emotion of which the human being is capable; that this element, though associated with pain in our vague opinion and "vague experience" of the matter, and often enough arising *from* pain, is nevertheless notably distinct from pain, and, for the mind's understanding, the *antithesis* of pain, and having a markedly different prognosis in the order of eternal determination. Whether or no this will then turn out to be the same as blessedness seems to me of minor consequence, even for Spinoza's case, which is the case we are particularly concerned with. The rhetorical habits and idiomatic commitments of one age of grace and its language, rather than some other, these considerations are not decisive for our question.

We have so far argued that our ethical conation toward the presumptive pain of the *other's body* is not properly expressed by the traditional notion of pity; it is for that reason that Spinoza regards the claims of that virtue with a sceptical, devaluing intention; that the ethical syndrome more proper to the observation of pain, *in oneself as in the other,* is the emotion called suffering; that this emotion lends itself quite easily to adequation as the love of God, whether that love be vast or small; and that in fact the emotion of suffering tends to be self-adequating, in Spinoza's high sense of adequation.

Some ingredients of this argument remain to be put into it.

First, we undertake to characterize more overtly what we have called "suffering." We do so in the first place by distinguishing it more specifically from the presumably self-characterizing, and apparently self-defining, syndrome called pain. Or, since we wish to entertain a category, which shall have pain as a "common notion" in it, let us speak rather of *painfulness*. This will do for the presumptive pain of the other, as well as for one's own.

We distinguish suffering from painfulness, in the first place, by noting that suffering might and does arise in the same context as joy (which is quite different from the context of pleasure, from which painfulness notoriously arises, or so it is said). So close is the empirical relation between suffering and joyfulness that one suspects a symbiotic relation here; more natural even than in the case of pain; so that one further suspects that the historical tendency of joyfulness to pass into the "Peasant Wedding" type of saturnalia and ecstatic gluttony may well be an attempt to flee from, or altogether to suppress, the suffering that is symbiotic to proper joy.*

Let us put the matter trivially enough to silence further argument on the point: Why, for instance, do people cry at weddings? Would a proper Benthamite cry? *Should* he cry if his calculus of prospective pleasures-and-pains from this particular union comes out +1? Bentham, or a proper Benthamite, mightn't, but J. S. Mill conceivably would; or could.

Language has no obligation toward tweezer-like precision in this matter, but it seems to me it would be clearly inappropriate to call this universal commonplace of "ambivalent" feeling by the name of pain. "Sadness" is the word sometimes used to point to it; and "sadness" let it be, if one prefers. *But then why is it that the same emotion, more or less imperfectly adequated, supervenes upon the emotion of mournful sadness or of grief at the death of one's beloved other?* If not at all the deaths.

The emotion of death-sadness, one recalls, has been found to be as "ambivalent" as the emotion of wedding-joy.

I submit that there is nothing esoteric here; the esotericism is merely psychological. Ethically and conatively, the ambivalence is one and the same: the notorious *rites de passage* of human existence—

*The body in its concreteness suffers. Suffering can be (among other things) a sublated form of pain. Pity, by contrast, is feigned suffering. The element of pain that admits of sublation into suffering is here called "painfulness." Joy as well as pain (whether confronted as one's own or as another's) admits of this element. HMR passes on, therefore, to a discussion of this form of suffering in *rites de passage*—whether ostensibly celebratory or ostensibly mournful. Henceforth he will call it "suffering/understanding" and it will be identical with blessedness.

which are by no means as sporadic and occasional as anthropology tends to see them, but rather endemic to the days of duration—give rise in the human body to a kind of more or less imperfectly adequated emotion which could easily have two names, as it has two faces: understanding and/or suffering.

They are not necessarily one and the same; nor need they be; neither are thought and extension one and the same.

But as thought and extension have only the one Substance between them, so to speak, so understanding and suffering have only the one *field* between them, namely, the *infinite order of determination*.

This is why, I suggest, people cry at weddings; that is to say, if their crying has any thought in it; it may, of course, be simply bad nerves. But it is not instructive to seize too quickly upon reductive de-explanations.

For by the same mode of counter-explanation one is required to account for the studied melancholy of Keats's *Ode on a Grecian Urn* as from the language syndrome of consumptive illness; penultimate warning signals given somewhat earlier than expected; but not too early; and perhaps complicated by venereal infection.

But the flaw in Keats's *Ode*, if flaw there be in this exalted poem, has nothing to do with the author's illness, both latent and most active: it has to do, rather, with the failure of the imagery's nerve; as if the problem of the "bride of quietness" is that she has been permitted by the ancient potter to arrest the law of the first infinite mode of extension, to wit, the law of motion and rest; whereas her true problem is not hers at all but the potter's, who was unable to suggest how she could more thoughtfully dance; that is, dance while weeping.

Perhaps, as Gotthold Ephraim Lessing once suggested, in his *Laokoon*, sculpture cannot really do this; perhaps the experience of sculpture is not "vague" enough, but that is not yet certain; and in any event poetry has abundantly demonstrated that it can do just that; namely, express the community of suffering/understanding with highest human joy. Innumerable examples come to mind; at which point examples from other arts crowd in as well. So that, for criticism's sake, one must conclude that the flaw in Keats's *Ode* is the flaw of binding knowledge of the third kind to an insufficient piece of clay. Knowledge of the third kind may well and truly reside in and arise from the "vague experience" of poetry; but not from poetry's conceits, no matter how well labored.

We return, then, to the suffering/understanding of human occasions, such as weddings, and funerals. We note, first, that these occasions, and the emotions of them, are quite removed from the un-vague human experience called pain; an experience which is precisely on the way to ceasing to be human. There is, of course, traditionally, and by rote, an affectation of pain in connection with a near-at-hand death; but it requires no particularly exquisite perception to recognize the ancient "ambivalence" of this affectation; in which ambivalence, the cheerfulness of liberation, and of overwhelming reminder of our infinitely *individuated* condition, is often smothered by compensatory hysteria.

No; we are speaking of normal grief, the grief of vague experience, as of normal, even if ritualized, rejoicing, as in the altogether vague experience of a human wedding.

In these polarized moments of duration the same quality of suffering/understanding may be observed to supervene upon the gestured style.

It may be easier to observe it in connection with the contained frivolities of a proper wedding.

It may be at once observed that the quality of suffering/understanding we are in search of has nothing to do with the tinsel dumbshow of prothalamium–epithalamium, and the rest of it; nor with Phoebus and Aurora, and the rest of them; in other words, nothing to do with some of the worst of tradition's corpus of poetry. These mythologized noises are strictly *political* in intention and significance; they are the trumpetings, or the brayings, of the social contract embarrassed for its members and therefore, to some degree, for itself.

But these emotions that cover, as well as underlie, the sentimentalities, or the failures, of the wedding, what do they seem to be?

Let us, then, construe the "wedding-emotion" as best we can, and take some speculative census of the sub-emotions that seem to be co-conative with it, in this vivid moment of the social contract at play.

Item: there is vicarious "lust," to use Spinoza's over-determined word; that is, one might contemplate, and therefore to some extent experience, the nature of another's pleasure, denied, in the nature of the case, to one's own body. Nevertheless, the body might admire, and give all due respect to that pleasure from which oneself is alienated, since the alienation comes, without prejudice, directly from the social contract. The sub-emotions of fantasy are born here; they may contribute to art and poetry.

Item: the poetic emotion itself. This enactment, these performative statements, of rubrics uttered, of rustling articulations and sussurations of dresses worn, of stiffened hopeless pirouettings of bridegrooms on trial and best men and second-best orbiting, monkey-like, all around him; these sudden mobilities and twitchings of usually paralyzed faces; these shuffling outbreaks of inhibited humor; and all the rest of it; out of these things high art and myth might yet be born; how these disguised, and thus sublated, coquetries are the necessary (or so it seems) prolegomena to every future parturition; although there might be an exception here and there, in durational time; that is, an instance of parthenogenic parturition, which would not seem to require a wedding at all; but which nevertheless usually does; and in any case is unable altogether to suppress the wedding-emotion, even though it does not know what to do with it.

Item: the biological emotion. As he and she from sperm and ovulation, so, in due course, thee, and thee; with dresses and trinketings as side-effects along the way; *and death and corruption as the end of it all*. For the biological emotion death is the one and only end; beginnings are exclusively contained within corruption, the only conceivable First Cause. When the biological emotion moves to contemplate a forward "regress" to the series—for instance, perhaps corruption leads to *another* wedding?—that emotion has already begun to transcend itself; it is gingerly approaching the adequated emotion of suffering/understanding.

Suffering/understanding: there is an order of infinite determination; and this couple, and these wedding guests, and any ancient mariner too, who might be there, are part of it; "caught up in it," so to speak; and so on.

But from the moment that the human mind—the mind, that is to say, of the wedding guest—has recognized and identified this cliché of its own existence, namely, that things are not what they seem, and that from the standpoint of something-or-other the death-emotion and the wedding-emotion, and the moments which they celebrate, have something, or even much, in common; from that same moment of recognition, the human mind at the wedding which it has been forced to attend, or at the death which it has chosen to witness, *rejects* the commonalty of the two emotions, and will insist on taking them one by one.

The human mind wishes to disentangle itself from the grip of the Ancient Mariner, who has made himself present precisely in order to insist on the universal validity of the "category mistake."

In the symbolism of this notorious poem the Ancient Mariner stands for the *human body*. The wedding guest stands merely for the human mind.

The classification of emotions, and their firm attachment to suitable durational episodes, belongs to knowledge of the second kind; the subjection, and sublation, of the classified emotions to the infinite individuation of *natura naturans* belongs to the adequation of the emotions, or to knowledge of the third kind. The mind, dutiful to the social contract, whose instrument it prefers to be, will say, as it should: rejoice, O wedding guest, keeping time with the loud bassoon; this, *indeed*, is a wedding. But the body knows better: this is an "intimation of eternity"; and since there is no such thing, except metaphorically, it turns out that this moment of confused emotion is simply an unrecognized moment of the highest form of knowledge: suffering/understanding. It is the body, the object of the idea that constitutes the human mind, that turns its own idea toward the proper knowledge of itself.

We have argued that the emotion of suffering/understanding is separable in principle, and therefore in empirical fact, from the distinctive durational occasions with which "painful" emotions and "pleasurable" ones are traditionally, and by formal habit, associated, respectively. The aim of the argument has been to separate the experience of "suffering" from the experience of pain; to suggest the cognitive character of the experience called suffering; to indicate the presence of that experience in the experience called pleasure, or even happiness; to propose that this cognitive significance of suffering is retained throughout the range of the pleasure–pain syndrome; to suggest the possibility that the emotion of suffering/understanding is near enough to what Spinoza calls "blessedness" as should suffice for all conceivable purposes of "vague" (i.e., durational) experience; to render explicit the sense in which the emotion of suffering/understanding is a form of body-knowledge; or, what comes to the same thing, a case-instance of *adequately understanding one's own body*, and therefore of knowing-loving God.

Is then the *intellectual love of God* a viable option in the extremity of the emotion called pain?

The following observations seem apropos:

1. We propose to the argument, first, that it henceforth keep in mind that Spinoza's "blessedness" is under no obligation to maintain a connection, however sublated, with pleasure.

2. In seeking, therefore, to locate the possibility of intellectual love somewhere, conceivably, in the spectrum of pain, we are no longer under the onus of trying to locate pleasure in its contradictory.

3. We are now face-to-face with a quite particular problem: what is the *body* of pain? What aspect of the *body-in-pain* can become the object of such adequated emotion that the emotion will pass into understanding, or intellectual love?

4. The empiric of pain suggests certain answers. Being truisms these answers are probably partial. For example: (*a*) The pain of childbirth is said to be bearable (or bearable/unbearable) because it is an experience, in ultimate intensity, of the social contract. It is said that many women, not all, welcome it again. This welcoming emotion, if it exists, does not locate itself in the intellect of the woman in labor but in her body. We now say: that insofar as she understands her body, and its fitness for many things, including the sharpness of these pains, she loves-and-understands the social contract, and its place in

natura naturans. One might say that she "loves" it, though as a matter of conative style it would be better not to use that word: she *has* loved the social contract, once and for all; she does not need to love it any more. (*b*) The case is different in the situation of applied torture. Nevertheless, even in this case, as Merleau-Ponty has pointed out,[20] the victim's ongoing relation to the social contract from which he issues (family, party, sect, nation, etc.) will help decide, for him, whether he "understands" the endured pain, and is a witness of its sublation into *suffering*. (*c*) There are well-known cultures—American Indian, African, Tibetan, etc.—where the social contract is *transmitted* precisely through the application of pain. Presumably, it is the American Indian's understanding of his body, acquired in the initiatory contract of pain, that enables him to sing the death-song when some unfriendly tribe undertakes to torture him to death.

5. So much for the empiric, or pseudo-inventory, of the body's pain.

One must altogether renounce any temptation to infer anything didactic for the culture from this inconclusive inventory of pain. Shall we train the young of the social contract to endure pain? Which pain? The pain of torture? of toothache? of cell aggrandizement? And by what means? What modifications of our inoculatory procedures—smallpox, typhoid fever, "polio," and the rest—shall become standard for pediatrics in order to teach the contracted and sub-contracted young to stand up and be counted for ethical conatus?

We are not authorized by the argument to divagate into such *paideïa* as that. It forewarns us of its essential and inevitable triviality. We are not to make of knowledge which is strictly of the second kind a *false* knowledge of the third kind. The proper characteristic of knowledge of the second kind is that it is, and should be, strictly *ad hoc*. The technologies of optimal amelioration, whether by injection or by trained auto-suggestion, are self-justifying; but they have, self-evidently and by definition, *nothing to do with the intellectual love of God*. The vector of eternity does not seem to leave its traces in such technologies.

What is the reason for that?

The reason lies in the relation of eternity to causality.

The technology of amelioration, precisely like pain itself, *localizes* the order of causality: in the one case to an illusory vanishing point, in the other to a point of no return, or death.

But the intellectual love of God, and its accompanying emotion of blessedness, if and when achieved, has projected the understanding of causes on to the proper screen of infinity. The causes of one's discomfort are always infinite. This is what knowledge of the third kind proposes to the body to understand.

It is this de-localization of causality—or the awareness, slow or sudden, of causality's infinite spread—that is responsible for the upsurge of suffering/understanding when the knowledge of the third kind reveals itself in the "vague experience" of the durational day. The word for it might or might not be "blessedness." Certainly it is both ultra- and infra- to the normal spectrum of adequated emotions. Therefore it seems appropriate to think and speak of it as the intellectual love of God; and to cultivate such sense as one can of its being *part* of the infinite love with which God loves himself. For what happens in such moments of "vague experience," whether the vagueness be occasioned by the wedding-emotion or the death-bed emotion, is that the body-and-mind of durational man becomes aware of the nature of Substance: that is to say, of infinite *individuation* in an infinite causal order; and to situate oneself in the knowledge of that order is, by the same token, to situate oneself as *co-determinant* of it.

Out of profound and immemorial linguistic habit the mind may at once reject its insight into the body-and-the-mind's co-determinate role in the matter. The mind is accustomed to think of such an insight as sinister; possibly as *hybris;* or possibly gnostic, and therefore sterile and useless, *ethically,* for all the lurid ontological excitement that it might seem to promise. The body, no doubt quite wisely, might prefer to read its own insight as an insight into a law of submissiveness, and of resignation; and such imaginary laws are plausibly more relevant to the ways of the social contract than any Promethean posture on a platform of air. But though the body's tactics in knowledge are and must remain its own business, the body's insight in the moment of suffering/understanding will remain indefeasible: *the infinite situation of the finite individual is not to be despised*. Not to despise it is to love God, in part, with the infinite love that he loves himself.

We now approach the absolute divide between pain, in its mereness and its atrociousness, on the one hand, and what we have called the emotion of suffering/understanding, on the other.

The metaphysical pride, so to speak, of pain—and it is quite a Luciferian pride—is that pain individuates absolutely and without compromise. Mme. de Sévigné erred, though her motives were no doubt "contractual" and therefore good, in claiming that she feels pain "in" her daughter's bosom (*"J'ai mal à votre poitrine"*). It is not modally given to us to do that; or to feel that. It is the somber glory of pain that nobody, but nobody, can take up the cross of it *for* us. But while bearing witness, with a commendable absoluteness, to the absoluteness of individuation, pain at the same time *denies infinity;* that is to say, denies the situation of the individual in God; and by so doing denies God. In the ultimate morbidity, and distortion, of pain, it can be pretended that *even death* will not stop pain, though it may interrupt it; and one may long for the interruption. This pretense underlies extremeties of punishment, as is self-evident when a "metaphysic" of pain translates itself into an organization chart of hell. The metaphysic of pain thus denies *eternity;* as the doctrine of immortality does as well.

But "we know and feel by experience" that *that part of the mind which is the essence of the body* is eternal. We know, therefore, by the same experience that our absolute individuation is situated in infinity; which is to say, in eternal Substance, expressed as *natura naturans;* and that that mode of an infinite attribute called thought, given to us, has a not-surprising but always luminous appreciation of the situation; capable even, in principle, if not in the preponderance of statistic, of sublating the anti-eternal experience of pain; by the willing retreat (if by no other means) from the durational order; a noble order, that needs no apology; and is, in fact, not worse and not lesser in its quality than the order of eternity; since what is in and of God is not less (or worse) than God himself, except in *effectiveness*. But God himself, though he is the first cause, and the immanent cause, of the social contract, as he is of everything else, including himself, is nevertheless content that the *efficient cause* of the social contract shall be the ethical conatus, eternally co-determinate, of the human order.

Postscript

Is it conceivable that one should *believe* that that part of the human mind which is the essence of the body *remains* and is eternal?

Of course not. One does not believe it.

Nor is it conceivable that one should here, addressing the attribute of thought, say to it, "O, eternal mind, I believe; help thou my unbelief." Eternal mind will not help one to believe. Eternal mind, so to speak, is not interested in *belief* at all.

"Intuitive science" no longer believes or disbelieves; and has succeeded, God willing, in making it clear to the human individual that he has never believed *anything;* and has lied when he has said "I believe"; or has been whistling in the dark, and in the infinite dark the whistle is not heard; or has merely, and awesomely, proposed to himself a move on the field of history; which is an important thing, and in some sense the only thing, to do; or has simply said to himself, like God himself, on at least one of his occasions, "I am."

For when a person says, and the person sometimes does say it when sufficiently provoked, "I *believe* that the sun will rise tomorrow," he knows in his heart, that is, with his better nature, already enlightened as it must be by knowledge of the third kind, that he is not saying anything, or is merely using in his own informal way the Cartesian expression, *sum:* I am. That is, I have a body; and, contrary to the claim of Descartes, I know it much better than I know my mind; for my mind does not exist to be known; but my body does. And when I say, as I already have, "my body," I am already saying that the sun will rise tomorrow; and it would be as meaningless to say "I *believe*" that the sun will rise tomorrow as it would be to say "I *believe* that I have a body"; in that anybody who says the latter meaningfully, that is, seriously, is already a little mad; and in grave danger. This is clearer if one applies it to the case of God: anybody who seriously says "I *believe* in God," and wishes to be taken constructively, is already a little mad. It is as if he said, "I believe I have eyeballs; and having read Dante, the *Paradiso*, or St. Paul, or somebody, I hope some day, seeing that it is already late, to see God; that is, to stand eyeball to eyeball with . . .?"

The eternity of a certain "part" of the human mind has nothing to do with belief; given the interesting tragedy of language, it may have a little bit more to do with unbelief. For human conatus and its ethic, like the intuitive science that properly guides the ethical conatus of human existence, adequates through "unbelief" rather than through belief; that is, through the "difficult and rare," rather than through the impossible and the commonplace.

"Determination is negation," it has been well said.[21] And all adequation is merely the rejection of the inadequate; including the inadequacy of "a" God, or of a conception of him, that has to be "believed" in.

But our own eternity is another matter. We do not so much mind being fooled by a God who is not—idolatry being a natural aspect of our haste to submit to the order of infinite determination, and thereby to escape the unpleasantness of the social contract—but we mind very much being fooled by eternity.

But this is absurd.

We have eternally agreed to die; so wherein could we be fooled? If fooled at all it would be *immortality* that would deceive us; and it is precisely here that the advantage, so to speak, of immortality over eternity lies. For immortality is at once *self-falsifying;* it is an irresistible invitation to disbelieve, and nobody has ever declined the invitation; therefore both the candor and the triviality of mythology; where everything is cheerfully acknowledged to be foolishness—the pretense of parable is very soon dropped in advanced mythology—but the triviality soon turns into prattle, as in Greek mythology, or into a snarl, as in the Norse, or into mere moral sweat, as in the Hindu.

And so mythological theology arises to sustain us in our unbelief; indeed warning us to hold fast to it; so that positive science can arise, by-passing altogether the wretched question of belief. The allegedly pure descriptiveness of positive science is transparent: one knows at once that nothing is "like this" or ever could be. *Nothing is like anything.* The world is "pure act," as the theologians have long been accustomed to say about God, and no action is like any other action; not even our own.

But eternity is in a somewhat different case. Are we asked, by the argument, to "believe" in it?

No. For what we "feel and know by experience" would be meaningless to believe in; or disbelieve. We do not "believe" in an action done, or in the sub-acts, generally called the means, whereby it becomes done, or self-insertive into the order of determination. We feel and know we have done it, by having done it. A question might arise as to whether it is *we* who have done it; and if so, in what sense, and to what degree; or whether it was perhaps another; another doer and another deed, not this one. But then we are merely practicing a metaphysical *refraction,* so to speak, on the infinite individuation of the order of determination, and trying to make it see by and through the corrective lenses of the social contract; that is to say, to see straight. For it goes without saying that seeing straight, like the question of who did what deed, is important only for the durational order; since in God there is neither straight nor crooked; that is to say, in God literally, or in God *un*individuated, as if that were possible. So we are reminded once more that the eternal social contract is responsible, or in Hobbes's words has authority, for the durational order, and for the uses of eternity that are made by that order, and by all that in it endures.

So that eternity is not an end; it is a *means;* or more plainly, it is a tool. To put it in terms of the first-order metaphor that Spinoza has employed: eternity is not a state or a condition or a *terminus ad quem:* eternity is the extensive aspect of God; or, to speak less bureacratically, it is God himself *extended;* and if extended, then, of course, "already" infinitely individuated. To love God, then, is to love extension, infinitely individuated; that is to say, to love our body; or to know and understand it. This we "feel and know by experience." We feel and know by experience that it is the only thing to do.

We are in that sudden case of M. Jourdain, discovering that he has always spoken prose.

And this eternal prose that we have always spoken—when we speak—has no ulterior motive; that is to say, no final cause; but is the cause of itself, as it were; that is to say, the mere exhilaration of being; or love of God; the same love with which he loves himself; the "bloom on the rose," as Aristotle, in another connection, said of happiness; the "bloom" being not the ("immaterial") substance of the rose, but its *natura naturans,* or that by which the order of determination is somewhat roseate.

And similarly the social contract, by which our human bodies have their being and occasionally endure, is for the co-determinate "glory of God," without which he could not be. We do not celebrate eternity, but eternity celebrates us. It is not life we love, for life, seen only from the standpoint of the second kind of knowledge, is mere extensiveness without thought; as if that were possible; but the social contract is what we love, in despite of ourselves; and the social contract gives us, as it seeks to exercise its finite authority over our eternal bodies, the various arts, visual, acoustical, erotical, and so on; astigmatic or otherwise paranormal; by which arts we cease to remember, but come instead to recognize what we have always known: that no man can hate God; that no man can hate his own ethical body; and that the suffering/understanding by which the five senses express their joy in the infinite order of determination—and there is no other way in which the joy and/or the determination could be expressed—is indeed the highest joy.

NOTES AND INDEX

Notes

Part One: Hobbes's Secret

1. The suggestion emerges from F. C. Hood's *The Divine Politics of Thomas Hobbes: An Interpretation of Leviathan* (Oxford: Oxford University Press, 1964). The thesis of this interesting book, which I do not wholly understand, may be too complicated and elusive for summary characterization. Thus, p. viii. "It now seems to be reasonable to view Hobbes as a Christian thinker. He is peculiar, in combining Christianity, materialism, scholasticism, and mechanism" (see further, e.g., pp. 70, 100, 227, 246, 253). This combination, for a respectable or nearly respectable seventeenth-century thinker, is no more peculiar than breathing. Whether the combination can be "sublated" into coherence is another matter.

2. Unless by radically disconforming and hazardous ways, as in John Bunyan's ecstatic dolefulness or George Fox's separating inwardness, or, more surreptitiously, in the dim enlightenment of Rosicrucianism. All of these movements promised much for the relief of despair, and one way or another delivered new burdens of uneasiness or hysteria; or necessitated flight.

As for the category "people," it is of course merely code language for localized or *ad hoc* expression of *Geist*. Every nominalist knows this; as, for that matter, did Plato. The Incorruptible Robespierre, who alone (after Rousseau) took the "people" for real—and therefore slaughtered them like flies—was the last of the "medieval realists."

3. Not only had his mother given birth to Thomas (her second son) prematurely "owing to her agitation at the reports of the Armada," the date being April 5, 1588, but also, when the Long Parliament met November 15 and impeached Stafford; "Hobbes took fright and went over to Paris, 'the first of all that fled.'" These reminiscent self-characterizations are cited by the *Dictionary of National Biography* (London: Oxford University Press, 1917), IX, 931ff., from the earliest memoirs of Hobbes's life by his friend Aubry and others. But Hobbes's respectfulness to the syndrome of fear is not so much anecdotally confirmed as it is illustrated by the roots of his argument, and its thrust.

4. Émile Durkheim's classic work is subtitled: "A Study in Religious Sociology"; tr. Joseph Ward Swain (London: George Allen & Unwin, 1915).

5. This formula may well enough stand for the whole thesis of Durkheim's book, illustrated on nearly every page, as his argument gathers way. See the

index references to "force," "causality," "logic," "totem," "time," "space," etc. This is how the *Elementary Forms . . .*, which purports to be an investigation of the "structure," as one would now say, of "totemism," turns out to be an essay in the sociology of knowledge, and a contribution to the understanding of philosophical ontology.

6. Richard S. Peters, ed., *Body, Man and Citizen: Selections from Thomas Hobbes* (New York: Collier Books, 1962), pp. 95f. Peters is excerpting from Hobbes's *De Corpore* (1655); Sir William Molesworth, ed., *The English Works of Thomas Hobbes* (London, 1839), I, 94f.

7. The "Marxist" thought referred to here is what we may think of as "Classic Marxism," from the *Communist Manifesto*, 1848, to the publication of Lenin's *Materialism and Emperio-Criticism*, 1909. After that, and more particularly after the Bolshevik Revolution, October 1917, Marxist thought may be said to have entered the state of nature, or the war of all against all.

8. Readers thus far, if any, will be aware that my use of the word "obligation" is indebted to Howard Warrender, *The Political Philosophy of Hobbes: His Theory of Obligation* (Oxford: Oxford University Press at the Clarendon Press, 1957), and to the writers there cited (Leo Strauss, M. Oakeshott, et al.), for the availability of a useful term. In Warrender, the term serves to link a real problem in the interpretation of Hobbes with abstract problems of the casuistry of categories in nineteenth- and twentieth-century moral philosophy. The category of "obligation" is stumbling block and trouble-maker for that more recent history. But I do not believe that it is so for Hobbes. (Warrender, of course, p. 10, takes a quite different view: "the obligation to obey God in his natural kingdom, based upon fear of divine power—is, we shall contend, the normal meaning of the term in Hobbes's doctrine and the proper subject-matter of the present inquiry . . . this type of obligation, as it is found in Hobbes's theory, presents some unusual features and there may be some difficulty in calling it *moral* obligation as the term is commonly used." But, etc.) I hold that Hobbes is not at heart interested in free-floating moral categories, like "obligation," seeking anchorage in the sky (divine law, etc.), or on earth in political sovereignty, civil law, and statehood. What he is interested in is *"obedience."*

In Hobbes, *"obligation" follows from obedience*, and not vice versa. Whom or what to obey? That is less important (in Hobbes) than one might think. Obedience as such takes the edge off *original fear*. (Obedience, from self-reflexive fear, is Hobbes's "reason.")

My own use of the word "obligation" refers to a crucial moment in the dialectic of Hobbes's *fear*. The usual distinction would be between Hobbes's fear as a psychological category and "obligation" as a moral category (when it is not a merely physical one). I suggest, however, that the fundamental ontological-moral category in Hobbes is *fear* itself. Fear is, so to speak, the creative principle in all the works of man. And it is trivializing Hobbes to specify this fear as "fear of violent death." What difference would it make to Hobbes's "metaphysic of morals" if the death be not violent but pacific? Is not death always psychologically violent, i.e., unwelcome? Therefore, I use the word "obligation" to suggest the self-reflexiveness of fear in its *flight from fear*—toward commonwealth. But flight from fear is still fear. Hobbes's social contract is *fear controlled*. Or, one could think of fear as Hobbes's "demi-urge," and of the social contract as its only-begotten-son.

9. If the Jeffersonian "liberty" with which we are endowed by our Creator refers to *natural liberty*, it is precisely that which we abjure and renounce in moving toward the social contract, or "instituting governments among men." If, on the other hand, the reference is to *civil liberty* (the postulate of such liberty is *inequality*), to speak of it as deific "endowment" is to render unto God that which belongs to Caesar. The splendor of the Declaration is not a philosophical splendor, which it could not be, since it is founded upon contradictions which it refuses to face, but the splendor of propaganda for beautiful intentions, partly justified by their subsequent history.

10. Hobbes in *Leviathan* has three things to say about religion. The problem obsesses him somewhat as the concept of the bogeyman might a sophisticated child: (1) the child does not quite believe in the bogeyman. What he is really afraid for, namely, his father—in Hobbes's case the possibly paradigmatic father had fled the town after an assault on the pastor—or for himself, is much more fraught with threat of ulterior harm than any bogeyman who ever lived. But the child assumes that he cannot grow up without a properly controlled bogeyman.

That religious history is some such complex of displaced fears and projective distortions we are almost persuaded to believe by the anthropological-sociological-psycho-historical account of religious notions, explanatory or purposive superstitions, fallacies of misplaced causes, anxieties of time to come, natural terrors of things and their absence that are always with us, rough-and-ready arguments to "first cause"—all of which hermeneutic is summarily and somewhat breezily given to us in the last three paragraphs of *Leviathan*, chapter 11 and in the whole of chapter 12.

This chapter—compare with it chapters 45 and 46 of Part 4—also pays Hobbes's respects, that is, his disrespects, to the illusory fancies of "incorporeality" and "invisibility" that are endemic to religious history.

But since (2) "the true religion and the laws of God's kingdom" are one and the same (chapter 12)—and these laws are the "laws of nature" that follow from the social contract—it follows, in chapters 39 and 43 of the third part of *Leviathan*, that the doctrinal requirements for peaceable conformity in religion are quite minimal (belief in God and in Jesus Christ as savior, chapter 43), and that, "The laws of God therefore are none but the laws of nature, whereof the principal is, that we should not violate our faith, that is, a commandment to obey our civil sovereigns, which we constituted over us by mutual pact one with another" (chapter 43, p. 386).

Hobbes could hardly make it plainer.

(3) Finally, in chapters 44 and 47 of the fourth part, entitled "Of the Kingdom of Darkness," Hobbes expresses his sense of scandal at the usurpations of religion, both doctrinal, as in the metaphysics of the Mass, and political, as in papist claims to authority in England, and in the perversions of history and exegesis and misunderstandings of the civil order (or social contract) upon which such claims would be based.

(We are incidentally invited, in chapter 46 of the fourth part, to contemplation "Of Darkness from Vain Philosophy, and Fabulous Traditions."

The objects of attack here are, e.g., "abstract" or "separated essences," "substantial forms," incorporeality and invisibility, "eternity" as a "*nunc stans*," or "standing still of . . . time," error as heresy, etc. Part of this is simply loyal nominalism, but the more serious part is Hobbes's conviction that "vain philosophy" has been accessory before and after the fact to the deceptions, usurpations, and other misdemeanors of politically invasive religion.)

Hobbes's "personal" or private religion, which is probably the religion of a chastened but not wholly convinced Job who has survived to be a witness of the Christian dispensation, is evidently *not* an "atheist" religion; but to what extent it is a "theist" one might have puzzled Hobbes as much as it does us. It would in any case be invidious to begrudge Hobbes the entertainment he seems to find in the chastisement of erroneous Scriptural exegesis that resounds throughout much of *Leviathan*. He sometimes speaks as if the spirit of Praisegod Barebones, Puritan Member of Parliament for London in the "Barebones Parliament" of 1653, were upon him.

11. I am using Rudolph Otto's well-known phrase from *The Idea of the Holy*, trans. John W. Harvey, 2d ed. (London: Oxford University Press, 1950), to suggest for the Hobbesian context the necessary awful *distance* (not a distance to be traversed but a distance to be conceded) between the citizen and his so-to-speak *alter ego*, that is, the "mortal god" as exercised sovereignty.

12. The distinction between "abstract" and "concrete" right is of course indebted to Hegel's distinction in the *Philosophy of Right*, though it is hardly the same as his distinction, which has to do with (*a*) what one might call "pre-literate" or "pre-political" morality; and (*b*) with the difference, as Hegel sees it, between his ethic and Kant's.

The distinction between "abstract" and "concrete" nature would also arise by implication from Hegel's argument in his *Philosophy of Nature*, when we consider that argument as an account of how *Geist*, or human history, arises by due sublation from the inorganics and organics of mere nature.

13. The kings are the Lord Protectors, if it comes to that. The Lord Protectors are a federal constitution, if it should come to that. Any one of these constructs of our political thought may serve as the point of ingathering of all the natural right that there is, when we come, as we must, to the politicization of man. This ingathered natural right is the *alter ego* of the sovereign, whoever he or it happens to be, as the sovereign is the *alter ego* of the citizen, and we know very well who he or she happens to be.

14. The kind that we have has been suggestively denominated "infantile" by Sigmund Freud.

15. As, for instance, in the further exposition of the third law, justice, in chapter 15; in the paragraph rubriced, "*Justice of manners, and justice of actions . . .*": "And so also in commonwealths, private men may remit to one another their debts; but not robberies or other violences, whereby they are endamaged; because the detaining of debt, is an injury to themselves; but robbery and violence, are injuries to the person of the commonwealth" (pp. 97f.). Hobbes's contrast of "manners" and "actions" corresponds to his contrast of "conscience" (or disposition) and "covenant." My argument has been that Hobbes's covenant is an "actualization" of his notion of conscience,

which does not come into being except in and after the social contract, and its *enforceability*.

16. With which may be compared Hobbes's allocutory paragraph on "*Vain undertaking from vain-glory*" in his chapter 11, "Of the Difference of Manners" (i.e., of human character). Hobbes's usage of "vain-glory" in chapter 15, as in chapter 11, suggests that what has taken place in his thought, behind the usage, is a subtle symbiosis of the notions of vanity, randomness or idleness, self-deception, *hybris*, moral duplicity, sadism, *schadenfreude*, cruelty, and cowardice. All these things enter into the "bad infinite" of "punishment-without-pardon." It leads straight back to, or is in itself, the state of nature.

Hobbes's definitions are often less like "counters" in a language-calculus, as is sometimes implied by simplistic misdetermination of Hobbes's place in the history of English positivism, and more like the half-baked actions which words purport to be in Ludwig Wittgenstein's *Philosophical Investigations*, tr. G. E. M. Anscombe (New York: Macmillan, 1953), or even like the gods in Homer's *Iliad*: that is, they are shadow-graphs of a human action about-to-take-place.

17. The historical speculation suggested by the possibility of a Southern victory comprises a number of political options. For example, would not the Confederacy have had to reconstitute itself as an indissoluble federal union in order to avoid the indefinite self-dismemberment by further secessions that would have been strictly in accordance with its own confederate principles? Further, since there is no natural ground (in differences of language, culture, and history) for the Balkanization of North America that would have followed upon a Southern victory, there would have been either indefinite civil war, or progress toward re-unification.

Part Two: Spinoza's Way

1. The nature of the epistemological-ethical "anxiety" that Spinoza alludes to in the early paragraphs of *On the Improvement of the Understanding* (sometimes referred to, more faithfully to the Latin title, as the *Emendation of the Intellect*) is necessarily obscure. The context's review of the empirical disillusionments which are the source and core of that anxiety is an implausible review: many people may have had those temptations and the corresponding disillusionments, but nothing that we know about Spinoza suggests that the temptations were ever his in any way worth remembering. Is the said "anxiety" a stereotype for the "*Angst*" (and its *nausée*) that some twentieth-century Franco-Germanic speculation has made a by-word? Or was it, conceivably, a side-effect of Spinoza's earliest efforts to look, as it were, "upon the face of eternity"? One does not expect H. H. Joachim's conscientious and scholarly *Commentary on Spinoza's Tractatus De Intellectus Emendatione* (Oxford: Oxford University Press at the Clarendon Press, 1940) to answer such a question; and it does not.

2. As Kant has long ago pointed out in the *Judgment of Taste*; and Plato too, for that matter, in the *Ion*!

3. In a paper so entitled, in *Proceedings of the Aristotelian Society* 2 (1910–11): 108–128.
4. As from chapter 10, "Performative Utterances," of J. L. Austin's *Philosophical Papers*, ed. J. O. Urmson and G. J. Warnock (Oxford: Oxford University Press at the Clarendon Press, 1961).
5. As, for instance, John Dewey, Merleau-Ponty, the Wittgenstein of *Philosophical Investigations*, and the Gilbert Ryle of *The Concept of Mind* (London: Hutchinson, 1949). Any technical meaning of "being," as of "in-the-worldness," might be quite alien to some of these writers, but the fundamental notion of knowledge as an aspect of the "performative" would be common to them all.
6. *Paradise Lost*, Book IX, ll. 412–612.
7. Spinoza's gloss on Scripture, in his Scholium to Proposition 68, Part IV, makes the point that the curious drama of Genesis 3:1–7 depends upon a special conception of the power of God. "In that history no other power of God is conceived excepting that by which He created man; that is to say, the power with which He considered nothing but the advantage of man." This is reasonably, if incompletely, orthodox; but not entirely enlightening. It could be just as true to say that the theology of Genesis 1–3 assumes that God did not altogether know what he was doing in the six days of creation; and played it by divine Ear; or, in other words, left it to man to find out. In Spinoza's vocabulary: God *infinitely thought* his creation, but by no means infinitely foreknew it. With *man*, and the advent of durational time, "foreknowledge" of advantage (and disadvantage) came into the world.
8. This question is made the most of in L. S. Feuer's *Spinoza and the Rise of Liberalism* (Boston: Beacon Press, 1958). A much more portentous investigation, from a different angle of approach, is Leo Strauss's *Spinoza's Critique of Religion*, tr. E. M. Sinclair (New York: Schocken Books, 1965). In a preface to the translation, added some thirty years after the German original of 1930, Strauss writes: "He [Spinoza] was the first philosopher who was both a democrat and a liberal. He was the philosopher who founded liberal democracy, a specifically modern regime" (p. 16; the thought is echoed on p. 20, and elsewhere in the essay).

In Strauss's essay, "Comments on *Der Begriff des Politischen*, by Carl Schmitt," published as an Appendix to *Spinoza's Critique of Religion*, pp. 331–351, much of the credit for the burst of "liberalism" into the world is given to Hobbes. Thus (p. 338). "Hobbes is to a much higher degree than, say, Bacon, the originator of the ideal of civilization. By this very fact he is the founder of liberalism . . ." etc.

It is evident that the foundations of this question—of liberalism—are categories of fluid sand. Nor is the question firmed up any when it turns out, in Strauss, as in other writers of the tradition of political science, that Machiavelli, in some paradoxical and devious sense, is responsible for *everything* political. Why a set of trivial utterances like *The Prince* should enjoy this grandiose role is not clear. Perhaps the discipline of "political science" is condemned to that kind of topicality in which the re-discovery of a current vulgarism of thought in an older text must be thought to have significance.

The general theme of relations (derivative, congruent, tangential, contrary, etc.) between Hobbes's *political* ideas and Spinoza's is commented on by Lewis Feuer, by Strauss (in *The Political Philosophy of Hobbes*, tr. from the German manuscript by Elsa M. Sinclair [Oxford: Oxford University Press at the Clarendon Press, 1936], as well as in *Spinoza's Critique of Religion*, pp. 104, 229, 242, 244, etc.), and more methodically by Frederick Pollock in chapter 10 of *Spinoza: His Life and Philosophy* (London: Kegan Paul, 1880). Spinoza himself refers briefly and somewhat cryptically to the difference between his view of "natural right" and Hobbes's, in the first paragraph of the Fiftieth Letter. It is hardly necessary to add that the historical-textual-categorical relation between Hobbes's "political philosophy" and Spinoza's is *not* the theme of this book.

9. The very existence of this question in a properly clarified form must be credited to H. F. Hallett's *Aeternitas: A Spinozistic Study* (Oxford: Oxford University Press at the Clarendon Press, 1930). This luminous book is central to the understanding of what can be learned from the *Ethic*, and suggestive of what Spinoza might have learned from it himself, had he read, or re-read, the *Ethic* not as its author, but as its student. With Hallett's *Aeternitas*, and the two smaller books that he has written on the same subject, one is equipped to disregard the reductionist commentation on Spinoza which tends to make him intellectually scandalous, or unintelligible, or both. Besides Hallett's book, all one might conceivably need for "improvement of the understanding" in this connection would be H. A. Wolfson's two volumes of *The Philosophy of Spinoza* (Cambridge: Harvard University Press, 1934). Wolfson's classic book does not do very much for Spinoza as philosopher, but it brings out very sharply the dense cross-hatching of influences, sources, and derivations which give to Spinoza's philosophic images the intensity that they have.

10. Spinoza puts the argument of these Lemmas in the "if" form, as a "hopeful conditional," so to speak, the matter being observable only in its result, as individuation, and not in its process. The conditional is made factual by the requirements of rational explanation. The truths of knowledge of the third kind devolve into the second kind under the pressures of explanation.

11. The notion of "agency" is extensively applied in H. F. Hallett's *Creation, Emanation and Salvation: A Spinozistic Study* (The Hague: Martinus Nijhof, 1962) to the general interpretation of Spinoza's doctrine of nature. My own briefer use of the term derives essentially from Hallett's. The principal difference is this: I do not believe that any *general* interpretation of nature is required by, or perhaps even possible for, Spinoza's philosophy. "Agency" comes into the world as a by-product or side-effect of human conatus within the infinite order of determination. Another way of saying this would be: "agency" is important only on the abstraction level of knowledge of the second kind. From the standpoint of knowledge of the third kind *agents* alone (having the inalienable individuation which we expect of them) are significant; and they are identifiable only by human conatus (since God does not bother to give invidious names); which is by no means coextensive with nature, or with Substance. And the *agents* that human conatus identifies, and perhaps endows with the authority of agency, are by no means exclusively human. For instance: his-

torical structures or institutions, or *sacral* objects like art objects or mountain peaks, or other non-human instantiations of Hegel's *Geist*, are non-human agents of a highly effective, not to say confusing, kind.

12. What I am assuming here is the necessary inter-connectedness of categories of language with sticks-and-stones, ellipticity of orbital motion, and other profiles of "objective reality." This follows inevitably from the conception of Substance (thus Part II, Proposition 7, of the *Ethic*: "The order and connection of ideas is the same as the order and connection of things"). But this basic Spinozistic assumption is comfortably shared, from a quite different point of view, by the neo-analytic, language philosopher Peter Zinkernagel in his *Conditions for Description*, tr. from the Danish by Olaf Lindum (New York: Humanities Press, 1962). Notably, chapters 3 and 5 of that book set forth an attractive argument for the necessary inter-connectedness of things-actions-subjectivities-of-thought-and-feeling (Spinoza's "affects") -and-*personal pronouns*. Zinkernagel's "language" or "describability" does service, in this mode of philosophizing, as a substitute conception of "Substance."

More specifically and avowedly Spinozistic is of course H. F. Hallett's discussion in *Aeternitas* (pp. 183ff.) of the problem "*where* is the redness of the rose?" Hallett's argument is to the effect that the stock problems of epistemology—e.g., where is the place (and/or time) of perception?—make sense only in terms of a conception of Substance. In this matter of what ordinary language does with "certain attributes of God!" two quite different philosophers, like Hallett and Zinkernagel, thus, at a distance, converge.

13. Psalm 116:11. In the context of the psalm, the saying was "hasty," or "impatient."

14. The expression occurs in the Scholium to Proposition 39, Part V, of the *Ethic*: "and, on the other hand, we consider ourselves happy if we can pass through the whole period of life with a sound mind in a sound body." (*a*) The contingency referred to is of the highest order of empirical improbability; which, of course, Spinoza must know as well as anybody. (*b*) The use of the Cartesian locution, "mind *in* a body," a locution entirely alien to Spinoza's fundamental views, but inextricably entrenched in language, suggests that Spinoza does not take too tragically these elementary truisms of hygiene.

15. To argue for the "infinite relatedness" of the mind, as against the body's, would be (*a*) to confuse relatedness with motility, or even lability; (*b*) to blur the distinction between the situation or fact of relatedness and the *understanding* of relatedness—thereby making too much of the no-doubt categorial fact, and making it prematurely, that understanding can itself be taken as a supreme form of relatedness; and (*c*) to arrive at a blurring of the difference of the attributes, and the difference of their modes.

In fact: the mind ranges across its own infinity, either (*a*) through the body, by way of its affects; or (*b*) by way of images, which, unless one is careful, are acts of *mis*understanding; or (*c*) by way of abstractions or "universals," which, at best, are knowledge of the second kind, and mere tools.

The mind's infinity belongs to mathematics; the body's infinity belongs to its life and death.

16. The corollary to Proposition 40, Part V: "For the part of the mind which is eternal (Props. 23 and 29, pt. 5) is the intellect, through which alone we are

said to act (Prop. 3, pt. 3), but that part which, as we have shown, perishes is the imagination itself (Prop. 21, pt. 5), through which alone we are said to suffer (Prop. 3, pt. 3, and the general definition of the affects)."

1. It is evident that the language of "parts," applied to the mind, is a sub-idiom of the "faculty psychology" language, which is Spinoza's heritage from Aristotle, the medievals, and Descartes.

2. The mind has no "parts," though the body has: and there is no reason in principle why all the *faculties* of the mind have to accompany its eternity. (For that matter, it is not generally demanded by an orthodox doctrine of resurrection that all the "functions" of the body should accompany its revival into "sempiternity.")

3. The "perishing" of the imagination, or of the body's-own-mind, is part of mortality (or *is* mortality itself) not so much because suffering ceases in our dying, but because we cannot paint pictures or write ballads when we are dead; nor do we then prove or enact theorems. That is a great pity. But it may not be too great a payment for the eternity, "neither before nor after," that we have already enjoyed.

17. The story, pregnant with suggestiveness, is told in Carl Sandburg's *Abraham Lincoln: The War Years* (New York: Harcourt, Brace, 1939), pp. 244ff., 261, and 279f.

18. In his Twenty-Ninth Letter (to Lewis Meyer).

19. Spinoza's explicit statements about "imagination" versus "intellect" are scattered throughout the *Ethic*. Typical formulations are Part II, Propositions 17 and 18, and Part V, Prop. 34.

The early-on statements in Part II are involved in the seventeenth-century psycho-physics of particle-mechanics and fluid-motion-displacements, combined. The hydrostatic model of the mind (or of the body's-own-mind), which Spinoza seems to be working with, raises more questions than it answers; but this would no doubt be true of an attempt, such as might be made today, to model the mind according to the "image" of quantum mechanics.

The ambiguities that result from the *modeling* of the mind are not resolved by improving the model.

20. In his *Phenomenology of Perception*, tr. Colin Smith (London: Routledge & Kegan Paul, 1962), the chapter on "Freedom," pp. 453ff.

21. The *locus classicus* for the familiar formula is Spinoza's Fiftieth Letter (to Jarig Jellis), with a somewhat qualified variant of it in the *Ethic*, Part I, Proposition 8, Scholium 1. But the purport of the thought runs like a red thread through the tradition, from its latency in Plato's *Parmenides*, its surfacing in the *Sophist* (as possibly in the *Timaeus*), and uninterruptedly thenceforth (if sometimes underground) to Hegel's master-dialectic in the *Phenomenology* and the *Science of Logic*, and to J. P. Sartre's celebration, the day before yesterday, of "nothingness" as the very substance of *self*-determination.

Index